WHISKEY WOMEN

WHISKEY WOMEN

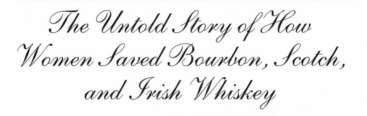

The Untold Story of How Women Saved Bourbon, Scotch, and Irish Whiskey

FRED MINNICK

Potomac Books

An imprint of the University of Nebraska Press

Library of Congress Cataloging-in-Publication Data

Minnick, Fred, 1978–
Whiskey women: the untold story of how women
saved bourbon, Scotch, and Irish whiskey / Fred
Minnick.
pages cm
Includes bibliographical references and index.
ISBN 978-1-61234-564-2 (cloth: alk. paper);
978-0-61234-565-9 (pdf). 1. Whiskey industry—
History. 2. Whiskey—History. 3. Distillers—History.
4. Businesswomen—History. 5. Women—History.
I. Title.
HD9395.A2M56 2013
338.4'766352082—dc23   2013024346

Set in Lyon Text by Laura Wellington.
Designed by A. Shahan.

To Jaclyn, my favorite whiskey woman

CONTENTS

ILLUSTRATIONS

A NOTE TO READERS

As you flip through these pages, you will see that I speak of both whiskey and whisky. Allow me to explain: *whisky* is the Scotch and Canadian spelling, while *whiskey* is the American and Irish spelling. I tried to respect these geographical indicators, because the proper spelling is important to whiskey drinkers. When generally referencing the spirits category, I used *whiskey*. Cheers!

INTRODUCTION

Although the evening was slightly cold, the sunset glowed over the blooming tulips and lush bluegrass on the grounds of the Kentucky Governor's Mansion. April showers had been kind, giving every plant vibrant life. Women dressed in their finest Derby attire strolled through the ornate grounds to the mansion's steps, under thick Southern columns. Two women stood at the doorway, looking out at Kentucky's First Garden, taking in the moment, knowing the significance of this day, April 14, 2011. The women were the founding members of the first American female drinking club to publicly kick off in a state's governor's mansion. The new organization, Bourbon Women, sought to take back something they had lost—a lady's rightful place in whiskey history. And of course, they did this while sipping Manhattans and whiskey on the rocks with the First Lady of Kentucky, Jane Beshear.

"We, ladies, love our bourbon, and we're here to show the world it's not just a man's drink," said the founder, Peggy Noe Stevens, who was a master taster for the spirits company Brown-Forman. Informal female whiskey clubs exist all over the world, but this was the first organization with national intentions to be created. Politicians, spirit brand executives, authors, and James Beard–nominated chefs joined the soiree to rub elbows with Mrs. Beshear, leaving one to ask an obvious question: What kind of drinking club launches in its state's governor's mansion with the First Lady as a founding member?

"Women have always been a part of the bourbon business, and it's a big part of our state's economy," Beshear said. Since 95 percent of bourbon, a form of American whiskey made mostly from corn, is made in Kentucky, there's strong state political capital behind this female club. Yet the notion of women and whiskey goes beyond the happenings of this small state. In boardrooms from France to New York, brand managers are discussing how to make a predominantly male-centric product more appealing to women. Whiskey, the Irish and American spelling, and whisky, the Scotch and Canadian spelling, have never taken such a strong stance toward women. According to a 2012 Simons

Market Research report, women represent 30 percent of the total whiskey-drinking population. Large publicly traded companies hope to increase this female demand.

Bottles and labels are becoming more feminine and elegant, while flavored whiskey targets female consumers in much the same way as flavored vodkas. Perhaps the greatest tribute to the growth of women and distilled malts is the fact the Glenfiddich's Janet Sheed Roberts Reserve, a fifty-five-year-old single malt Scotch named after the founder's granddaughter, sold for $94,000 at auction in 2012. Although other whiskies have sold for more, Glenfiddich's extremely limited edition (only eleven bottles were made) is one of the highest-selling all-time whiskies. The Reserve sold just two weeks before Sheed Roberts passed away at age 110.

Whiskey was once the lady's staple beverage for guests. In the 1700s and 1800s, Scottish and American women mixed whiskey with tea and sugar in punch bowls, while Irish women used poitín, Irish moonshine, to keep their families healthy. They continued enjoying whiskey during Prohibition and up until the late 1950s. But a woman's whiskey-drinking habits of yesterday are not why I pursued this book. Something Stevens said at the Bourbon Women founding meeting stuck with me: "Women were the first distillers."

First Lady Beshear explained the contributions of women: "Women have been involved with bourbon for many, many years. If you look back, you would see so many women in all parts of the business, from the actual preparation to the bottling to working on the Board of Directors." If women have been so important to whiskey, why are we just now talking about them? Flip through any magazine covering whiskey over the past fifty years, and you'll see drastically more coverage of men than women. When women are used in whiskey brand promotions, they are sexually objectified to allure potential male drinkers with their short skirts, long legs, and busts. In addition, whiskey is almost exclusively named after men.

For a business steeped in tradition and history, whiskey has forgotten its better half. Women have always been a part of whiskey history; they've just never received credit. As I pursued the story of women's role in the whiskey industry, I discovered that women contributed greatly to the evolution of alcohol.

Nearly four thousand years before whiskey was first distilled, Sumerian women invented beer. An Egyptian woman created the alembic still around 3 AD, giving moonshiners an early prototype for the stills they use today. Medieval European women worked in apothecaries, distilling everything from rosewater to potatoes. They called these early distillations *aqua vitae* (Latin) and *Usque-, Uisce-,* or *Uisge-Beatha* (Gaelic), both meaning "water of life." Although the word *whiskey* had been used in the 1500s, it did not become a common term until the 1800s. Even some mid-nineteenth-century American accounts show that rum, tequila, and brandy were frequently mistaken for whiskey. This categorical confusion may explain why early female distillers are often left out of whiskey history; they were distilling anything and everything before *whiskey* became a popular term. But their contributions should not be overlooked. This book explains how 1600s Scottish aqua vitae makers were accused of witchcraft and why 1800s Irish tax collectors targeted female whiskey makers.

Whether they were beaten down by their respective governments or they simply chose to conform to their expected societal roles, women liquor makers became fewer as distilling became big business. They typically only owned distilleries after their husbands died. In Ireland and Scotland, more than thirty women owned legitimate tax-paying distilleries. Some women drove their companies into the ground; others planted the seeds for future whiskey empires. From the 1700s to the 1950s, these women distillery owners were among the most influential people in the entire spirits industry. Laphroaig, Dalmore, Bushmills, and Johnnie Walker might not be here today without a woman owner in the brands' history.

Today women are CEOs of liquor companies with large whiskey portfolios, and they compete with men for management positions. Despite the often sexist usage of women in advertising, the whiskey business has mostly embraced the growth of women in the working ranks. Making and marketing a good whiskey are the primary concerns; gender should be secondary.

This book gives credit to the women who perfected the recipes we enjoy today and helped build iconic brands worth billions of dollars. They may not have a whiskey named after them, but the world of whiskey owes them a debt of gratitude.

WHISKEY WOMEN

1

Before Whiskey

When people think of whiskey, they often picture its alluring color, ranging from a soft shade of straw in a single malt Scotch to the deep russet of bourbon. The color variations depend on the aging process in oak casks, but the flavor starts with grains soaking in hot water that become a rudimentary beer or wort, the extracted liquid from the fermented grain mash.[1] The fermented grains are distilled and aged in a barrel until bottling. This process varies by region but has remained mostly the same for two hundred years. Long before industry perfected triple distillation or steam-powered engines, Sumerian women invented the first step to creating whiskey: they made beer.

The first evidence of women making beer is found on Mesopotamian cuneiform tablets dating around 4000 BC.[2] Many anthropologists believe women cultivated barley for beer, not bread. In 1950, A. Leo Oppenheim, a distinguished Assyriologist, published a tablet from the Metropolitan Museum of Art in New York that included 160 terms about beer manufacturing. "The Brewer's craft is the only profession in Mesopotamia which derives divine protection and social sanction from a goddess—in fact from two female figures of the pantheon: Ninkasi and Siris," Oppenheim wrote.[3]

Sumerians used beer for religious rituals, medicine, and a normal beverage, drinking through large straws in jars. According to recovered plaques thought to be from 2550 to 2400 BC, women sipped beer during the sorrow of funerals and through the orgasmic enjoyment of sexual intercourse.[4] Gods and goddesses enjoyed beer, too. At one banquet, deities were seated before the beer jug, and to not know how to drink beer meant one was uncivilized. Enki, the "Lord of Wisdom," occasionally became intoxicated, and his daughter, the goddess Ninkasi, presided over all beer manufacturing.[5]

The Sumerian women sang songs to Ninkasi and wrote poems about how she "holds with both hands the great sweet wort."[6] They worshiped her likely because beer was safe to drink. Even though nobody still bows to her image, Ninkasi remains a fascinating beer figure. In 1989 legendary San Francisco microbrewery Anchor Brewing re-created the 4,000-year-old recipe outlined in the "Hymn to Ninkasi." Anchor used *bappir* (twice-baked bread), malt, honey, and dates to replicate the Sumerian beer. The alcohol level was 3.5 percent and did not contain hops or other bitter ingredients. Reviews applauded Anchor for making the beer and said it was appealing, albeit much sweeter than modern beers.

Egyptian women also made beer. The Egyptian goddess Hathor was the "inventress of brewing" and the "mistress of intoxication." Her temple at Dendera was known as the place of drunkenness. Despite Hathor's power among the Egyptians, ale received widespread blame for town drunkenness, leading to the suppression of beer shops in 2000 BC. "While those disturbing members of the Egyptian community were waxing wrath over the beer shops, our savage ancestors probably contented themselves with such drinks as mead made from wild honey or cider from a crab tree," John Bickerdyke wrote on the first page of the 1886 *Curiosities of Ale & Beer*.

Even if Egypt's politicians tried their own Prohibition of sorts when closing down beer stores, the attacks focused on the retailers, not the women who made the brew. Middle-class and upper-class women crafted several types of beer by experimenting with grains, herbs, and spices. The women soaked grain in water for a day, rolled barley, left it to dry, and then wetted it again. They then filtered the soupy liquid with a cloth and set it aside for maturation. If they did not have grain, the Egyptians mashed stale bread in a pot of water, leaving it to ferment.

The Sumerians air-dried malts, while the Egyptians crushed malt into cakes. H. S. Corren writes in the 1975 *History of Brewing* that the Egyptian method of preparing wort from beer cakes remains a mystery. Malting would later become a specialized process for "malters" soaking the barley in water and tricking premature germination. As for the ancient processes, it has been widely assumed that both Egyptians and Sumerians made beer mainly from barley. Recent studies offer evidence that Sumerian beer was nonalcoholic, while early hieroglyphics indicate that Egyptians used yeast, a living organism that feeds on the sugar from liquid grain, to create alcohol. These techniques would be used by women in different cultures for centuries to come, but not the Greeks or Romans.

The Greeks and Romans forbade women to make wine or to drink alcohol. The Greeks viewed drinking wine as a cultural event for the highest ranks and did not approve of women drinking, but did not show the same fervor as the Romans for punishing women. The Roman elder Cato publicly stated he would punish his wife if he caught her drunk.[7] In the second-century book *Attic Nights*, Aulus Gellius wrote: "Women were not only judged but also punished by a judge as severely for drinking wine as for committing adultery."[8]

If a woman committed adultery, the Roman law allowed the man to kill her with impunity. And in some cases, women were sentenced to death just for being near alcohol. A matron's relatives starved her to death because she was found to have broken the seals of boxes that held the wine cellar key. Ironically, the Roman Empire was partially conquered by German barbarians, who allowed their women to drink and even make beer. Viking and Nordic women could drink, but their level of imbibing is not clear.[9]

In ancient Cerra Baul, Peru, from 600 to 1000 AD, the Wari Empire women made the drink *chicha*, a fermented corn brew.[10] Elite Wari women milled sprouted corn kernels with grinding stones and placed the milled corn in 150-liter vats for boiling. The mash was then transported to a fermentation area and aged three to five days. To this day, chicha is a celebrated Peruvian drink.

In several ancient cultures, beer was used as medicine and entertainment, as well as a complement to rituals. They buried their dead with jars of beer and wrote about its significance. Sumerians, Egyptians, and Peruvians all trusted their women to make the liquid that kept people alive.

In the Middle Ages, female brewers remained important to their societies. Dutch women were considered better brewers than men. "In 1300, brewing was a ubiquitous trade that required little specialized skill or equipment. . . . As such, it was accessible to women," and in the mid-1400s, women in London counted for 30 percent of the brewers' guild.[11] Those who made beer were called ale-wives and brewster wives, but were most commonly referred to as brewsters. These women perfected beer and ale from the 1200s to the late 1400s for the same reasons as the women thousands of years earlier: Beer was the safest drink and simple to make. It also became one of the best antidotes.

For a severe spider bite, one physician recommended cracking an egg into ale and rubbing the concoction into the wound.[12] When a soldier was injured in battle, a popular remedy called for a mixture of serpent's fat and beer. There was always a shortage of serpent's fat.

Women owned their own breweries and were often employed as lead brewers. When men died, they frequently bequeathed their breweries to wives, daughters, and female employees. In his 1306 will, Stephen de Barnade of London left his wife, Agnes, all his wooden brewing utensils with cistern adjoining.[13] In 1333 and 1334, Elizabeth de Burgh, Lady of Clare, maintained a large London brewery, making sixty gallons of ale each week.[14]

When making ale, the typical brewster dumped her grain of choice in a vat and ladled water over the grain, letting it soak. Then she ground the malted grain until it looked like coarse mill. The mill was placed in a wash tun—a large container similar to a clothes-washing bin—with boiling water. She added herbs, yeast, or other ingredients to the mash to make her recipe special. One woman added loaf sugar, spruce, and fresh yeast for a sweeter beer.

Women faced the same regulations as the men. Under the reign of Henry VIII, infamous for killing his wives, brewers and brewsters were forbidden to make their own barrels. The king's law stated that beer brewers had damaged the craft of coopers. Towns also mandated the aging process of beer as well as taxation. Local governments regulated grains and required certified ale tasters to sample the product before it could be sold. These regulations kept unsafe products from entering the market, while ensuring that the government received its taxes, a process that is repeated throughout alcohol history.

If they did not follow the rules, female brewers frequently found themselves in the courtroom to address litigation and criminal concerns. In a case brought to court in the late fifteenth century, Johane Wynde sued Margaret Clark of Ramsey for unpaid wages in Clark's brewing business. Wynde had worked for Clark for six years as an apprentice. The judge ruled in favor of the employer.[15] If found guilty of making bad beer, brewsters suffered corporal punishment, including flogging.

The court records of Wakefield, West Yorkshire, indicate that between 1348 and 1350, 185 women violated brewing regulations.[16] One woman was cited for failing to send beer to an ale taster before selling it, a minor offense that would not earn the notorious nickname "brew witch" or "ale witch." These ominous titles were reserved for those practicing sorcery.

Alice Huntley was accused of witchcraft in the late fifteenth century. According to the Chancery Rolls, between 1475 and 1485, Huntley practiced witchcraft and sorcery against the laws of the Church and the king. It is not clear if bad beer was the main reason for the accusations, but she was among the many brewsters who were accused of witchcraft. Chaplain John Knight complained that she hid liquor, which was often considered evidence in witchcraft trials. While searching her house, investigators found materials "for wychecraft and enchauntements with other stuff beryed and deeply hydd under the erthe."[17] While this report could mean she was hiding fiery satanic potions in snake pits, it is more likely that she was just keeping her beer cool. Brewers were known to keep barrels in caves. Despite the discovery, Huntley was not arrested. Instead, her accuser, Chaplain John Knight, was arrested, likely for false claims or harassment.

Knight's claim against Huntley illustrates the beginnings of opinion turning against brewsters. As witchcraft became a greater concern, female brewers were targeted. According to the Essex Witch records, from 1566 to 1589, one of the top five witchcraft complaints was that women had spoiled the beer.[18] Witches were frequently said to defecate in and "bewitch" beer, leading to a general intolerance of brewster-made beers. In 1623 Dr. Cyrial Folkingham, who prescribed ale for curing maladies, wrote that women were the quacks of the brewing profession.[19]

Many brewsters may have received a reputation as witches because they were bad brewers or bad businesspeople. Women did not typically use hops, which were widely used for flavoring and as a stability agent. Hops, which are not used for whiskey wort, can greatly ameliorate a beer's flavor. But seventeenth-century author Thomas Tyron wrote that "beer high boiled with hops" can lead to the gout and consumption. "The boiling of hops two, three or four hours in beer is a thing of pernicious consequence, giving a grosser, fuller and stronger taste in the mouth. It lies longer in the stomach, sending gross fumes and vapors," Tyron wrote in his 1690 book, *A New Art of Brewing Beer, Ale, and Other Sorts of Liquors*. Perhaps female brewers did not think hops' stronger taste was worth the bodily consequences. Nonetheless, if they were making beer from spoiled oats, and a consumer tasted it next to a brewer's hopped-up beer, the brewster beer would taste terrible in comparison. Plus, many brewsters cheated customers and ran disorderly establishments, offering sexual services along with a pint. These unsavory business tactics certainly hurt the overall brewster standing.

In seventeenth-century London, just 7 percent of the brewers' guild members were women. Women continued leaving the brewing picture in the eighteenth century, when men greatly outnumbered female brewers. By the nineteenth century, the term *brewster* had been all but forgotten.

Several scholarly texts have resurrected the brewster's place in beer.[20] In fact, beer and research seem to be synonymous these days. From the University of California Los Angeles to the University of Chicago, researchers appear determined to learn beer's impact on ancient cultures, a fascination stemming from both archaeological and agricultural research. "There can be no doubt that the emergence of agriculture was closely related to the processing of grain after the harvest and that beer brewing soon belonged to the basic technologies of grain conservation and consumption," wrote Peter Damerow of the Max Planck Institute for the History of Science, Berlin.[21] Archaeologist Alexei Vranich told *Smithsonian Magazine* that beer is more important than armies when it comes to understanding people.[22]

Lost in this brew quest is how beer's discovery impacted whiskey. According to the U.S. Alcohol and Tobacco Tax and Trade Bureau, whiskey is "spirits distilled from a fermented mash of grain." It should never be overlooked that Jack Daniel's, Jim Beam, Johnnie Walker, and every other whiskey begin in the grain fields. Farmers pick the corn, barley, rye, or wheat and ship it to the distillers, who mix grains with hot water to begin fermentation. Although regions' style varies, this one basic principle of fermenting grains remains the same.

Without Sumerian women fermenting barley, would modern whiskey exist? The Sumerians also grew wheat. If they had discovered fermentation of wheat instead of barley, would wheat have become the primary grain for beer and whiskey? These are impossible questions to answer. Perhaps researchers will uncover new evidence about the Sumerian women making beer or learn that another culture altogether discovered beer.[23] But there's no denying that Sumerian and Egyptian women gave future distillers the fermented base for whiskey.

Meanwhile, other women were taking the next step in making whiskey, distillation. Many scholars believe the first chemists were two Mesopotamian women, Tapputi-Belatekallim and [——]-ninu (the first half of her name is unknown).[24] Because most chemistry apparatuses were derived from kitchen utensils, it makes sense that women were the first chemists. The two Mesopotamians created perfumes around 1200 BC through plant extraction and distillation.[25] Tapputi was the female overseer of the Royal Palace and in charge of all perfume products, an important position in the Mesopotamian culture. Dead kings were prepared for burial with oils and perfumes, while women of rank rubbed oils into their skin to keep it silky smooth.

Women would be stripped of their freedom thousands of years later in other cultures, but the Mesopotamians treated women with great respect. In fact, the female chemists continued perfecting distillation for centuries. After Tapputi and [——]-ninu's breakthrough, Egyptian woman Maria Hebraea invented the distillation processes still used today.[26]

HYMN TO NINKASI

Translation by Miguel Civil

Borne of the flowing water . . .
Tenderly cared for by the Ninhursag,
Borne of the flowing water . . .
Tenderly cared for by the Ninhursag,

Having founded your town by the sacred lake,
She finished its great walls for you,
Ninkasi, having founded your town by the sacred lake,
She finished its great walls for you

Your father is Enki, Lord Nidimmud,
Your mother is Ninti, the queen of the sacred lake,
Ninkasi, your father is Enki, Lord Nidimmud,
Your mother is Ninti, the queen of the sacred lake.

You are the one who handles the dough,
[and] with a big shovel,
Mixing in a pit, the bappir with sweet aromatics,
Ninkasi, you are the one who handles
the dough, [and] with a big shovel,
Mixing in a pit, the bappir with [date-]honey.

You are the one who bakes the bappir
in the big oven,
Puts in order the piles of hulled grains,
Ninkasi, you are the one who bakes
the bappir in the big oven,
Puts in order the piles of hulled grains,

You are the one who waters the malt
set on the ground,
The noble dogs keep away even the potentates,
Ninkasi, you are the one who waters the malt
set on the ground,
The noble dogs keep away even the potentates.

You are the one who soaks the malt in a jar
The waves rise, the waves fall.
Ninkasi, you are the one who soaks
the malt in a jar
The waves rise, the waves fall.

You are the one who spreads the cooked
mash on large reed mats,
Coolness overcomes.
Ninkasi, you are the one who spreads
the cooked mash on large reed mats,
Coolness overcomes.

You are the one who holds with both hands
the great sweet wort,
Brewing [it] with honey and wine
(You the sweet wort to the vessel)
Ninkasi, . . .
(You the sweet wort to the vessel)

The filtering vat, which makes
a pleasant sound,
You place appropriately on [top of]
a large collector vat.
Ninkasi, the filtering vat,
which makes a pleasant sound,
You place appropriately on [top of]
a large collector vat.

When you pour out the filtered beer
of the collector vat,
It is [like] the onrush of
Tigris and Euphrates.
Ninkasi, you are the one who pours out the
filtered beer of the collector vat,
It is [like] the onrush of
Tigris and Euphrates.

2

The First Distillations

During distillation, heat boils the fermented grain mash and separates the water from alcohol, which is cooled or condensed to form clear drops of distilled spirits. This distillation process has become an industrialized spectacle of efficiency with each major whiskey category using its patented stills. But long before bourbon makers implemented towering stills or Irish whiskey lovers romanticized about their pure pot stills, Alexandrian Egyptian women practiced alchemy from the first through the third centuries AD, essentially creating the distillation mechanisms that would lead to spirited liquors.[1] In the 1930s, German scholar Adam Maurizio theorized in *Geschichte der gegorenen Getränke* that early distillation was used to prepare a wide range of drinks, including mead (fermented honey and water) and beer.[2] If this is true, women may have created an early form of whiskey shortly after the death of Jesus Christ. But Maurizio's theories received little support, and most believe early Egyptian distillation was used to create perfumes and solutions of sulfur, mercury, and arsenic sulfide.

The most important figure among the Alexandrian chemists was Maria Hebraea, also known as Maria the Jewess.[3] An alchemist, Maria's writings were lost, but her influence lived through alchemists who followed. Most notably, the legendary fourth-century alchemist Zosimos Panopolis credited Maria with devising new heating and distilling apparatuses constructed of metal, clay, and glass.[4] Maria created the *balneum Mariae*, a water-bath that consisted of a double vessel, the outer one filled with water and the inner vessel with the substance to be heated to a moderate degree.[5] Practicing in the third century, Maria was the first to prepare copper burnt with sulfur for gold preparation, and she theorized that all matter was one. According to Zosimos, Maria believed: "One becomes two, two becomes three, and by means of the third the fourth achieves unity, thus two are but one."

Maria invented a still consisting of two gourd-shaped vessels connected by an alembic. As the most important piece to her still designs, Maria's alembic carried a tube leading to the receiver and became the common term for the still. Liquid was poured into the boiler, fire heated it from below, and the vapors passed through the alembic to the receiver.[6] Moonshiners in the hills of West Virginia and Kentucky still use distant prototypes of her invention, while brandy makers use antique French alembic stills for small quantities.

Maria's still includes the *kerotakis*, a cylinder with a hemispherical cover used to heat pigment mixtures and wax, and the three-armed still known as the *tribikos*. When distilling in the tribikos, the liquid was heated in an earthenware vessel and the vapor was condensed and cooled. A lip inside collected the distillate and carried it to the three delivery tubes.

Although her discoveries had much wider implications than whiskey, including the creation of transmutation, Maria's quest to combine her theories of alchemical science with chemistry gave future distillers the basic tools to create liquors. Later Alexandrian female alchemists also made great contributions in mathematics and distillation. Cleopatra was even thought to have contributed to distillation. But Egyptian female-led alchemy died in 415 AD, when Hypatia, the daughter of the author Theon, was hacked to pieces by Christians. Egyptian historians believe she was murdered because she was an outspoken female scholar.

In the Dark Ages, women were excluded from religious orders and lost the opportunity to read, write, or study Latin and scientific texts. With the exception of Chinese alchemists, who practiced their profession openly and continued to influence cultural advancements, women during the Dark Ages were forced to practice distillation only in their homes or in hiding. However, when the demand for distilled medicines increased in the fourteenth and fifteenth centuries, doctors called upon women to run apothecaries.

During the Middle Ages, women quietly contributed to medicinal advancements. Known as *Wasserbrennerinnen* or Aquavit-women, they created alcohol-based medicines in apothecaries, distilling ale, rosewater, potatoes, and anything else they could get their hands on.[7] These women created distilled spirits that would commonly be referred to as "hard water" or aqua vitae, *uisge beatha* in Gaelic, *akvavit* in Scandinavian, and *eau de vie* in French. From the fifteenth through the seventeenth centuries, the term *aqua vitae* meant distilled wine, beer, or potatoes, and it was applied to any and all ardent spirits. This lack of early spirit definition has sparked debate among Shakespearean scholars. Aqua vitae was used six times in Shakespeare's plays, but it is unknown whether the bard was referring to whiskey or brandy. The argument leans toward whiskey, likely because of *The Merry Wives of Windsor*, where the character Ford mentions an Irishman with his aqua vitae. The Irish grew very few grapes to make brandy, but had been making a form of whiskey since the eleventh century.

Shakespeare scholars have good reason to debate the drink, because the aqua vitae formula was not consistent. The thirteenth-century Italian medical professor Taddeo Alderotti wrote that aqua vitae was produced from wine alone.[8] "Its effects are marvelous against all cold affections," Alderotti reported. The fourteenth-century *Red Book of Ossory*, a Latin register of the Irish diocese, states that the best aqua vitae was distilled four times and that aqua vitae was the best defense against brain fevers, weakness, cold, shortness of breath, sores, and even gray hairs.[9] Like Alderotti's preference, *The Red Book of Ossory* mentions wine as the base source. But other aqua vitae recipes from that time called for distilling lemon and orange peels, rosewater, cowslip flowers, beer, and onions. Herbs were sometimes added, as well as animal parts or blood. A female distiller was expected to know many recipes. The sixteenth-century writer Gervase Markham proscribed in *The English Housewife*: "She shall distill all sorts of waters for the health of her household."[10]

Although recipes varied, aqua vitae was the aspirin of the Middle Ages. Midwives made sure women in labor drank plenty of aqua vitae to ease the pain. In 1663 the Countess of Newcastle was prescribed a cassia, saffron, and borax powder in a "burnt white wine" for general pain.[11] Aqua vitae was prescribed for bronchitis, mercury poisoning, and gout. It comforted the heart, revived the spirits, and prevented swooning fits. Aqua vitae was also a remedy for the plague, wrote Lady Catherine Sedley in her 1686 "receipt book." One Sedley recipe calls for distillation in a limbeck, another name for Maria the Jewess's alembic still: "Take a gallon of Gascoyn wine, then take ginger, galingall, camel, cinamint, tollianders, nutmegs, cloves, aniseed, of each one drahm, then take sage, mint, red roses, thyme of the moor, pellitory of the wall, rosemary, wild marjoram, pennyroyal, thyme, lavender and avens. . . . The virtues of this water be these: It conforteth the spirits vitall, and preserveth greatly the youth of man, and helpeth the inward diseases coming of cold, and against shaking of palsy, it cureth the contraction of women that be barren, it killeth wormes in the body, and killeth the cold gout, and helpeth toothache, it comforteth the stomach very much."[12]

This demand for good aqua vitae made aquavit-women highly employable. Apothecary manager Thomas Foxe of London hired Agnes Miller as a servant in 1618, saying that he placed "great trust" in her abilities to sell his products and help him invent brews.[13] But this was not an accepted practice throughout Europe.

In Nuremberg, Germany, during the sixteenth century, the city council created legislation to ban in-home aqua vitae production in an attempt to prevent women from making spirits.[14] This movement spread across Europe, and doctors began dismissing aqua vitae made by women and warning that their products might cause serious adulterations. Just as naysayers ousted brewsters as witches, aquavit-women were linked to witchcraft. Accusers claimed that aqua vitae turned people into demons.

In *On the Demon-Mania of Witches*, Jean Bodin wrote, "When poisons and spells are found on the witch who is arrested with them, or in her room, or in her chest, or she is discovered digging beneath the doorway of a stable, and the poisons are found there that she was caught hiding, and the livestock dies, one can assert in this case that it is a clear and concrete fact."[15] Authorities considered possession of a vial of aqua vitae not prescribed by a doctor to be proof of witchcraft.

In 1418 Joan of Navarre, the second wife of Henry IV of England, was imprisoned for four years for plotting to poison her stepson, Henry V, through witchcraft.[16] The evidence against her included a bottle of aqua vitae. Similarly, Eleanor Cobham, wife of the Duke of Gloucester, was accused of trying to kill Henry VI in 1441. Eleanor confessed to witchcraft and to practicing alchemical magic after authorities discovered aqua vitae in her possession. After Cobham's trial and other trials of so-called witches, the *English Chronicle* declared that women were most disruptive when not sexually productive, encouraging men to draw links between menopause and witchcraft.[17] The anti-witch mentality led to the mass executions in the sixteenth century.

In 1515, 500 accused witches were burned at the stake in Geneva, Switzerland, and 1,000 were killed in Como, Italy.[18] Between 1500 and 1660, historians believe Europe executed between 50,000 and 80,000 alleged witches. Eighty percent of these victims were women, many of whom had been caught with aqua vitae. Ireland and England had the lowest death rates because the judicial system lacked the legal framework to execute witches.[19] Furthermore, the Irish did not trust the legal authorities and tended to unite against their English suppressors, rarely accusing neighbors of witchcraft. In Scotland, however, James VI made eradicating witches a top priority. In the 1590s, he encountered terrible seas on his voyage to and from marrying Princess Anne of Denmark. The ship's captain blamed witches for the storms, and Danish women confessed to creating the North Sea tidal waves that instilled great fear in the king. After this incident, James wrote the book *Daemonologie*, in which he supported the witch-hunting practice that would kill 4,000 in Scotland.[20]

But during these witch hunts, women were also making aqua vitae for intoxication purposes and selling in the public market. Although it is possible that an angry neighbor accused a woman whiskey distiller of witchcraft, most aqua vitae–related witch convictions came from women concocting folk medicine remedies. In 1623 in Perth, Scotland, Janet Ross was executed for prescribing a feverish patient an egg with a little aqua vitae and pepper. The Perth editor wrote that witchcraft charges were "generally connected with cures wrought or attempted for some severe disease."[21]

The fear of being labeled a witch drove many aqua vitae women to practice their craft in secrecy. Not even connections with royalty could protect a woman from witch charges. Anne, princess of Denmark and Norway, electress of Saxony (1532–85), created a distillery house complete with walls and moats. It would have taken an army to penetrate her production site. Anne, whose slender body was the epitome of medieval beauty, sought out trusted sources and famous doctors to find the best distillation formulas. She was curious about medicine and nursed her husband through a painful illness. Anne also trained young girls in herbal medicine and founded a church to care for refugees, pregnant women, and the infirm. In 1869, a memorial was built by

Robert Henze in Dresden, where it still stands, to honor the kind princess who gave so much to Denmark. But imagine if Anne could have practiced her medical interests openly, without fear of being labeled a witch. Removing women from the educational equation drastically thwarted advances in medicine.

Yet somehow aquavit-women snuck through the cracks to make apothecary-approved spirited remedies. From 1617 to 1669, sixty-four women owned apothecaries in London and distilled spirit for medicinal purposes.[22] Because they frequently distilled beers, aquavit-women most likely made unaged whiskey without even knowing it.

3

Tough Irish Women

When English soldiers invaded Ireland in 1172, they found the Irish drinking an alcohol called *uisge-beatha*, Gaelic for "water of life." Barley flourishes in Ireland's damp climate, so this twelfth-century uisge-beatha was almost certainly whiskey. It's unclear how Ireland distilled whiskey so early. According to legend, around the fifth century Saint Patrick brought distillation to Ireland. But in 1858 Dr. Andrew Ure theorized that northern European "barbarians" introduced distillation when they attacked the island.[1] Another argument gives credit to the Moors, and the first Irish *Annals* mention of Irish whiskey appears in 1405: "Richard Magranell, chieftain of Moyntyreolas, died at Christmas by taking a surfeit of aqua vitae."[2] As with many historical debates, Irish whiskey's origins remain a mystery.

However the art of distillation found its way to the Emerald Isle, women used the process to make uisge-beatha at home, with a pot and hurdle, a brass pipe that acted as the worm condensing the liquid. The distiller started with around twenty quarts of good strong beer or ale and distilled it down to fourteen quarts of powerful whiskey that would have ranged from 95 to 120 proof by today's standards. According to one 1671 recipe, Irish distillers added licorice and occasionally saffron or anise seeds to the mash before distilling.[3] Almost all early accounts of Irish whiskey call for a minimum two times distillation; today's Irish whiskey standard is triple distillation. Once the distilled spirit was made, women mixed it with sugar and mint, even butter, to reduce the alcohol burn. According to a letter written by a butler traveling through County Fermanagh in 1760, the Irish drank whiskey to intoxication and "are never sick after it neither."[4]

They also made the unaged spirit poitín, known in England as poteen.[5] Outsiders referred to it as Mountain Dew because poitín was made in the mountains, and tax collectors called it illicit whiskey. However, poitín was drastically different than the recipes of legitimate tax-paid whiskey. Some recipes called for potatoes and oats, while the traditional whiskey was mostly made of barley and corn.

Women made poitín in the hills and snuck it into weddings, funerals, wakes, and fairs. They created cocktails with poitín, using creamy goat's milk and mint leaf. They added butter and honey to the spirit. These likely wretched mixtures won't be appearing on a modern menu any time soon, but the poitín mixing illustrates the spirit's importance for country social gatherings.

The more refined English acquired a taste for top tier Irish whiskey. Sir Walter Raleigh was the spirit's most important supporter. After the First Earl of Cork gave Raleigh barrels of whiskey he fancied, Raleigh shared the whiskey with Queen Elizabeth. Raleigh called the Earl of Cork's 32-gallon keg of whiskey "a supreme gift." In general, Irish nobles were quite fond of their country's whiskey and frequently gifted barrels to the English. In 1585, the mayor of Waterford sent Lord Burleigh a "rundell of aqua vitae."[6] When Lord Justice Cork sent his daughter to London in 1622 to meet Captain Prince at Durham House, he sent with her a harp and whiskey as gifts to her possible future husband: "Drinke a little of this Irish Uskebach, it will help to digest all raw humours, exell wynde and keep his inward parte warme all the day after, without any offence to his stomache."[7]

The seventeenth century was a time of Irish whiskey enthusiasm for the English, but the increased English demand for Irish spirits spurred a transition from small, at-home operations that sold whiskey at local markets to businesses intent on expansion. Newspaper advertisements for Irish-made "usquebaugh" began appearing in London and later New York as early as the 1720s.[8] An ad for Bowden's Usquebaugh in the February 8, 1750, edition of the *Whitehall Evening Post* described the whiskey as an absolute remedy for gout and rheumatism. The ad encouraged the public not to be fooled by imposters: "To prevent the public from counterfeit, a label will be put on each bottle with these Words, BOWDEN'S USQUEBAUGH, with the name sealed on the top of each cork."

As their increasing thirst for Irish whiskey was changing the production scales, the English also influenced the name of uisge-beatha. Phonetically pronounced "isk'ke-ba-'ha," *usage-beatha* became *whiskey* because the English could not pronounce the Gaelic word. The new term *whiskey* also applied to Scotch whisky and frequently appeared on the society pages of London newspapers. Whether from Scotland or Ireland, it became a drink for virility and strength. In 1737, a sixty-eight-year-old London woman publicly blamed her husband's whiskey drinking for her pregnancy at such an old age.[9] Another Englishwoman wrote in 1738: "Were we but as wise as we're poor, I should think good . . . whiskey might serve us for drink."[10]

This interest in whiskey, from England's destitute all the way to the queen, had much wider implications than a change in the spirit's name. Lawmakers realized the Irish and British governments were losing significant taxation money on whiskey. On Christmas Day 1661, the Irish government imposed its first whiskey tax at 4 pence per gallon. The taxes essentially made poitín illegal and forced one-still women to either go out of business or sell the whiskey illegally. But these Irish taxes were nothing compared with the effect in Great Britain.

ILLICIT FEMALE DISTILLERS AND TAX COLLECTORS

Conflicts really began under Henry VIII in the 1530s, as he sought to gain control of Ireland. Even though the island represented little monetary gain, Henry received royal decrees from Pale, four counties near Dublin, to allow him to control the region. In the king's quest to build Protestant faith, he saw Ireland as a strong Catholic country worth conquering. The Fitzgeralds, the earls of Kildare, were Ireland's most powerful family, and they fought back with their armies. After many bloody skirmishes, the rebellious Irish were no match for England and their own countrymen who supported Henry. In 1541, the Irish Parliament declared Henry king. Henry dissolved several Catholic monasteries to spite Ireland's deep-rooted connection to Rome, and so began the centuries of battles between Protestants and Catholics and between the English and Irish rebels.

As England took more control of Ireland, it siphoned Irish industry revenues, but whiskey stayed off their radar for the first two hundred years. The country distillers proved beyond the reach of the English tax collectors. By the 1780s, Irish whiskey was too profitable for England to ignore. When the whiskey taxes increased from the 1661 4 pence mandate, the policies favored larger distillers and greatly limited a smaller distiller's ability to compete in the marketplace. For example, in 1782 there were thirty-nine small legitimate tax-paying distilleries operating in County Donegal.[11] Fifteen years later, there were none. The revenue laws set license fees, prohibited distilling after dark, and were not accommodating to female home distillers whose stills were the size of a standard barrel.

In England's attempt to tax Irish distillery revenue, the country failed to realize how poor the Irish distillers were. Rev. Edward Chichester of Cloncha wrote, "Disregarding the inferior capital of Ireland, small stills were suddenly prohibited from working, while those of the largest description alone were licensed. It is obvious that so sudden a change could not have been easily acceded to, especially after the duties on spirits became excessive, for Ireland abounds in fuel and mountainous districts, affording the greatest facility to illicit distillation."[12] Small distilleries just couldn't make enough whiskey to pay the taxes. Margaret Elliott was forced to give up her distilling operation in 1768 after paying a £5 fine.[13] Elliott was one of the casualties before the English greatly targeted the revenue of Irish whiskey makers.

When Ireland became a part of Great Britain in 1800, Ireland's taxation systems were brought in line with England's, and England deployed aggressive tax collectors. It pursued militant operations against any distillers who did not pay taxes. Excise agents—also known as Gaugers, still-hunters, dochill-stabbers, and eventually the Revenue Police—tracked sales of barley and surveyed water sources that could potentially be used for distillation. If they found anything resembling a still or whiskey operation—even a bucket of malted barley—the agents arrested landowners or commandeered property to pay for the fine.

In 1818, a Carlow County informant swore he saw "hot potatoes" cooking in a black pot at a woman's house.[14] This was enough evidence to convict her of illicit distillation even though she could have been making potato soup. The informant claimed the boiling potatoes would be distilled. If hops were not present, the excise agents assumed the cooking mash was used for distilling illegal poitín and not for making beer. No matter how little evidence existed, excise agents seized all distillation equipment, levied fines, and even confiscated property not related to distillation. They wielded Gestapo-like power with similar government support.

Excise agents could levy fines of £60 against Irish parishes found to have one of several stated articles used in distillations.[15] If a parish had a body of a still, a head, worm, potale, singlings (first distillation off the still, known today as low wine), or wort (beer) in any amount, the excise agent fined the parish even if there was no other evidence of production. When six illegal stills were discovered in 1813 in Roscommon County, the owners could not be found, so the judge levied equal fines against the six parishes. This would be the equivalent of a state judge forcing a county to pay the fines of a wanted meth dealer.

Excise agents were allowed to enter houses at any moment and tear rooms up from top to bottom in search of illicit whiskey. They were not responsible for damages caused in the search of poitín. If a property owner posted a claim against the Excise Agency, the judges and witnesses often worked with the excise agents. A satirist wrote of an excise judge hearing the cases of accused illicit distillers: "The judge knocked them off at the rate of one in a minute."[16]

Agents had great discretion in determining what was legal. If during the search they found an unlabeled can filled with whiskey, agents would smell the liquid and determine whether it was illegal poitín. But a can of poitín would have smelled the same as legitimate unaged whiskey she purchased at the market. Even today, if you ask any police officer to smell moonshine and vodka, it's doubtful he or she could tell the difference. This subjective, on-the-spot judgment only added to an agent's power.

In 1814, the excise agents formed an army of three hundred to raid the poorest area of Ireland, Innishowen, where they seized anything they could carry home.[17] These large organized efforts placed a magnifying glass on all women. The evil of poitín would not be eradicated if people believed women would be allowed to escape the heavy penalties inflicted on men, a judge said.[18] Another Irish judge said, "In my experience . . . . the women are worse than the men."[19] Perhaps this government-instilled fear of female poitín makers explains why the Revenue Police targeted women.

A military party showed up on the property of Mrs. Bramhall, an eighty-year-old Innishowen widow, and stole her furniture. Her sick daughter lay on the bed; the men forced her off onto the floor. Until she paid her fines, Mrs. Bramhall would not receive her property or even her daughter's bed. Though Mrs. Bramhall cooperated with the authorities in hopes of saving her daughter's life, her daughter died during her legal appeal.[20]

Rather than have her life dictated by agents, Margaret M'Aleny fought back. M'Aleny slit her only cow's throat to prevent excise agents from taking it.[21] It's more likely the police would have sold the bovine for personal profit than put the money toward her fine. Agents always wanted more.

After an older widow could not pay the illicit still fine, the agent took her cow and said the decrepit animal would not cover the fine. The agent's mentality was that everybody near the still was guilty of harboring an illegal distiller. When the distiller could not pay, agents took the neighbor's goods. This agent stripped the widow's neighboring girls of their best dresses. Innocent and poor, the young girls had their best clothes taken. How did this help Great Britain collect whiskey taxes?[22]

Outraged against the indecency of the excise men who constantly patrolled their streets and farms, the townspeople fought back. They no longer stood idly by or allowed their children to be harassed. Fueled by hatred for the English, the Northern Irish killed excise agents with bullets, fire, and blades. In several skirmishes between 1810 and 1815, agents retreated when distillers and residents outnumbered them. Speaking about the violence between agents and distillers, Aeneas Coffey, a surveyor of excise and acting inspector general of excise, told the House of Commons: "From the several attacks that had been made upon the revenue parties, who attempted to make seizures in that place upon former occasions, and whose efforts had failed (the parties sometimes having even been obliged to enter into terms of capitulation with the smugglers to surrender their seizures upon condition of being allowed to depart in safety), it was considered necessary to send a large force . . . whenever an attack was to be made upon it; great difficulty existed in procuring such a force to act in the matter that was necessary to accomplish the object." Coffey also described a skirmish in which an estimated 50 to 60 distillery workers fired 200 bullets at the tax collection party.[23]

This bloodshed did not scare Great Britain, but it did make the government realize that the smaller excise agent teams supplemented with military were not strong enough to handle Ireland's poitín distillers. In 1819, the Revenue Police became a formal arm of the Excise Department. Instead of employing a handful of agents and informants, Great Britain's Ireland had a powerful police force with the "expressed purpose of suppressing illicit distillation." From the government's view, collecting taxes was all that mattered. When renewing the Revenue Police's budget, the Excise Department approved the £40,000 expenditure in 1834 because the police force greatly exceeded duty and fine collection goals.[24] But what was not mentioned in this budget review was that the Revenue Police considered themselves above the law and in a holy cause. They carried muskets and still-killing tools, such as a pointed five-foot-long iron rod called a dochill-stab. They apprehended, beat, and even killed any distiller who opposed them.

The Irish whiskey battle with Revenue Police was a small fight in the greater island struggles. But for those women who made their living with whiskey, the spirit was everything.

In 1835, a Mayo County woman who retailed illicit liquor told the Commission of Inquiry on the Irish Poor that whiskey was her sole dependence. "I have no means on earth to keep my children inside the door with me, but to borrow money from one neighbor or another and buy a drop of poteen to sell again," she said.[25]

Meanwhile, Ireland's potato blight, *Phytophthora infestans*, caused widespread famine and killed 800,000 people, forcing another 2 million to emigrate.[26] In his journal, when docking in Cork to pick up passengers bound for America, Captain Forbes of the USS *Jamestown* wrote in 1847: "Here a large boiler containing rice, meal, etc., was at work while hundreds of spectres stood without, begging for some of the soup which I can readily conceive would be refused by well-bred pigs in America. Every corner of the streets is filled with pale, worn creatures, the weak leading and supporting the weaker, women assail you at every turn with famished babies."[27]

This dire time showed the gentle side of Kate Kearney, Ireland's most famous poitín distiller. Considered a beautiful woman, Kate lived in a quaint cottage at the entrance to the Gap of Dunloe.[28] She distilled a mixture of grains and herbs, which she gave to anybody during the Famine. In 1840 one traveler, Edward Newman, wrote that he had received a cup of poitín mixed with goat's milk from Kate's own hand, and it was "a very comforting mixture."[29] Her illicit hooch was never confiscated by the law, probably because Kate Kearney wooed any lawman who attempted to arrest her. Her beauty and poitín were so legendary that travelers twenty years after her death showed up for a taste. *Baptist Magazine* wrote in 1872: "Kate Kearney is one of those weird, half real, half mythical characters around whose name has gathered much that is romantic. If such a person ever lived, it is certain that she never dies."[30] She became a symbol throughout the Famine, an idea that good can come of illicit whiskey. There were probably many other Kate Kearneys helping the poor and giving the sick homemade liquor to ease their suffering. But the relentless force of the Revenue Police did not give history many pleasant stories of poitín during the Famine. Even in the national crisis, the Revenue Police still hunted distillers.

In 1853, Revenue Police detected illicit malt in Carlow County in the village of Naas. As the ranking officer and his sergeant investigated the illicit malt, his men awaited them in the village streets. A townsperson threw a rock at the Revenue Police. Without hesitation and without a superior's order, the men leveled their muskets at the houses and fired, killing a woman cooking potatoes at her hearth. "That I called a cold-blooded murder," a Colonel Brereton testified before the House of Commons in 1854. Brereton said the fights between Revenue Police and smugglers were caused by a lack of understanding. "In perhaps all the cases, the collision had arisen from two causes; first, the total ignorance of the use of arms, and the total want of discipline of the parties; and, secondly, total ignorance of what was called danger, and how that danger might be most sensibly avoided," Brereton testified. Shortly after this murder, two revenue agents walked up to Ellen Mason's house requesting drink. She said no. An angry policeman pulled his bayonet, piercing her cloak and back bundle. As she ran to safety, the lawmen destroyed everything in her home with no probable cause. These incidents could no longer continue. Ireland faced too many other problems to allow the Revenue Police to target women. One incident would be enough to cause concern, but their antagonizing nature seemingly happened on every street corner.[31]

The Revenue Police was disbanded in 1857. But women feared them for decades, and Revenue Policemen even replaced the Boogey Man. Little girls feared being left alone because the Revenue Policemen might come get them. "My poor mother used to set a light in the upper window that you could see far out off-shore whenever the revenue men were on watch," wrote Katharine Tynan in her 1899 book, *The Dear Irish Girl*. Women were scared to death of Irish Revenue agents.

This fear was well earned. Irish lawmen would never have the power that the Revenue Police wielded from 1819 to 1857. Nonetheless, the strife between tax collectors and the illegal distillers lasted well into the 1940s, and women were right there in the thick of it all. In 1923, three Dublin women carried rifles outside the Oriel House. When they were spotted by a member of the Intelligence Department, agents looked inside the hotel and found twenty bombs, twelve revolvers, six rifles, one hundred rounds of .45 ammunition, fifty fake CID badges, and thirty gallons of poitín.[32] In operations like this, the women sold poitín for extra cash to fund other causes, such as the revolution.

The more poitín they sold, the bigger and more infamous they became. In Scotstown, a village in County Monaghan, Ireland, authorities were constantly searching for a woman simply known as the "Poteen Queen of Scotstown." She supposedly supplied the area with the best illicit whiskey money could buy in the early 1900s. A drunk smelled of poitín and told police officers he bought liquor from the Poteen Queen. A sergeant scoped out Mrs. Mary McAree's home and found two gallons of ale and a suspicious fireplace buried under fresh sod.[33] Mrs. McAree was arrested but swore she knew nothing of the jars found on her property or the buried fireplace that allegedly heated a large still. The officer did not have the smoking gun he had hoped for, that's for sure, but this was certainly enough material to convict a woman in the 1930s. When the judge asked if she was the Poteen Queen of Scotstown, Mrs. McAree simply said no. The case was dismissed without prejudice, and nobody ever confirmed the Poteen Queen's identity. Perhaps the Poteen Queen wielded the kind of power that gets cases dismissed.

Although the Poteen Queen and Kate Kearney stories have been few, cloak-wearing, whiskey-making Irish women broke the law to make a spirit they loved. Whether they called it whiskey, Mountain Dew, or poitín, Irish women were pioneers. They opened customer channels in spite of being targeted by Revenue Police and sold liquor to put food on the table. This popular 1830s ballad says it all: "When I was at home I was merry and frisky, My dad kept a pig and my mother sold whiskey."[34]

As impactful as women were in illicit Irish whiskey, they were even more important on the legitimate side. In the 1800s, women helped build many of the brands still on liquor shelves today.

WOMEN GROWING MAJOR IRISH WHISKEY BRANDS

In 1608 King James I granted Sir Thomas Phillips, a landowner and governor, a license to distill in Atrim, Ireland. This would eventually become Bushmills. More than 130 years later, illicit distillers started making whiskey at the Atrim distillery, developing a product that was smuggled throughout Ireland. Bushmills even bragged about its origins in bootlegging. "One thing has always remained pre-eminently the same, and that is the excellent quality instituted by the bold smuggler band of 1743," according to an 1889 advertisement in the newspaper *Colonies and India*. In 1784 Hugh Anderson officially registered the Old Bushmills Distillery, and the area of smuggled whiskey created legitimate duty-paid product.

Since then, Bushmills Irish Whiskey has been known as Ireland's Protestant whiskey, an accolade given more for its northern proximity than for the company's religious preference. Of all the places in the world to make whiskey, the Old Bushmills Distillery is one of the best spots, located on a small plot of fertile land with great water access. Although it is no longer grown on the property, barley sprouted around the distillery as early as the eleventh century.[35] Bushmills' water source, St. Columb's Rill from the River Bush, runs through the land and is naturally filtered over basalt rock. These God-given circumstances quickly made Bushmills one of the world's best distilleries. In 1860, Dr. Sheridan Muspratt wrote that Bushmills was one of the world's preeminent distilleries and certainly better than the Holland gin distilleries.[36]

As critics like Dr. Muspratt were falling in love with Bushmills, the distillery built its foundation by an equal opportunity ethos that was extremely rare for the time. The distillery employed women and purchased barley from widows. And when owner Patrick Corrigan died in January 1865, he confidently left Bushmills to his "loving" wife, Ellen Jane, who took the Irish whiskey to new heights.

Usually listed in business correspondence as E. J. Corrigan, widow of Patrick Corrigan, Ellen Jane wielded great power. She ran the company with distiller James McColgan, but she handled most of the business affairs while James made the whiskey. When Ellen Jane negotiated the terms of her lease in 1874, she ensured that the Bushmills Distillery property was described in the deed exactly as it was in life: "malthouse . . . a straight line along the old country road 120 feet . . . extending northward behind the distillery 30 feet at each end and 40 feet in center be said measurements more or less."[37] She also made sure nobody used their water, protecting their sole access for a favorable supply.

When Ellen Jane took over, Bushmills was an extremely successful operation that produced around 80,000 gallons of whiskey a year and was already considered "the best Parliamentary whiskey in the north of Ireland," said a major-general in 1830, while the editor of the *Fishing Gazette* said: "We can safely say that Old Bushmills is unquestionably the finest Irish Whiskey we have ever tasted."[38] Ellen Jane turned this already successful distillery into a limited liability company, transforming it from a Northern Ireland distillery into a serious international company that produced 100,000 gallons a year. She helped introduce electricity to the distillery and fought the old guard on past business procedures.

At the time, distillers often sold unaged bulk whiskey to blenders and other distillers in need of supply. This clear liquid would have lacked the nutty and sweeter characteristics that Bushmills delivered after aging in the barrel. Every drop of Bushmills was barrel aged on the property and obtained its rich barrel flavors and color. This move represented a line in the sand with growingly important blenders, who could make or break Irish whiskey brands. By not selling the cheaper product for quick revenue, Ellen Jane helped solidify Bushmills' quality standing.

When she sold Old Bushmills in 1880 for £3,000, Ellen Jane even negotiated a voting spot on the board of the new company. The board seat demonstrates her male peers' respect in a country that typically did not offer women leadership positions or company board seats. During Ellen Jane's tenure as owner and board member, Bushmills grew in size, developing the ability to ferment in 1,200-gallon pots, and in stature, winning awards in Cork, Liverpool, and Paris. Ellen Jane initiated the first steps to making Bushmills the international whiskey powerhouse it is today. And although she was not the distiller, Ellen Jane would have been the chief executive officer by today's corporate hierarchy. The only traces of her Bushmills life are in wills and business correspondence. Not much is known about Ellen Jane Corrigan outside of Bushmills, but every business move she made helped build the company's foundation.

Today Diageo, the world's largest spirits company, owns Bushmills, and the Irish whiskey brand's master blender is Helen Mulholland. Bushmills is also one of the whiskeys most widely enjoyed by women.

Another significant Irish whiskey in today's market, Tullamore Dew, was owned by Mary Anne Daly in the late 1800s. But she essentially turned operations over to her son, Capt. Bernard Daly. The slogan

"Give every man his Dew" was developed during her ownership, and Tullamore became a popular Offaly County distillery. Yet there's little mention of Mary Anne's contributions.

Similar to Tullamore Dew, not much is known about the female owners of the Cassidy Distillery in Monasterevin, the Venice of Ireland. But two women owned the distillery in the late eighteenth century and just before U.S. Prohibition. Perhaps these records were lost or nobody cared to keep them, but Irish women business ownership was not consistently documented. The largest Irish distillery collection and its female association belongs to the Locke family and its women's ownership of the famous Killbeggan Distillery, also known as the Locke Brusna Distillery.

Established in 1757, the Locke's Distillery sat on the Brosna River and was powered by an old watermill. Like Bushmills, Locke encouraged the development of women with forty women employees in October 1874 and female merchants accounting for fifteen out of forty customers in December 1901. The distillery's goodwill toward women came after John Locke bequeathed the business to his wife, Mary Anne, in 1868.

Mary Anne had good "business sense," but left the distilling and technical duties to the company distiller.[39] She was a numbers woman, looking for ways to increase production. Distilling was seasonal, between October and May in Ireland. The summer heat disrupted the malting and fermenting. If a distiller tried to ferment in the heat, a bacterial infestation could ruin an entire batch. So the only way to increase production was to increase the number of final distillations. This meant adding more labor, always checking the mash, and running the pot stills for distillation nearly every week during the busy season. With so much usage, older stills could explode, but that was a risk Mary Anne was willing to take.

Under Mary Anne's leadership, Locke's Distillery went from producing 60,000 gallons a year in the late 1860s to 78,000 gallons a year by the 1870s and 157,000 gallons in 1886.

Always pennywise, Mary Anne increased revenues and avoided as much tax as possible. In one legend, she hid barrels in her home to decrease the inventory count at the distillery. Excise men caught on to this scheme and searched her home, but she had them so well hidden that they never found them.

Mary Anne's greatest contribution to Locke whiskey was establishing trade partnerships with blenders in Belfast and Ireland. When she relinquished control of the distillery to her two sons, John Edward and James Harvey, in the early 1900s, the Locke name equaled the prestige and marketing power of Jim Beam in today's whiskey world. Locke whiskey was smooth, mellow, and downright consistent—three qualities that whiskey drinkers always look for. Mary Anne gave Locke its golden years.

John Edward passed away in 1920 and James Edward seven years later. The distillery was left to Mary Anne's granddaughters, Florence Eccless and Mary Hope Johnston. They were rich heiresses and unfamiliar with the day-to-day distillery happenings. They also inherited the company in dire times.

The U.S. Prohibition, the Irish War of Independence, and the trade war against Great Britain decimated Locke's outreach in the 1920s and 1930s. Bad counterfeit product showed up in the United States, lessening the brand's quality reputation, while other Irish whiskey brands were developing new strategies, even smuggling whiskey into the United States, to make ends meet. Florence and Mary Hope became owners of the distillery at the worst possible time with the absolute worst scenarios against them. After running Locke for two decades, the sisters clearly did not want to carry on the family business. The board voted to sell in 1946.

At the time, there was a trend in Irish whiskey of business-minded foreigners purchasing struggling distillers and selling to English brokers. The short sale of whiskey to London brokers was a way around the 1930s Control of Manufactures Act, which mandated 51 percent Irish ownership of Irish industries. If a distiller was financially hurting, they sold to these brokers but never relinquished control of the company. On the other hand, for Locke, the Irish ownership mandate reduced potential buyers.

When Locke advertised in trade journals for tenders, suitors cared not about the Control of Manufactures Act, as offers trickled in from New York to Switzerland. An employee even tried to bring in angel investors to buy the distillery, but secretary Joseph Cooney could not compete with the £305,000 offer from a rich Swiss group. To get around the 51 percent Irish ownership requirement, the Swiss partnered with the high-ranking Irish senator William Quirke.[40]

Mary Hope Johnston accepted the offer, but the distillery never received the deposit because, as one of the Swiss representatives said, "Deposits always lead to trouble." In this case, the lack of a deposit led to trouble. The Justice Department discovered an alleged proposal of somebody trying to sell 60,000 gallons of whiskey on the English black market at £11 a gallon. As the Justice Department looked into the matter, the culprit was one of the Swiss partners wanting to buy Locke's distillery, indicating they were planning to avoid duty after purchasing Locke's and selling a massive quantity to the English market. They also learned one Swiss man was really Russian and had a fake passport; another was wanted in England for an unknown criminal charge. This, of course, put the magnifying glass on Senator Quirke, who had been in office since 1931 and had been the Leader of the House and Leader of the Opposition. Quirke also owned an auctioneer company and was retained by a "Swiss Syndicate" to help purchase the distillery. His commission was £22,000, and the Swiss leader gave the senator an exquisite gold watch, leaving a deputy to wonder if he had misused his privileges to make the sale happen.

These potential improprieties led to a two-week tribunal on the sale of the Locke Distillery to learn if government officials abused power to influence the sale. Quirke's opponents believed they had caught the popular politician with his hand in the cookie jar. In addition to the connection to a high-powered politician, the Irish government showed concern over the longtime Locke employees and the potential lost excise revenue. "There was further danger that the whiskey might be utilized for blending into an inferior product," said the chairman of the tribunal.

For sure, this was embarrassing for anybody associated with the distillery, but the Tribunal of the High Court could not find enough evidence to imprison anyone. The court decided that the speculation did not incriminate Quirke or the minister. It also scathed the deputy in charge of the investigation for contradicting himself during testimony. The judges said the investigation "was made with a degree of recklessness amounting to complete irresponsibility."

The government officials may have been exonerated, but some believe the Locke scandal was the beginning of the fall of the Irish government in 1947. It was a black eye for all of Ireland, but the Locke Distillery endured negative corporate corruption publicity every day.

It was absolutely devastating and leaves one to wonder if this could have all been avoided if the Locke board had done a better job of vetting potential buyers.

As it turned out, even if the deal had gone through, the Swiss Syndicate would have just sold Locke's matured stocks on the English black market and probably sold off the distillery. A woman known as Mrs. Chapelle represented a London partner to the Swiss and was setting up the distribution channels before the deal went sour. If Locke's deal had been finalized, Mrs. Chapelle and her Swiss friends would have made £660,000. This indelible mark on Locke's legacy could have been avoided if Mrs. Johnston had considered the other offers more seriously.

In his testimony, despite being ordered not to discuss other tenders, the senator let it, "slip" that there was another offer on the table for £225,000 from a "Mr. Murphy." Nobody has confirmed Murphy's identity, but it's likely that it was the same Murphy who ran the Middleton Distillery in Cork County until 1975. There was also the unknown-in-amount offer from within the company. Why didn't the board take less money to keep the brand in Irish hands or those of a Locke worker? If the sisters had cared about their family legacy, they never would have considered the Swiss offer.

In the end, Locke's fate was all about the money. "We came to the decision . . . that we would sell the business to the highest of these two offers," Mrs. Johnston said at the tribunal.

During the tribunal, the distillery operated in limbo with former customers moving on to other brands. "I could not guarantee the fulfillment," Patrick Cooney said. The bad publicity, poor management, lack of capital, and retreating customers led to Locke's demise in 1953. Today Jim Beam owns the Locke brand and has been distilling at the Killbeggan Distillery since 2007.

The original Locke buildings were restored in the 1980s with an emphasis placed on creating a museum that tells the Locke story. Jim Beam plans to continue producing Locke's eight-year-old Irish Single Malt Whiskey, but the Kilbeggan Irish Whiskey is the driver as Locke continues to fill a niche demand, says Stephen Teeling, Jim Beam's global marketing director of Irish whiskey. From the Locke perspective, the facility is merely a museum, a fraction of what it once was and a glimpse of what it could have been.[41]

4

Early Scotch Whisky Women

Like Ireland, Scotland's whisky history personifies the country's heritage. The most concrete evidence of Scotland's whisky beginnings surface in the late fifteenth century. According to the Exchequer Rolls, in 1494 Friar John Cor received eight bolls of malt for the making of aqua vitae by order of the king.[1] Between 1495 and 1512, the Exchequer Rolls and the Accounts of the Lord High Treasurer show nineteen references to aqua vitae and somewhat map out the country's direction for whisky making. On two occasions, according to the Lord High Treasurer's accounts, James IV twice paid a Dundee barber for aqua vitae.[2] Only three names were given in the early rolls and accounts, and they were surgeon barbers. The Scottish king only trusted astute gentlemen for aqua vitae supply, granting a 1506 aqua vitae monopoly to Edinburgh's Guild of Surgeon Barbers: "That na persons man nor woman with this Burgh make nor sell any aqua vitae . . . except the said Masters Brethren and Freemen of the said crafts."[3]

Similar monopolies were granted to other Scottish burghs. Since women were not the primary surgeon barbers, these laws forced them to make aqua vitae illegally. While Scottish authorities were killing "folk medicine" women for owning aqua vitae in fear of witchcraft, "intoxication" aqua vitae women were punished for illegally making or distributing the spirit.

In 1556 Edinburgh authorities ordered Bessie Campbell to cease from vending aqua vitae in the burgh except on market days, based on the 1506 monopoly.[4] On March 20 the town council said "that Bessie Campbell had been complained of for violating these privileges. . . . It will be observed that the prohibition in this judgment against manufacturing whisky was absolute while the prohibition against its sale tacitly permitted 'Bessie' to sell on the market-day."[5] The town council decided that the monopoly for surgeon barbers should not restrict Bessie and traders like her from supplying "country people" living beyond the city limits. This ruling indicates that women could sell the spirit but not make it in Edinburgh.

Scottish medical historians believe surgeon barbers outsourced aqua vitae production, and the monopoly gradually ended, leading to the conclusion that regulating the sale of liquor was not a priority in 1556.[6] So, if nobody really cared, how did Bessie become the first known person arrested for whisky bootlegging?

The surgeon barbers partnered with distillation-savvy churches, and Bessie probably just stole a friar's customer and was turned in. But her circumstances demonstrate the Scottish government's attitude toward women making whisky. In 1579, an Act of Parliament declared that no one except earls, lords, barons, and gentlemen could make brew or sell aqua vitae.[7] But much like the monopolies before, this act was not really enforced.

The Scottish Parliament introduced a malt tax in 1644 and joined England in 1707 to create the United Kingdom. Whisky duty was based on still production in gallons, and in the 1790s England required a rate of £0.09 per gallon. By 1814 stills smaller than 500 gallons were prohibited in the Highlands. These laws forced many distillers into hiding and gave all of Scotland a common enemy—the tax collector. Scottish poet Allan Cunningham wrote in 1840: "Gaugers were . . . so cordially disliked in Scotland, that to cheat them was almost considered a duty."[8]

The cat-and-mouse game between illegal distillers and tax collectors made illicit distiller arrests front-page news. After police busted an illegal distiller, the *Edinburgh Advertiser* wrote on January 23, 1816: "Illicit Distilleries—One of them was a very large scale, the still (entirely of copper) of no less content than sixty gallons, with other utensils corresponding. They also destroyed a great quantity of wash and low wines."

These arrests were also rare. An 1820 Inland Revenue report concluded that illicit distillation made up more than half of the consumed spirits in Scotland.[9] Instead of increasing tax collection efforts, as Great Britain did with Ireland, Scotland decreased its duty by one-quarter in 1824. The goal was to decrease illegal booze and hope that smugglers would pursue legitimate licenses. The plan worked. In Scotland, there were 14,000 prosecutions for illicit distilling and malting in 1823, but that number dropped to 48 in 1856.[10] This also opened the door for one of the greatest women in whisky history.

Johnnie Walker is the world's best-selling blended Scotch whisky. It sells in nearly every chain restaurant and is synonymous with a wide range of quality from the Red Label, full of versatile character, to the Blue Label, an intense multilayered expression of greatness. But before it was the popular brand known today, women ran Johnnie Walker's most-important distillery, Cardow.

In the early 1800s distiller/farmers worked together to conceal their illicit whisky from the excise agents. In Knockando, Helen Cumming lured agents into her Cardow farm and offered them food and shelter. There was no hotel, so they took the offer. While agents ate her bread, Helen hoisted a red flag over the barn to alert other distillers of the agents' arrival. Unfortunately, the agents became aware of her scheme and caught her husband, John, three times in 1816. Despite being fined £200 and £300, the judge let him off with nominal excise duty. Scotland authorities later realized there was just no stopping illicit distillation, so they eased the excise laws, and John Cumming became a "distiller of genuine malt whisky" in 1824. But that didn't mean the government trusted him. An excise officer took residence at the Cardow farm, paying Helen eight shillings a week for bed and board. He kept a close eye on the Cumming operation, making sure every drop of whisky was taxed. There was no way around it—the Cardow farm was making legitimate, tax-paid whisky. It also became the area's most important employer and philanthropic company.[11]

Lewis Cumming took over his father's operation in 1832, but Helen still contributed to Cardow, the "smallest distillery in Scotland." In 1854 Cardow had two employees, a brewer and a maltman, earning £30 and £15.2s.0d, respectively. By 1860, Cardow had a weekly output of 200 gallons of whisky with an annual profit of £50. Helen, often referred to as "Granny Cumming," sold whisky at a shilling a bottle through the kitchen window. When Lewis died in 1872, Helen was ninety-five and encouraged her daughter-in-law, Elizabeth, to take over the business.

Elizabeth was twenty-four years younger than her husband, Lewis, and when he and their five-year old daughter died within three days, she had two small sons and was pregnant with her third. Even then, in a time when women worked on farms, carrying on a business while trying to raise a family would have been difficult. In probate, the distillery was valued at £1,836.18s.8½d, including £593.7s.½d for the distillery equipment alone. Elizabeth could have sold this equipment and the existing whisky stocks to live comfortably. But the daughter of a Knockando farmer chose the harder route and became the new owner of the Cardow farm and distillery. She was much more than a business-woman, however; she also became the moral compass of the area. One legend puts her in the middle of a domestic dispute. She listened to both sides and then walked up to the man and slapped him in the face, ordering him to be a better husband to his wife. The couple never publicly squabbled again. Elizabeth was a "true friend of the poor," giving out loans at zero interest. She was also a brilliant businesswoman.

Under Lewis's leadership, the Cardow distillery underwent a slight overhaul in 1870, but the buildings were still "straggling and primitive," wrote Alfred Barnard in the 1880s. Barnard said the whisky, in contrast, was the "thickest and richest description . . . admirably adapted for blending purposes."[12] Blending whisky was becoming increasingly popular, and Elizabeth saw their well-suited blending whisky losing market share. Her distillery could not keep up with the demand due to its lack of facilities.

In 1884, Elizabeth acquired four acres of land within 300 yards of the old buildings. Over the next year, she built a new distillery, adding massive stone walls and slated roofs. The new facility consisted of a malt bar, barley lofts, malt kiln, malt house, mill room, combined mash house and tunroom with six washbacks, and a still house with two pot stills. The distillery had an eighteen-foot water wheel that powered heavy mill machinery. Instead of carrying both distilleries, Elizabeth sold the Old Cardow Distillery for £120 to William Grant in 1886.

The Old Cardow could produce 20,000 gallons annually; the new distillery boasted a capacity of 60,000 gallons. This increased production only bolstered Elizabeth's already outstanding relationships with her trade agents, especially Charles Mackinlay & Co., which acquired several major traders over a five-year period.

When a longtime blending customer, the Distillers Company Limited of Edinburgh, wanted more whisky, Elizabeth refused to meet their demands, writing on January 4, 1886: "I note what you say about disposing of my Distillery. I could not possibly entertain such an idea, being that I have three sons to provide for. I shall be very glad to guarantee a weekly supply of 600 or 700 gallons to the Distillers Co. I have had several applications from intending purchasers, but it has always been my own opinion that it would not be justice to my family."[13]

Later in 1886, Elizabeth transferred most of her duties to her son, John Fleetwood Cumming, a medical school student, and remained the proprietor and an important figure for the company. But she was stepping away. John immediately faced adversity, agreeing to price cuts with the Mackinlays and steep discounts to a London whisky trader. Demand for blended whisky continued, and in 1892 John could not fill all the orders. "It is impossible to please everyone," he wrote to Mackinlay.[14] Meanwhile, the blenders were growing, inflating prices, and buying up distilleries. One, in particular, was becoming quite powerful.

Listed in a trade press advertisement as "distillers, brokers, blenders, and exporters," John Walker & Sons Limited, later named Johnnie Walker, engaged in negotiations to purchase the Cardow Distillery in 1893. Before she agreed to the deal, Elizabeth negotiated the completion of a fourth warehouse under construction and cottages for the workmen to ensure her long-standing and loyal workers remained employed. She did not want the people working for her to lose their jobs. Elizabeth also ensured that her son, John, was appointed to the Walker's board with a substantial shareholding. With property and whisky stocks valued at £20,500, Johnnie Walker purchased the Cardow distillery in September 1893. The move allowed Johnnie Walker to eliminate the distiller, blender, and sales agents, effectively removing the middlemen and allowing them to begin building the empire it has today.

When Elizabeth Cumming died May 19, 1894, less than a year after she had sold the distillery, her will stated that John would keep the Cardow farm. This required the approval from the Walker board, to which they replied: "By all means respect her wishes as far as possible." John appointed his cousin, Lizzie Cameron, to be the farm overseer, and she lived on the property rent-free. Elizabeth would have approved of this act, as the unwed Lizzie needed a place to live.

Elizabeth's death was felt around the parish, but her family continued giving back, and her lineage remained on the Johnnie Walker board. Her grandson, Sir Ronald Cumming, became chairman of Johnnie Walker and later chairman of Distillers Company Limited. As his brands accounted for 53 percent of the world's Scotch whisky sales in 1965, he was the Bill Gates of the liquor business, commanding authority and greatly impacting the future of the industry. During his reign, nobody was bigger or better at managing spirits brands. Fortunately for Sir Ronald, he did not need to hang a red flag outside the barn like his great-grandmother.

Although she was the most prominent Scotch whisky woman between 1700 and 1890, Elizabeth Cumming was not the only significant woman to inherit a distillery. In fact, Scottish wills and archival records indicate more than thirty women in Scotland managed legitimate distilleries, such as Dalmore, Glenmorangie, and Ardbeg.

WOMEN WILLED DISTILLERIES

More so than any other whisky country, Scotland's regional *terroir* and philosophy give the whisky its aroma, richness, and bold character that cannot be found in any other place in the world. Every region derives much of its flavor from Scotland's longtime use of peat, an energy source from decayed vegetation. Peat, often from 1,000-year-old dead plants, is used in Scotland barbecues and whisky making. It is pulled up from the ground and stacked to dry, forming briquettes similar to charcoal. Whisky makers kiln-dry their barley over peat fires, giving Scotch whisky its distinctive smoke and tangy notes. But each region has a different method for using peat and a different unaltered water source that gives the Islay Lowlands, Islands, and Highlands, as well as their respective subregions, their patented flavor profiles. And within each major whisky-making region, women have been there since the beginning.

The Lowlands is a 100-mile stretch in the southernmost depths of Scotland. Its light whisky is often complex with a trickling of herbal notes. It's also where the earliest Scottish women managed whisky. From 1795 to 1799, Mrs. Whitehead operated the Cowie Distillery, four miles southeast of the town of Stirling. Elizabeth Harvey and a Mrs. Somerville operated the Gallowhill and Linlithgow distilleries in 1798 and 1799. And perhaps the most important Lowlands whisky woman, Jan MacGregor, ran Littlemill for fourteen years. From 1825 to 1839, MacGregor helped refine the Lowlands' triple distillation style.

Most women became legitimate distillery owners after their husbands passed away. On August 12, 1777, Margaret Watt inherited her husband's Lowlands distillery in Canongate, a small district in Edinburgh. Margaret does not appear to have greatly impacted the whisky world, but her name does appear in a dispute with a brewer. Margaret was accused of mistreating a brewer's sister and in turn causing his suicide. She was absolved of any wrongdoing, and her distillery went out of business.

In most cases, women took a male-run distillery and either maintained status quo or improved the situation. The Highlands region, which ranges from the sandstone-laden northern portion to the western foothills, found many women with bequeathed distilleries in the 1800s. Dunmore, Glenturret, Ord, and Stromness were all operated by women in the 1800s.

When Alexander Conachar bequeathed the Eastern Highlands Blair Atholl Distillery to his wife, Elizabeth, in 1858, she inherited a distillery with thirty competitors in Pitlochry, a beautiful small town bordered by the Tay Forest and the Tummel River. The distillery received outside investors, but Elizabeth remained co-owner and carried on as the Blair Athol Distillery. The Conachar name meant something in Pitlochry, whose people thought Mr. Conachar was a descendent of the chivalrous young Conachar, who was an early companion to the Fair Maid of Perth, Catherine Glover, in the novel by Sir Walter Scott.

Elizabeth's title was farmer and distiller, and she was in charge of the daily operations, managing a 130-acre farm with a distillery that employed three boys and three men, including her son, David, the distillery manager. Her daughter, Margaret, was also listed as a distiller for an operation that consisted of copper stills and an iron mash-tun.

Elizabeth died in 1882, and the distillery was sold to Peter Mackenzie. She may not have transformed whisky-making processes, but she kept the Blair Athol Distillery alive long enough to pique interest. Mackenzie, who purchased several other brands, grew the distillery to the point where it could make 1,500 gallons a week. After being purchased and renovated by Arthur Bell in 1933, the distillery became Bell's Blair Athol.

Much like with Elizabeth Conachar, a woman who obviously greatly impacted her distillery but left few traces of her business dealings, not much is known about the McDougall sisters, Margaret and Flora. They inherited their brother's interest in the Ardbeg Distillery in 1853. Flora died in 1857, and according to the 1861 Census, Margaret was living at Ardbeg as a distiller employing fifteen men. She died four years later, and Ardbeg is now owned by Glenmorangie, which was run by a woman in the 1800s.

When William Matheson died in 1862, he left his distillery to his wife, Ann, and their son, John. The mother and son worked well together, creating a new company called John Matheson and Co. to continue the family distillery business. But John became more interested in farming, and the company was dissolved in 1875. Ann continued making whisky under Matheson & Co. with her youngest son, William, working as the distillery manager. However, the distillery was showing signs of wear and tear, and Ann could not afford to modernize facilities. In 1887, she sold the business to the Glenmorangie Distillery Company, a consortium formed by some local businessmen (including her son-in-law, a local banker), but Ann kept a significant shareholding in the new company until her death in 1896.

Throughout their tenures, the McDougalls and the Mathesons had brothers, sons, and longtime employees helping to run the business. There were no legal brawls to indicate families did not get along. This was not always the case.

When somebody inherits a great deal of money, this sometimes leads to jealous family members. It's as true today as it was in 1850, when Dalmore Distillery's Donald Sutherland died.

Dalmore Distillery, the iconic brand in Ross-shire, suffered a great loss when Sutherland passed on.[15] Although he left the distillery in the capable hands of his loving wife, Margaret, Donald could not anticipate the actions of his unsavory brother-in-law or bankrupt father-in-law. The Sutherland name had already suffered ridicule when the first Duke of Sutherland displaced thousands of people for his sheep farms in the 1820s. Donald had at least brought the name back to good esteem by operating a successful distillery.

Dalmore was worth £3,668.0.2d ($250,000 in US dollars), including £1,000 in crops and £400 for existing whisky stock. Margaret's total share of her husband's estate was around £4,000. She could have sold it and moved to the city or hired people to continue the Dalmore name. Instead, her father persuaded Margaret to dip into her inheritance to finance his dream farm. He also demanded that Margaret's brother, Charles, run the distillery despite not having any distiller experience.

Between her father poorly running a money-losing farm and Charles practically giving away whisky, the distillery haemorrhaged money, racking up steep debts shortly after Donald died. The business spiralled into bankruptcy. Dalmore owed area barley farmers significant money, and the whisky's value had plummeted. If found guilty of financial impotence, Margaret could go to debtors' prison.

In court proceedings, Margaret admitted to being strong-armed into heeding her father's wishes even though she gave "considerable personal attention to the business." Margaret claimed Charles entered a partnerlike agreement when finances started disappearing. But her brother denied any such partnership:

> In May 1854 I went to Dalmore to manage the Distillery. . . . I think the Distillery of Dalmore paid the first year. It was a favourable year and I think we made money. I never balanced the Distillery Books. The monies from time to time required for the Stocking of the farm of Parks were taken from the Capital of the Distillery. . . . After the farm of Parks was taken and so much money withdrawn from the business of the Distillery, I became embarrassed in the management of it and the business was completely injured. . . . I can give no account of the money which I sent over from Dalmore to Park of Inshes. . . . To keep a Distillery like Dalmore in proper working position there should be in addition to the Plant and Machinery about 5000 Gallons of manufactured Whiskey always in Stock and about £1000 engaged in Malt and Barley and Cash to nearly £2,000 to carry on the business. . . . We kept a Book called the Barley Book in which was entered the Barley which came into Stock and which was given out to steep. . . . I swear positively that I did not with Mrs Sutherland's money assist in retiring it and it was not renewed so far as I know.[16]

Later interviews would show that Charles understood the banking, debts, loans, and credit affairs of Dalmore. He also sent whisky to Newcastle, England, on consignment instead of selling barrels outright. It also appears he forged Margaret's signature for a Glasgow Bank loan that would have been the equivalent of $37,000. Dalmore's near-fall rested solely on Charles's shoulders. The courts accused the brother of financial incompetence. Before he could be arrested, Charles fled the country.

Meanwhile, Margaret was forced to promise future crops to creditors to avoid debtors' jail, but the sheriff exonerated her and placed the majority of the blame on her brother and father. Still, with her relatives out of the picture, the Dalmore Distillery debts were hers to pay. But this could not be considered Margaret's fault. In this Victorian time, women were not empowered, and a strong-willed father could easily sidestep a daughter's feelings to access her inheritance. She went from being a rich and important woman to a lady stripped of her inheritance by her own father. Judging by her testimony in the bankruptcy proceedings, Margaret appears to be an intelligent woman with an interest in the distilling business.

Nonetheless, the business was in shambles, a mere shell of its former self. The brand still carried significance with Donald's existing whisky stocks being exported to England and Australia. When the Mackenzie brothers purchased the bankrupt brand in 1867, they started keeping track of vintages, and a little of the 1868 was used in the Dalmore 64 Trinitas, a blend of 1868, 1878, 1922, 1926, and 1939 vintages. Only one bottle of the Dalmore 64 Trinitas is still available, and it is for sale at £100,000.

Dalmore's run of bad luck continued long after the Sutherlands. In 1911 a fire destroyed £100,000 in Dalmore whisky. A 1933 fire caused by a butler depleted even more whisky.[17] But not even bankruptcy or two fires could keep Dalmore down. The 1990s was the decade of exposure, and the Dalmore demons were soon forgotten. Today it's one of the world's most prestigious whisky brands with bottles regularly selling for $20,000 or more. The highest recorded Dalmore whisky sale was £175,000 at auction.

The Sutherland name, however, has never recovered. The First Duke of Sutherland 100-foot statue towers over the village of Golspie, a not so subtle reminder that he displaced so many people for sheep farming. To this day, people want to tear it down. In 2010 and 2011, vandals painted graffiti on the statue and sparked a debate among the Scottish diaspora. Dalmore's master distiller, Richard Paterson, believes this is why the Sutherlands are more of an eyesore than a history to the Dalmore brand. "They are just not liked," Paterson told me. "People here do not forget."

5

Early American Women

In the 1700s and 1800s, the voyage to America was nothing glamorous. At every turn a child was looking for his mother or father and begging for food. The ships were overloaded; the available food was vermin ridden, and the water was stagnantly scummy. People died drinking saltwater and urine, and many wasted away into an insane oblivion until somebody threw them off the ship. One remedy on the ship was whiskey. If a woman's child was sick, a mother took a small seashell, filled it with her whiskey, and forced her child to drink the "medicine." Ship crewmen even told Irish women to bring a bottle of whiskey just in case they encountered rough seas to ease the green around the gills.

Using whiskey for medicine continued long after they docked. Much like aqua vitae was used for treatments from the 1500s to 1700s in Europe, whiskey was the chosen remedy for coughs, runny noses, rashes, chills, fevers, and just about everything else. American pregnant women dosed up on whiskey to ease the pain of childbirth and to relax after labor. Early settlers bathed in whiskey to rid their skin of tiny insects and bacteria.[1] People suffering from foot pain rubbed a teaspoon of whiskey on their heels, soles and in between their toes. The 1837 book *The Female's Friend* advised women to use a glass of whiskey to cure the inflammation of the bowels.[2] Doctors prescribed opium mixed with whiskey so that the narcotic was more easily absorbed. They also prescribed it for depression and tuberculosis. For pneumonia, a housewife would administer whiskey with milk and eggs every two hours.

Whiskey was a woman's weapon in the battle against sickness and death. Some doctors theorized women were hypochondriacs and drank whiskey to cure whatever problem they had, but the medical journals of the mid-1800s only reinforced the woman's medicinal eagerness to include whiskey in everyday life. In a published case study, a sixty-five-year-old woman under the care of a Dr. Andrews had a "most interesting" recovery from poisoning after mixing grains in whiskey.[3] The *American Practice* instructed family physicians to use the best whiskey for skin problems, like blisters and ulcerations, because the spirit "affords immediate relief." For curing mosquito venom lodged in the glands, the *St. Louis Medical Journal* wrote: "The reason why whiskey cures is because it enters the blood without chemical decomposition and whenever the whiskey globules comes in contact with venom globules the venom is neutralized and made harmless."[4]

Even religious and lifestyle journals promoted whiskey use for good health. To cure colic, the magazine *Faithful & Christian Instructions* instructed readers to take two ounces of rye whiskey and a pipe full of tobacco. "Put the whiskey in a bottle, then smoke the tobacco and blow the smoke into the bottle, shake it up well and drink it," the magazine offered in 1850.

The *Faithful & Christian Instructions* gave many more whiskey remedy recipes, including for "good Eye Water": "Take four cents worth of white vitriol, four cents worth of prepared spicewort, (calamus root,) four cents worth of cloves, a gill of good whiskey and a gill of water. Make the calamus fine, and mix all together; then use it after it has stood a few hours."[5]

Perhaps the need for medicinal liquor is why women made alcohol at home in the first place. While the men worked on the farm, early American women made butter, clothing, and alcohol. In a 1773 edition of the *Virginia Gazette*, an essayist wrote that liquor-making women "will ripen the seeds of virtue in men."[6] The woman's alcohol skills were so attractive that men paid for women to move to America just to make liquor. Creating what may have been the first true mail-order bride industry, men needed women to make good drinks for health and pleasure. Educated women followed the *English Housewife*'s cookbooks and were reminded of their role in making alcohol by women equal to today's Martha Stewart. In her 1788 *Lady's Complete Guide*, Mary Cole wrote: "The housekeeper cannot be said to be complete in her business, without a competent knowledge in the art of brewing."[7]

Instead of barley, early American women made whiskey with rye, wheat, or corn and distilled it with a pot still similar to those in Ireland. According to her 1818 handwritten recipe, Catherine Spears Frye Carpenter filled a 100-gallon tub with grain bushels, hot water, and meal.

She stirred, sprinkled a handful of meal in the mash, and let it sit for two hours. "Then pour over the mash two gallons of warm water. Put in a half gallon of malt, stir that well into the mash. Then, stir in a half bushel of rye or wheat meal. Stir it well for 15 minutes. Put in another half gallon of malt. Stir it well and very frequently until you can bear your hand in the mash up to your wrist. Then, put in three bushels of cold slop or one gallon of good yeast. Then, fill up with cold water. If you use yeast, put in the cold water first and then the yeast. If you have neither yeast nor slop, put in three peck of beer from the bottom of a tub." Catherine called this her sweet mash recipe.

Her sour mash called for placing six bushels, very hot slop, and corn-meal into the tub. She stirred and sprinkled a little meal over the mash, let it stand for five days, and added three gallons of warm water with one gallon of rye meal and one gallon of malt. "Work it well into the malt and stir for three quarters of an hour. Then, fill the tub half full of Luke warm water. Stir it well and with a fine sieve or otherwise, break all the lumps fine. Then, let it stand three hours then fill up the tub with Luke warm water."[8]

Once distilled, Catherine's sour mash recipe likely immediately entered the market. In the early 1800s, most American whiskey was made for immediate use, and distilleries sold barrels to local markets, taverns, and traders in Pennsylvania, Virginia, Maryland, North Carolina, Tennessee, and Kentucky.

American women made social occasions around whiskey. The *Southern Literary Messenger* instructed young women to use "wassail bowls" for whiskey punches, eggnogs, and apple toddies.[9] In railcars, women drank whiskey before and after supper. Poor women drank whiskey, and so did the rich.

At the Washington DC social scene, Kentucky corn whiskey was winning over politicians, with statesman Henry Clay famously saying he used it to "lubricate the wheels of justice." Virginian Letitia Tyler, a senator's wife and future First Lady to President John Tyler, entertained guests with whiskey, hog meat, cornbread, and friendly conversation.[10]

Whiskey has always been strongly tied to Washington. President George Washington is frequently called America's first distiller, albeit many women likely distilled before he did. And even though he preferred wine for himself, Thomas Jefferson purchased whiskey for his slaves. In fact, one of Jefferson's contracted distillers was a woman. On

May 3, 1783, Jefferson ordered "Rye carrd. to Mrs. Meriwether's to be distilled 119. bush. from Shadwell. 58. bush. from Monticello."[11]

As Jefferson did, plantation owners frequently gave slaves whiskey. After a hard day's work in the corn and cotton fields, their backs sweaty, their muscles aching, slaves walked into their quarters and received a nice glass of corn liquor to celebrate harvest. Catherine Spears Frye Carpenter, the author of the sweet and sour mash recipes, owned nine slaves, and their values ranged from Little Bob at $350 to Bob at $700. In one of the few times they could feel equal to their owners, slaves and masters often drank the same whiskey. Andrew Moss, a slave on a Tennessee plantation, remembered being served corn liquor regularly: "Every night our marster give us one glass o' whiskey. Dat's to keep off disease."[12]

AMERICAN WHISKEY WOMEN AT WAR

During the Revolutionary War, some women cut their hair and pretended to be men to enlist in the Continental army. One woman who signed up to fight the Brits was freckled-faced, hot-tempered Nancy Morgan Hart, who grew corn in her small Georgia estate to make whiskey for family. Her family migrated from Pennsylvania to South Carolina and finally to the banks of the Broad River in Wilkes County, Georgia.

Hart became a formidable frontier nurse, placing bandages on deep cuts, making whiskey cough syrup, and making sure her travel party remained clean of bites and sores. When the war broke out, Nancy stayed behind with her husband and served as a spy for the local militia. She frequently entered a British camp disguised as a man and procured information for Gen. Elijah Clarke to help win the battle of Kettle Creek. One day her husband was working the fields when six Tories appeared on her doorstep demanding food. It would not have been out of character if the cross-eyed, six-foot-tall woman lost her temper at that very moment and taken her chances with a musket and fast legs. But she remained calm, made them a meal, and at some point asked, "Would you boys like some of my homemade corn whiskey?" They said yes.

The Americans loyal to the English liked her whiskey enough to lose track of the situation and become drunk. According to legend, Hart seized their rifles, killing one and wounding another. The others were captured and hung.[13]

While no Revolutionary whiskey woman tale will ever live up to Hart's heroic moment, women and whiskey played a major role in the war. George Washington understood the medicinal value of whiskey: "Lives of our men depends upon the liberal use of spirits in the judgment of the most-skillful physicians."[14] Soldiers were issued a rum or whiskey gill (four ounces) before battle. But Washington's operative phrase was "most-skillful physicians." He and his officers associated women selling liquor with prostitution, a stigma that would follow whiskey women for centuries.

At Valley Forge, from 1777 to February 1778, soldiers consumed 500,000 issued gills of whiskey and rum. They were also going to nearby saloons and deserting their posts. American soldiers were simply consuming too much alcohol.

Contrary to the British punishment of several hundred lashes for drunken incidents, Washington's army only gave up to thirty-nine lashes for unacceptable drunkenness. Seeing his men too frequently drunk, Col. Joseph Reed of Pennsylvania wrote: "To men of this stamp thirty-nine lashes is so contemptible a punishment that it is very frequent for them, in hearing of their comrades, to offer to take as many more for a pint of rum."[15]

Washington restricted whiskey shops near camps from selling to soldiers and restructured liquor licenses to favor men. Since camp whiskey sales and women were often tied to prostitution, which was detrimental to good order and discipline, Washington limited women in the camp to relatives and nurses.

The Continental army medical corps authorized one female nurse for each ten sick or wounded patients. Nurses used whiskey for all the typical prescriptions of the day—dysentery, bug bites, toothaches, stomach pain, etc.—as well as to maintain cleanliness of the surgery area and as an anesthetic, even though whiskey would not become a physician-accepted anesthesia until the mid-1800s.

With a typical wounded patient, the nurse applied dressings over the wound. Then she placed a wet water-and-whiskey cloth on the dressing. This would evaporate inflammation and "reduce the morbid heat."[16] If the patient continued to experience pain, nurses applied a bread-and-milk poultice over the dressings. Whiskey was viewed as an important medicine and was purchased from distillers throughout

Pennsylvania. But as soon as the Revolutionary War was over, the new nation needed to pay its debts.

In 1791, at the suggestion of Secretary of the Treasury Alexander Hamilton, Washington and Congress placed an excise tax on whiskey. If Scottish and Irish history tells governments anything about taxing whiskey, it is that distillers do not care much for paying them. Distilleries in large cities made few objections, and some even saw it as a chance to weed out smaller whiskey producers in the hills. But the whiskey families west of the Allegheny Mountains, making rye whiskey commonly referred to as Monongahela Rye, saw the tax as a personal assault. Whiskey was their drink of choice, medicine, and primary source of trade. They even supplied George Washington with whiskey for his troops, and now this new country wanted to tax them.

When tax collectors showed up in the early summer of 1794, fifty armed men attacked the home of John Neville, regional supervisor for the collection of the federal tax in western Pennsylvania. So-called whiskey rebels also attacked Pittsburgh, Fort Pitt, and destroyed federal property throughout Pennsylvania and Maryland. Making matters worse for the new government, rumors indicated that rebels were negotiating with the English and Spaniards for support. In response, George Washington, a whiskey maker himself, activated 12,950 militiamen from New Jersey, Pennsylvania, Maryland, and Virginia. This was the first time a federal army would be used against U.S. citizens, many of whom fought during the Revolutionary War.

For every woman in western Pennsylvania, standing over her pot still, she had to ask herself: Is this really happening? Are we really waging war over making whiskey? She might have been on her second or third husband after losing previous spouses to illness and war. Now her current husband or male relative was ready to fight for the sake of liberty and, of course, that pesky whiskey tax. What would come of this?

President Washington saw the rebellion as a major blow to the growth of the country, while Thomas Jefferson believed Alexander Hamilton had created the tax to justify a federal army. The 1793 yellow fever outbreak in Philadelphia coincided with Pennsylvania whiskey producers trying to avoid capture. Physicians said whiskey and brandy were the best treatments against the yellow fever, which killed 5,000 people. With Pennsylvania's distilleries in the foothills, hiding from taxmen, physicians were presumably low on whiskey to fight the fever.

In October 1794 the federalized military entered western Pennsylvania and within a month captured 150 rebels. Washington pardoned them, and the violence turned into peaceful protest and vigorous political debate. In 1802 Congress repealed the distilled spirits excise tax, and the federal government relied on import tariffs until the War of 1812. A brief excise tax existed between 1812 and 1817, but distillers could make whiskey tax-free until 1861, the beginning of the Civil War.

Although the woman's contributions to the Whiskey Rebellion are not well documented, the War of 1812 and Civil War greatly needed women making whiskey and treating the wounded with whiskey medicine. During the Civil War, especially, when whiskey-making men enlisted, women were important for the production and distribution of whiskey. Female traders would show up at Southern camps, selling whiskey at a discount. According to Confederate officers, the drinking greatly impacted the Confederates' ability to fight. Confederate general Braxton Bragg said: "We have lost more valuable lives at the hands of whiskey sellers than by the balls of our enemies."[17]

There may have been some medical truth to the general's opinion on whiskey. The nonmedicinal Civil War whiskey recipes included disgusting ingredients like tobacco, bacteria-laden river water, and rattlesnake heads. The Confederate general probably also noticed that many of those liquor-selling women prostituted their bodies. In 1862 Washington DC boasted 450 bordellos with approximately 7,500 full-time prostitutes.

Prostitutes gave the boys a cup of whiskey, which was so bad the soldiers called it "Bust-Head," "Nockum Stiff," "Oh! Be Joyful," "Pop Skull," and "Bark-Juice." In his letters home, Illinois soldier John M. King wrote: "Someone at headquarters got the idea that a quantity of whiskey issued to each man in the evening would be beneficial to the general health of men. There was not enough given each man to make him drunk, but there was just enough to make the men boisterous, excitable, talkative and foolish. After the drinks there was a sort of pandemonium in nearly every tent."[18]

Although one out of every ten Union soldiers came down with a venereal disease, whiskey wasn't just used by women to get men to pull their pants down. Nurse Phoebe Yates Pember regularly treated patients with whiskey and had to fight to keep her whiskey rations. In November 1862 Pember became the Confederate administrator of

Chimborazo Hospital, the largest military hospital to that date, supervising some 15,200 soldiers during her tenure and becoming the first female administrator there. Pember kept a pistol handy to deal with resentful men trying to steal her whiskey. Pember wrote in her memoir, *A Southern Woman's Story*, "Daily inspection . . . convinced me that great evils still existed under my rule, in spite of my zealous care for my patients. For example, the monthly barrel of whiskey which I was entitled to draw still remained at the dispensary under the guardianship of the apothecary and his clerks, and quarts and pints were issued through any order coming from surgeons or their substitutes, so that the contents were apt to be gone long before I was entitled to draw more, and my sick would suffer for want of the stimulant."[19]

Young surgeons attempted to take the whiskey barrel from her room, even though she had her noncommissioned officers' support and the congressional law on her side to be responsible for the whiskey. Pember considered maintaining the whiskey barrel among her most important jobs. "The monthly barrel was an institution and a very important one," Pember wrote. "Indeed, if it is necessary to have a hero for this matter-of-fact narrative the whiskey barrel will have to step forward and make his bow." Whiskey helped keep men alive, and Pember did everything within her power to make sure the "tempted" surgeons never got their hands on it. History remembers Pember as one of America's greatest nurses, and her whiskey trials are a small subchapter to a great career and life.

THE FEMININE TOUCH OF EARLY DISTILLERIES

In the late 1780s Mary and Jacob Beam were a part of the great whiskey migration, when whiskey makers were leaving the Northeast for the hills of North Carolina, Tennessee, Kentucky, and Georgia. In some cases, they were escaping the federal excise taxes and seeking harbor in remote states that would not be accessible to Washington's army. But there were already an estimated 500 distilleries set up in Kentucky at the time of the Whiskey Rebellion, so it is as likely the Beams were just looking for a new home just as others were discovering the American frontier. Nonetheless, the Beams were listed in the first Census of Kentucky as Lincoln County residents.

Between 1792 and 1803, Mary Myers Beam inherited 100 acres from her father, Jost Myers. Instead of bequeathing the property to Mary directly, Jost gave it to her brother, Jacob Myers, who parceled 100 acres to the Beams for £40. This backwards transaction has left Beam descendants baffled. Did Jost Myers purposely leave his daughter out of the inheritance? In the brother Jacob Myer's will, he wanted his niece, Rebecca, to "have nothing out of my estate if she marry Burkett." Did Mary's father dislike Jacob Beam as much as Jacob Meyer apparently disliked Burkett? Could this be an indication of a deep-seated family dispute over the Myers woman marrying a Beam? Whatever happened between the Beam and Myer families, Mary's brother apparently liked her husband, and they were able to begin the Beam bourbon legacy.[20]

Jacob Beam knew the distilling business, but he had no means to buy land. He could farm and mill and was a good whiskey maker, but what good were those skills if he couldn't buy land to plant corn or to set up a still? Without Mary and the awkward inheritance scheme, the world's current best-selling bourbon might never have been.

More than a decade after the Beams were settled, whiskey making had become a strong business with hundreds of distilleries in Kentucky alone. Kentucky whiskey makers were floating barrels down the Ohio River to other river towns, while North Carolina and Northeast distillers sold in the larger nearby towns. American whiskey's only competition was rum. In the Northeast, whiskey sold for 28 to 30 cents a gallon, while West Indies rum cost 200 percent more. However, rum was becoming increasingly popular with fishermen who had access to the spirit, and Congress sought to add a 15 cent duty on all foreign spirits and a 2 cent tax on New England rum to make sure American whiskey remained the preferred drink. The New Englanders, who had developed a powerful import business with West Indies rum distillers, did not appreciate the tariff bill. The congressional enthusiasm toward passing a tariff on rum and not taxing the country's more popular spirit showed how important whiskey had become to the United States by 1828. "Whiskey has come into almost universal use throughout the United States, except those sections of the country which carry on a direct and barter trade with the West Indies," said U.S. Representative Samuel F. Vinton (Ohio–Whig) in 1828.[21]

Congress avoided whiskey taxes for much of the first half of the 1800s, preventing the antagonizing of the whiskey rebels again. This allowed the United States to become a new haven for distilleries and let distillers operate as businesses without paying taxes. The government still kept track of distillers, though, with each state requiring licenses. By 1840 nearly every county in the country had a distillery. Virginia claimed 1,454 distilleries that produced 865,725 gallons of spirits, while Kentucky possessed 889 distilleries that produced more than 1.76 million gallons of spirits a year. With the few exceptions, like location of the current Buffalo Trace Distillery in Frankfort, Kentucky, these distilleries are no more, but the sheer numbers and production show America favored whiskey to other distilled liquids. Even New Jersey boasted 319 distilleries with the capacity of 334,017 gallons of spirits compared to only six licensed breweries. Most of these operations were making whiskey and brandy from small home-based pot stills, but many employed dozens of men and women.

A Distiller Wanted

Wanted at the distillery of the subscriber living at the Salsbury Mills, two miles from Williamsport, a distiller. One who can come well recommended, for sober steady habits, and who understands business well (none else need apply) will meet with constant employment and liberal wages—apply to George Sprecker, Washington County.—*Hagerstown Mail*, Hagerstown Maryland, 1828

American whiskey distillers enjoyed tax-free manufacturing with demand from two major target audiences—the medicinal and thirsty drinkers. This made the distillery business one of the most profitable concepts in the country. Licensed women distillers were right there in the thick of it, too, although they were the minority.

Just as Bushmills' Ellen Jane Corrigan listed herself as "E. J." on contracts, American women often only published initials. Perhaps they feared their land and equipment would be confiscated because some states did not allow women to own property. It makes determining the exact number of women distillers impossible. Thus no true record of American female-owned distilleries will ever be known. Still, in major whiskey-producing states, more than fifty identifiable female names were associated with distilleries.

In 1817, Mily Stone received a "License to work a Still for distilling Spirits from Domestic Materials," signed by Kentucky governor John Adair, a future U.S. attorney general, and John Breckinridge, a former U.S. attorney general. With the license to operate three stills, Mily made 298 gallons a year with a recipe of corn, rye, and a touch of barley.[22]

Virginia's Marion Radford and N. H. Sisson, Pennsylvania's Lavinah Knight and Mitilda Werkheiser, Tennessee's Louisa Nelson and Josephine Brown, and Georgia's Ida Weldon, as well as more than twenty Kentucky women, are listed in tax or state license records from 1880 to 1914.[23]

In most cases, women married into the distilleries. Lidia Rodgers inherited the J. H. Rodgers Distillery in 1890 and closed it, but the *Wine & Spirit Bulletin* indicates she or a relative reopened it on December 1, 1902. When Florence Ellen Wathen married Thomas A. Medley in the early 1900s, she combined two powerful Kentucky bourbon families. The Wathen family began its American whiskey story with Hudson Wathen, who operated distilleries in Maryland. His son, Henry Hudson, moved to Kentucky in 1787, and Florence was born into one of Kentucky's premier whiskey names. She was essentially whiskey royalty, and of all the boys she met, she fell for a young man with a similar whiskey pedigree. Like Florence's ancestors, Thomas Medley's relatives first distilled in Maryland and moved to Kentucky sometime in the 1700s. Thomas became a sixth-generation whiskey maker and was producing some of the best bourbon. They were among the few family-owned distilleries in the 1940s, and today Wathen's bourbon enjoys a respectable following in popular whiskey markets. But there's nothing to indicate that Florence had anything to do with the modern Wathen's bourbon popularity. By all family accounts, Florence just fell in love to merge two whiskey names.

Sometimes the women named the distilleries after themselves. From 1815 to 1848, the Catherine Spears Frye Carpenter Distillery supplied much of Case County, Kentucky, with its sweet and sour mash whiskeys. Angel L. Wood managed a distillery named after herself in the early 1880s. In the early 1900s, the Susan Johnson Distillery had a small mashing capacity, but still produced forty barrels filled with whiskey a year. Perhaps the most important of the female-named distilleries was the Mary Jane Blair Distillery Company. In 1908 Mary Jane Blair's family managed the distillery five months a year, maintaining four warehouses storing 9,000 barrels. After Prohibition, it reopened as the Blair Distilling Company, producing Colonel Blair, Nick Blair, Marion County and Blair's Old Club bourbons.

The Mary Jane Blair Distillery was the most successful woman-owned and operated American distillery, but the only woman-owned

American whiskey still standing is George Dickel. In Tennessee, George A. Dickel created a liquor wholesale company in 1861. Dickel blended and bottled whiskeys, procuring most of his whiskey from the Cascade Distillery in Coffee County, Tennessee. Dickel eventually purchased the distillery, where the Cascade Spring water made beautiful whiskey that developed a large following with Spanish American War soldiers because Dickel opened trade alliances in duty station San Francisco.

In his 1894 will, Dickel instructed his wife to sell the business at the "first favorable opportunity." After he passed away, Augusta Dickel did not listen and maintained her husband's share of the George A. Dickel & Company, but she did not participate in the day-to-day operations. She mostly traveled throughout Europe, likely bringing her whiskey to guests in France. "All the women folks were spoiled like the Devil," said Paul Davis of Augusta's hospitality. "Like all German folks, they were good feeders and always had lots of parties."[24] When Augusta died in 1916, she left her entire estate to brother-in-law V. E. Shwab, who had operational control of the distillery since George's death.

Today George Dickel Tennessee Whiskey is a favored brand among bartenders because of its affordability and quality. Although Augusta was only an owner on paper, she could have sold her shares to a competing whiskey company or interfered with operations. She may not have changed the whiskey world, but Augusta certainly made an impact by not listening to her husband.

BOOTLEGGERS AND MOONSHINERS OF THE 1800S

Women were more influential in the illegal sale of whiskey than the tax-paid versions. In 1799 Marian McLain was a victim of the first wave of American whiskey tax. She was arrested in Georgia for illicit distillation. Two hundred years later, Marian's great-great-grandson Trey Zoeller founded Jefferson's Reserve bourbon.[25] Shortly after Marian's arrest, the whiskey tax was repealed, and the government only initiated a short whiskey tax period during the War of 1812. So women were free to distill as much as they wanted to, tax-free. Then the Civil War broke out, and each side tapped whiskey distillers differently.

For the North, the Internal Revenue Act of 1862 placed excise taxes on liquor, tobacco, playing cards, pool tables, and jewelry. The U.S. federal government whiskey tax started at 20 cents per proof gallon in 1862 and rose to $1.50 per proof gallon and $2 per proof gallons in 1864 and 1865, respectively. The Confederate States commandeered most distillation equipment to melt and use in the war effort.

After the war, tax-avoiding whiskey distillation was as prevalent in the hills of Tennessee, South Carolina, and Kentucky as the streets of New York, Philadelphia, and Baltimore. And women were some of the most notorious.

In 1869, after Irish distillers in Brooklyn refused to pay a revenue agent, twenty policemen showed up but were driven back. A few weeks later, 800 federal troops arrived in the area known as Irishtown. The *New York Herald* reported that the soldiers were met with a powerful force, especially "the Irish women collected at the upper windows . . . particularly violent, and made a bedlam of the place with their ferocious demonstrations." But not even a gang of Irish women could hold off 800 armed men.

After they busted the distillers, revenue officers confiscated whiskey and sold it at auction at $1.95 per gallon. Sometimes the proceeds went to the city, or the revenuers just drank the whiskey. Some confiscated barrels had tax stamps, but the officers argued that the barrel was in its second use of one stamp, a $1,000 first offense fine and imprisonment the second time. For general distillation arrests, the first charge was $100 in New York; the second was a month in jail and $1,000. Jail time didn't detour whiskey makers from perfecting their craft.

In 1876 the commissioner of Internal Revenue said there were 3,000 illicit stills operating in the South, and the government believed it was cheaper for the distillers to be legitimate than illicit. "The average product of illicit distillation costs, through deficient yields, the necessary bribery of attendants, and the expenses of secret and unusual methods of transportation, from two to three times as much as the production of legitimate and legal distillation," said economist David A. Wells in 1876.[26]

From 1876 to 1883, the Internal Revenue seized 6,731 stills and arrested 8,620 people for illicit distillation. Most illicit whiskey makers were, according to the *New York Evening Post* in 1883, "raw-boned, swarthy-looking, muscular, with bronzed skin, piercing coal-black eyes, and long wavy hair that falls in tangled masses over his low forehead." Women moonshiners did not meet these descriptions; they were poor and made whiskey to survive. But they faced the same severe punishment as the men.

When Bettie Smith of Fentress County, Tennessee, was arrested in 1885, the judge asked why she went into the business. "Because I wanted to make whiskey," Bettie said. The woman had been making whiskey since she was sixteen, the same year her father died and her uncle moved to Texas. Somebody had to make the whiskey she loved. Her humorous tone toward the judge shows a woman with no fear.

JUDGE: What did you do with the whiskey you made?
SMITH: Sold it.
JUDGE: Who bought it?
SMITH: Well, judge, it would be rather hard to tell who bought it all. Some time ago, a party of gentlemen came into my neighborhood to hunt deer. The party got out of whiskey, but found it difficult to buy any. After a while, I told a man if he would put his jug down on a dollar and go away, he might, when he came back, find the jug full of whiskey. He did so.
JUDGE: Would you know the man?
SMITH: Oh, yes, sir I recognized him in a moment. You are the man, Judge.[27]

Illegal whiskey makers like Bettie Smith risked everything and were often armed and ready to defend themselves against arrest. The Jasper County, Georgia, women were known to kill anybody who stood in their way, a fatalistic attitude indicative of the female whiskey traders. Mollie Miller ran one of America's bloodiest whiskey-making gangs in Poke County, Tennessee, killing three revenue men and five informants. Twenty-four-year-old Lucy McClure was a darling West Virginian woman great at using a pistol and making moonshine.[28]

Tennessee's Betsy Mullens, who weighed 600 pounds, gave whiskey to anybody with a few coins to rub together. Despite being bedridden, she managed the distribution for all illicit distillers in the Newman's Ridge area. When lawmen threatened to arrest her, she jokingly said, "Carry me out if you can."[29] Mrs. Malinda Shrewsbury, an eighty-year-old moonshiner, operated in the West Virginia mountains, storing thirty barrels of corn liquor a year and maintaining a bank account of $11,000.[30]

In the South, they distilled in the mountains, hidden by miles of trees and brush. The Northern women distilled in the woods, too, but mostly made liquor in the attics or spare bedrooms. Unless they benefited from their own distribution system, women distillers sold to middlemen who transported by horse, rail, or boat.

Many Wild West women packed their satchels with whiskey and filled wagons with barrels. They supplied Native American tribes with "fire water" and helped establish whiskey's importance in the frontier's bartering system.

Although introducing whiskey in Indian Territory was a federal offense, Belle Starr, "the Bandit Queen," stole whiskey from the whites and sold it to Native American tribes. Starr, whose black-and-white photographs show a soft beauty under her hardened exterior, ran the Starr Gang, which specialized in stealing and hiding along the Canadian River. She used her money to bribe officials to release her gang members, and if this didn't work, she batted her long eyelashes and flirted until she got what she wanted. In 1889 unknown gunmen killed the whiskey-trading "Bandit Queen" in an ambush. Most thought it was her third husband who killed her for "whiskey" money.[31]

6

The Targeted and Early Marketers

As America became more entrenched in whiskey, political figures began whispering and then yelling about Temperance. In 1857, Republican Sara T. D. Robinson, wife of Kansas's first governor, described Missourians as "whiskey-drinking, degraded, foul-mouth marauders."[1] Thanks to the support of the likes of Robinson and other big names, the temperance movement was gaining widespread attention along with the suffrage movement. In many Christian women's opinion, whiskey was no longer a medicinal measure; it was evil and destroyed good men. In their 1888 book, *Woman and Temperance* by Frances Elizabeth Willard and Mary Artemisia Lathbury, the Woman's Christian Temperance Union made an effort to show how whiskey was especially infiltrating the youth. A quote their book used from a fourteen-year-old Pennsylvania girl: "Our town is in a dreadful state; it seems as if whiskey almost ran along the streets, and the boys and young men all drink. Yesterday I saw a boy of fifteen lying under a rail fence, dead drunk."

Their Temperance cries caught the attention of the whiskey business, with George Garvin Brown, a young pharmaceutical salesman who founded the Brown-Forman Company, encouraging the industry to practice responsible marketing and not to market to women in the late 1800s. By then, Brown's message may have been too late.

Since doctors still prescribed whiskey to patients, some manufacturers made the strategic decision to market their products for medicinal use. Of course, whiskey reps were just falling in line with other medicines, claiming the whiskey could cure everything from cancer to ugliness. In an 1884 ad for Dr. Bull's Cough Syrup: "That fat man, who the ladies declare is the handsomest man in Washington, used to be an invalid, but he took to hard drinking; not of whiskey, but of Dr. Bull's

Cough Syrup, and now he walks right over the very slenderest dudes, and don't care at all."

The most notorious whiskey maker targeting women, Duffy's Pure Malt Whiskey, purchased full-page advertisements that looked like legitimate newspaper articles. Many believed Duffy's laughable claims, such as a 148-year-old Waco, Texas, man signing an affidavit that Duffy's Pure Malt Whiskey was the only medicine to keep him alive. Duffy's also received endorsements from 116-year-old Frances Burton, 101-year-old Susan Baker, and 84-year-old Annie Rentz. A mother even claimed that Duffy's Pure Malt whiskey saved her 9-year-old daughter's life. The whiskey also helped husbands when their wives were having female issues. "Duffy's Malt has been my steady companion for twenty-five years. I am waiting on myself, and feel that so long as I can get some Duffy's Malt Whiskey I will live twenty-five years longer. It's wonderful the way it keeps my strength and vigor. It keeps my digestion perfect, so that I can get almost anything. Truly Duffy's is a godsend to old people, and I recommend it with all my heart, and will never be without a bottle in the house," said Mrs. Burton of Buffalo, New York, in a *Boston Globe* advertisement.

According to Duffy's, almost every one of the 3,536 centenarians in 1903 drank its whiskey. This pure malt whiskey cured colds, catarrh, consumption, malaria, bronchitis, asthma, and all diseases of the throat and lungs. Dr. Willard H. Morse, who was a world renowned physician, said Duffy's threw off germs and prevented after-effects because it was "chemically pure and contains great medicinal purposes." A so-called Temperance doctor, Dr. T. P. Palmer of Tennessee, even endorsed Duffy's: "I endorse Duffy's Pure Malt Whiskey as a medicine . . . and for nothing else."

For female consumers, the fact that these ads ran in legitimate newspapers probably made them trust Duffy's claims. An 1897 *New York Times* ad: "What is a cough? It is an irritation of the throat and lungs. What causes it? Congestion. Stop the congestion, the irritation ceases, and the cough is cured. . . . Some doctors give cod liver oil, others cough syrups, but the most advanced prescribe stimulants. . . . Duffy's pure malt whiskey contains no deleterious or injurious qualities." A 1903 *Boston Globe* advertisement: "Duffy's Pure Malt Whiskey not only kills germs, but it stimulates the blood, aids digestion, and tones the action of the heart."

These false claims gave the anti-whiskey leagues another like-minded group to join their fight—doctors. After Duffy's published a letter from 106-year-old Nancy Tigue of Lafayette, Indiana, saying she felt like she was not a day over 60 and she could see better than she had in ages, her son made it public that his mother had never even heard of Duffy's. "Mother is almost blind . . . never drank any intoxicating drinks at all," her son, Michael G. Tigue, wrote. Tigue's comments were included in a 1905 *Journal of American Medical Association* article that alarmed the medical community about Duffy's fraudulent testimonials. Although the journal admitted that whiskey had "wonderful virtues," it encouraged doctors to discontinue subscriptions to medical journals carrying Duffy's false testimonials. This was merely a fraction of Duffy's problems. Internal Revenue mandated only medicines containing more than just alcohol were tax-exempt. Duffy's filed for bankruptcy in 1911. Duffy's medicines were lumped with the snake oil salesmen and contributed to the truth-in-advertisement and false claims laws. The brand became the laughingstock of whiskey history, but their gimmicks worked. Women drank Duffy's whiskey to cure everything. Meanwhile, whiskey-packing women of another ilk were targeting men with barrels of whiskey.

As the American settlers traveled west, whiskey became an important currency in the fur trade. Pioneers swapped whiskey for coonskins, buffalo pelts, horses, grease, meat, timber, and just about anything else that was necessary for 1800s living. The spirit's currency status has been well documented, but whiskey-trading stories often omit an important reason whiskey traveled west: sex.[2]

During the Gold Rush, taverns, brothels, and casinos popped up all over California, New Mexico, Colorado, and Wyoming, and they all employed women to "please" men and sell whiskey. In what Wild West historian Cy Martin called the "Great Whore Invasion" of 1850–51,[3] California bar owners ordered prostitutes from Chile, China, Mexico, and France. More than 2,000 women arrived in San Francisco in 1850 via New York, New Orleans, Paris, Marseilles, South America, Australia, Asia, and the Pacific Islands. An August 1850 *New York Herald* article: "A speculator of Paris has just arranged the departure of two hundred women for California, and these whores of our harems of Paris, Rouen, Lyons, and Havre, will sail for the gold country within a fortnight. Be it understood that these beauties are not diamonds of the first water. But no matter, they leave France with a strong resolution to be good girls. I hope they will stick with it."

Once they arrived at their employer, depending on the establishment, the women became waitresses to serve prospectors working the streams and mines with gold to burn. The average waitress/prostitute earned $15 to $25 a week, but she also made a commission on selling whiskey. At San Francisco's Bella Union, thirty "pretty waiter girls" worked in the upper and lower sections of the casino and encouraged men to buy liquor, while arousing them. The more they drank, the more she earned. One French prostitute earned $50,000 in a year, likely thanks to her ability to keep men drinking. Collectively, the income of these women probably exceeded many states' gross revenue.[4]

In 1859 Dr. William Sanger surveyed 2,000 "working" women and learned that "destitution" and "inclination" were the top two reasons they joined the profession—a near even split between women forced and wanting to sell their bodies for sex. "Drink, and the desire to drink" was number four, indicating that about 10 percent of prostitutes performed sexual duties to feed their alcohol addiction. Ninety-nine percent of the surveyed women said they consumed intoxicating drinks before performing acts with customers, but their bosses typically did not permit drunkenness.

Sanger learned some tribes forced Native American women into prostitution to earn whiskey wages. "To this degraded condition the women seem perfectly reconciled, and expertness at the assigned employment is a source of pride to them," Sanger wrote. As degrading as prostitution was to the woman, Sanger could not deny the money. In 1857 New York, sex-hungry men spent more than $7 million at brothels or "nearly as much as the annual municipal expenditure of New York City." Visitors spent nearly as much on wine and liquor, $2.08 million, as they did on the prostitutes, $3.1 million.[5]

The liquor and prostitution business rivaled any moneymaking venture of its time. If a tavern did not offer sexual services, it stood to lose customers. The sexed-up taverns were becoming so common that this led to Sanger polling every major city about its prostitution levels. Many mayors were in denial or unwilling to admit prostitution publicly. "We have no houses of ill fame in our city; none of assignation; there are no public prostitutes," wrote Newark, New Jersey, mayor H. J. Poinier in 1856. The Newark mayor's sentiment was the general "hear no evil, see no evil" consensus. Politicians gained significant excise tax revenue from brothels and were frequent customers.

After the Civil War, the law seemed more concerned over whiskey taxes than prostitution. If taxes were not paid, local excise departments would break into the brothel and revoke its license to sell liquor—the strictest penalty that could be imposed on the proprietors, and the brothels went out of business. Without liquor, men did not walk into sexed-up saloons. This kept tavern owners paying the taxes, but many tried to keep all the money they could for themselves and their girls.

Brothel boat owner Nancy Boggs managed to evade taxes with her whiskey scow for most of her career as a madam. Arrested in 1877 for running a bawdy house, Boggs escaped this charge and suffered a $100 fine in 1880 for the same offense. However, these bawdy house charges were not really what concerned Portland and East Portland; they wanted their tax share of the liquor sales.

To avoid liquor taxes on her moving bordello, Boggs floated up and down the Willamette River between Portland and East Portland. Small canoes went to the city docks to pick up customers, mostly lumberjacks and prospectors with money to spend. Boggs kept a small double-barrel pistol in her garter hose and pulled it out any time a mean fella refused to pay her women for services rendered. The ladies serviced hundreds of men a month, filling their gullets with whiskey, with little risk of getting caught. Other brothels existed in Portland, but Boggs's riverboat had to be the most profitable. Her lack of taxes helped her pay the women better wages and keep profits for herself.

Whenever the law came close to her docked boat, she pulled up anchor and drifted to another shore away from their reach and jurisdiction. The two Portlands hated one another, creating little legal cooperation. This run back-and-forth method worked until 1882, when the two towns set aside their differences with the common goal of taking down the prostitution ship in Oregon's first interagency whiskey sting. It also became one of the first major steps of cooperation between East Portland and Portland. The two eventually merged into one city in 1891.

Nancy fought the cops off with a high-pressured hose, but they returned at nightfall and cut her anchor. The ship sailed adrift, heading toward the Pacific Ocean until it hung up along the shoreline near Linnton, Oregon. The boat sprung a leak. The girls' combs, dresses, and all that precious whiskey would have fallen into the river if a steamboat captain had not saved them and the boat. That event was apparently a moment of clarity for the madam. The crafty Nancy Boggs realized she could not outrun the two Portlands forever, so she took her prostitutes and whiskey to the land and started paying taxes. The law never pursued her again, even though she continued running a prostitution ring.[6]

Around the time of Boggs's great escape, towns across the country were filled with wives losing husbands to liquor and brothels. The country's mood toward the saloon became a "social evil" where wild women forced men into intoxication and adultery. The likes of the Boggs's bordello and the $50,000 French prostitute gave the temperance movement the platform it needed to garner serious respect. At the same time, it was much easier for society to blame the women, often forced sex slaves, and the whiskey than to hold the men accountable for their actions. When answering to their wives for their infidelity, the men would say, "The whiskey made me do it."

This growing concern led to cities cracking down on prostitution and passing prohibitive liquor laws. In 1892 the San Francisco City Council passed a law prohibiting liquor sales in theaters, effectively destroying Bella Union's ability to attract clientele. Newspapers ran front-page editorials, calling prostitution a "parent of evil. It is not only a social evil, it is a sanitary evil, and is even becoming a political evil."[7] Using Nancy Boggs as an example of a "flesh peddler" in the early 1900s, Portland mayor Doc Harry Lane pursued prostitution reform, and all Portland buildings were required to have a "tin plate" plaque indicating ownership in front of their businesses. The best governmental fight against prostitution was temperance.

Stopping the saloons and the ladies of the night became the battle cry for the temperance movement. It was also a marketing point for the suffrage movement, with the *Woman's Journal* calling woman suffrage a cure for prostitution. Legislators attempted bans on gambling, lotteries, and increased the policing of prostitution, but the steady drum beat to illegalize liquor was often fueled by the studies of intemperance. In the 1840 book *Magdalenism: An Inquiry into the Extent, Causes, and Consequences of Prostitution in Edinburgh*, Dr. William Tait wrote: "Many of the unhappy beings pass days without tasting victuals, every penny which they can procure being spent on ardent spirits. Their desire for intoxicating liquors is, in many instances, much more powerful than that for food, and is always first indulged. Some might live a week without participating in an ordinary meal, but none pass a day without drinking whiskey."[8]

Sex sold more liquor than any other American tavern in the 1800s. For as unsavory, unethical, and downright disgusting as many of these establishments were, bordellos created a demand for whiskey that made the spirit an important American currency and commodity. New York prostitutes sold more liquor in 1847 than the net revenues of Indiana, Illinois, Iowa, and Missouri combined.[9] Women of the oldest profession were arguably the most important whiskey retailers in the 1800s, but their unsavory nature tarnished the whiskey industry and forced cities to ban women from taverns.

7

Temperance Women

The debauchery of the saloon gave many women and religious figures sincere motivation to stop the flow of alcohol. But temperance was not popular, and it needed a powerful figure to lead the initial charge. Nearly 100 years before U.S. Prohibition, an Irish priest created the strongest foundation for the temperance movement. At a small gathering in 1838, the Very Reverend Theobald Mathew signed a temperance pledge and said, "Gentlemen, if only one poor soul can be rescued from the intemperance and destruction, it will be doing a noble act and adding to the glory of God." From that day on, Mathew dedicated his life to temperance. He called the Irish's drunkenness the root of his country's problems and worked to rid Ireland of alcoholism.

Mathew held temperance meetings in Cork twice a week, where he signed 156,000 persons to pledge temperance from April 10 to December 31, 1838. The next year, he visited Limerick and pledged 150,000 in four days. He earned similar results in Waterford, Lismore, Ennis, Conmel, Cashel, and Galway, as well as thousands in England and Scotland. Mathew's labors led to the disappearance of drinking houses, as well as distillers pitching their illicit stills into bog pools and women dragging their husbands to his events. Called the "Great Apostle of Temperance," Mathew even negotiated a peace between rival families who hated one another and found a common ground with Protestants who took arms against Catholics.[1] In a rather cynical view, the *New Yorker* wrote in 1840 that Mathew was so successful simply because neighbors witnessed the improved health of those taking the pledge. Other critics said all previous temperance movements had failed and gave Mathew little chance of succeeding. But Mathew's 1840s trip to America set the Volstead Act of 1919 in motion.

Throughout the United States, temperance organizations existed. In the 1830s, about one-tenth of the U.S. population belonged to a temperance society. The Daughters of Temperance maintained about 30,000 members. But the American temperance movement lacked a consistent fundamental message, and many temperance advocates publicly blamed the Irish for the new country's drinking problem. Newspaper ads looking for workers added the caveat that Irishmen "need not apply" because of the fear they would show up drunk, if they showed up at all.[2] The fact that Father Mathew could debunk the drunken Paddy stereotype gave so many sober Irish immigrants hope. And his tactics of love meant so much to a country that hoped to avoid bloodshed. Said New York mayor Caleb Smith Woodhull to the reverend: "Your victories are not made up of the dead and dying left behind in your path, but to living thousands, whom you have rescued from a fate more remorseless than the conqueror's march. Your trophies are seen in the smiling faces and happy homes of the countless multitudes whom you have won from the deepest abyss of wretchedness and despair."[3]

Congress invited Mathew to sit in a December 1849 session. Mathew was so revered that he even gained respect from Congressman Henry Clay, who owned a distillery in Kentucky and whose constituents would be economically hurt if Mathew's ideals came to fruition. Mathew, who also spoke frequently against slavery, was a man who appealed to many. Clay said Mathew "has achieved a great social revolution—a revolution in which there has been no blood shed, no desolation inflicted, no tears of widows and orphans extracted."[4]

Mathew visited 25 states, 300 cities, and pledged 600,000 people to temperance. He drew people with a simple message: "Come, my friends, there is room, plenty. I promise you, you will not regret this step. It will be the foundation of your happiness here, and your eternal happiness hereafter." His words make as much sense today as they did then. "There are people in this world, who if they have no real troubles to vex them, will create troubles for themselves by their own folly," Mathew said in Sand Springs, Arkansas. His enthusiasm motivated iconic Americans and future temperance leaders.

Frederick Douglass took the pledge and wrote to American abolitionist William Lloyd Garrison when he become number 5,487,496 of Mathew's "temperance children." When Mathew reached 5.8 million pledges worldwide, the *Weekly Wisconsin* wrote, "Who can estimate the good which he has done!" His pledges included millions of women, future members of the Women Christian Temperance Union, members of the Protestant American Temperance Union, and the founding members of several Catholic total-abstinence societies. Mathew became one of the first public figures to endorse Prohibition: "The Principle of Prohibition seems to me the only safe and certain remedy for the evils of intemperance. This opinion has been strengthened by the hard labor of more than twenty years in the temperance cause," Mathew wrote.

Mathew tugged on the heart of every woman who had lost her man to drink. Lady Emeline Stuart Hartley wrote of his American visit: "More hallowed far thy deathless titles are, Friend of mankind—O sainted Theobald! . . . A peace-apostle 'twixt two worlds of peace, Thine is the triumph that can never cease! . . . Echoes man's voice of praise and reverence now, Where raged the battle thunder's deafening roar; Thrill, softly thrill, though gracious western air, With all the meek omnipotence of prayer."[5]

After his passing in 1850, Mathew's beliefs remained alive in the American temperance movement. Women realized sobbing about their drunken husbands would never change intemperance. They needed to take action. Although they could not vote, women pursued legal efforts to stop intoxicating liquors.

In 1850 1,500 Buffalo, New York, women petitioned the Common Council to not license the sale of intoxicating drinks.[6] The next year a petition with 2,200 signatures went before the New York Legislature. In Oswego County, New York, women appeared before a grand jury to complain about liquor dealers violating laws. The president of the Woman's New York Temperance Society, Elizabeth Cady Stanton, pressed the state legislature to allow women divorces from drunken husbands, arguing that the failed marriage was directly tied to the drinking. The *Troy Journal* praised the idea, but it drew harsh criticism from many in the male temperance movement. Reverend Dr. Mandeville denounced the Women's New York Temperance Society, saying its members were a "hybrid species, half man and half woman belonging to neither sex." He said they handled women's rights without gloves. This type of criticism only seemed to strengthen the women's resolve.

In the greatest to-date victory for temperance, the "Maine Liquor Law" banned alcohol for the state in 1851. Citing as precedence, Maine legislators noted Muhammad prohibited intoxicating liquors; an ancient German tribe banned wine in their territory; the Society of Friends disowned members in the liquor business; and Congress enacted the 1802 Indian tribal Prohibition. "These are a few of the precedents for the Prohibitory Liquor Laws of Maine. . . . A careful examination of them will lead to the conclusion that they are all not only the same in principle, but in purpose or design."[7]

Before the state's Prohibition became law, the Maine legislature was inundated with petitions year after year, including one petition that was fifty-nine feet long with 3,800 signatures. Even though they could not vote, women used all their legal power to stop their husbands from shaming families with alcohol. They also sought equal rights.

Salem, Ohio, women procured 7,901 signatures for an equal rights petition and 2,100 for the right of suffrage. Even if they did not get exactly what they wanted, their efforts were making an impact. In 1857 the Ohio Legislature passed a bill that stated no married man shall dispose of any personal property without having first obtained the consent of his wife and that she shall be entitled to his wages if he deserts the family.[8]

In every state, women pressed legislators with petitions and sob stories. After one mother lost her son in a shooting with drunks, she wrote in the *Union Signal*, "I'd rather have the sweet memory of my pure temperate boy to cherish, than to have a living son who would touch intoxicants or advocate their use. My sorrow cannot be half so bitter as the sorrow of a drunkard's mother."[9] Temperance women linked whiskey use with robberies, infertility, murders, petty crimes, vagrancy, and debauchery.

The Woman's Temperance Crusade closed more than 30,000 saloons with public prayer in the 1870s. Still, their voices were not as strong as if they were male. They could not vote, and women seeking voting rights saw an opportunity to pool the temperance efforts with the suffrage movement.

Temperance women wanted reform in alcohol, slavery, and suffrage. Strong activists, such as Elizabeth Cady Stanton and Susan B. Anthony, made it their life's mission to pursue women's rights. They were also lobbying married women to possess their own wages and guardianship of children. The mere audacity to seek such rights put these women under incredible public scrutiny. One Rochester, New York, minister said: "Miss Anthony, you are too fine a physical specimen of woman to be doing such work as this. You ought to marry and have children." The reformer simply replied: "I think it a much wiser thing to secure for the thousands of mothers in this State the legal control of the children they now have, than to bring others into the world who would not belong to me after they were born."[10]

By the time the Woman's Christian Temperance Union (WCTU) was created in 1874, the country's mood toward Prohibition and women's rights was changing. Anthony and Stanton had already impacted significant women's right changes. In 1848, the New York State Legislature passed the Married Women's Property Act, which allowed married women to receive property for their own use and it did not belong to their husbands: "The real and personal property of any female who may hereafter marry, and which she shall own at the time of marriage, and the rents issues and profits thereof shall not be subject to the disposal of her husband, nor be liable for his debts, and shall continue her sole and separate property, as if she were a single female."

The Married Women's Property Act became the standard for states seeking to implement similar laws. Anthony and Stanton's National Woman Suffrage Association enjoyed a powerful following and the attention of Congress, state legislators, and even the Supreme Court. Anthony empowered women to stand up and fight for their beliefs, leading to women zealously fighting for temperance.

Women's voices became so loud that some lawmakers made Prohibition and suffrage their main platform. In his October 1874 speech, "Prohibition and Woman Suffrage," the Honorable Albert Williams blamed the Republicans and Democrats for dishonoring the Constitution. "Indeed, when a party becomes so corrupt that it can only be preserved in whiskey better let it rot," Williams told the Prohibition Reform Party.[11]

With the help of Prohibition parties and other like-minded organizations, including the Anti-Saloon League and the National Intercollegiate Prohibition Association, the WCTU became the thought leader for Prohibition. The organization admitted only women, turned conservatives into progressives, and built an army of 150,000 women with the motto of "Do everything." The WCTU managed to influence nearly every American school to add temperance education, while influencing laws in every level of government. They lobbied and won dry counties in Kentucky, Arkansas, and Texas—three significant whiskey-making states. They were even in the White House, with President Rutherford B. Hayes's wife, "Lemonade Lucy," belonging to the temperance movement.

Not even the First Lady, however, could match the force of WCTU's greatest asset—a Kentucky-born woman with a checkered family past. Carrie Nation, a devout Christian, came from a family riddled with mental illness and alcoholism. Her mother believed she was Queen Victoria. She was widowed at the age of twenty-four when her first husband, Dr. Charles Gloyd, drank himself to death. She later married David Nation, a lawyer and preacher, and moved to Missouri. When she became ill, she remained in bed and studied the Bible for six years, healing past wounds with God's words.

Nation became famous for cracking saloon windows with rocks, opening barrels, and breaking down doors with her hatchet and doing whatever it took to stop drinking—all in the name of God. Nation wrote: "In all ages it has been true that God's messengers have been unpopular because they are sent to combat the prevailing evils of their day and generation. Therefore, Christ said: 'Blessed are ye when men shall revile you, and persecute you, and say all manner of evil against you, falsely, for My sake. Rejoice and be exceeding glad for great is your reward, for so persecuted they the prophets before you' (Matt. 5:11, 12). . . . I represent the distracted, suffering, loving motherhood of the World. Who, becoming aroused with a righteous fury rebelled at this torture." Nation endured severe public ridicule, death threats, and significant legal troubles for her actions, but nothing would stop her.

In February 1901 at Topeka, Kansas, Nation was led by a woman who pretended to be her friend but "was a spy and traitor." When she realized the temperance imposter was just wasting her time, a boy showed her the tavern she wanted to hatchet. Once there, Nation lifted her hatchet to smash the "Senate" saloon door, but a woman and man grabbed it. "The bartender ran towards me with a yell," Nation wrote, "wrenched my hatchet out of my hand and shot off his pistol toward the ceiling; he then ran out of the back door, and I got another hatchet. . . . I ran behind the bar, smashed the mirror and all the bottles under it; picked up the cash register, threw it down; then broke the faucets of the refrigerator, opened the door and cut the rubber tubes that connected the beer. It began to fly all over the house."[12] When the cops showed up to arrest Nation, beer dripped from her clothes. She faced a $100 fine and a "conspiracy" to keep her behind bars, but she never stayed for long.

Nation went from town to town, often bringing women hatcheters. Because the temperance women believed the saloons were "murdering their sons," Nation saw many volunteers, but they didn't always bring hatchets.[13] In a gang of four women, including a Catholic nun, Mrs. Julia Evans brought a hunk of iron and smashed the bar to pieces, while Nation threatened to hatchet the bartender if he ran toward her. They were all arrested.

Nation did not always use violence, likely because she was running out of bail money. At a hotel in Racine, Wisconsin, she told a packed audience that God cursed the liquor traffic, "the bitterest foe to humanity. This traffic is like a burglar," but it causes more tears and destroys more homes. For the play *Ten Nights in a Barroom* at the Frederick, Maryland, Opera House, Nation appeared in the second act for a long liquor lecture and sold hatchets. When passing through Elyria, Ohio, she saw old veterans gathered in front of a cigar store playing cards. Carrie stopped at the store and yelled, "Gambling! Gambling! Get the police!" One of the men told the local newspaper, "I do not know who this woman is, but if she has any family she ought to be home looking after them instead of making herself obnoxious in cigar stores."[14] While many dismissed Carrie Nation, her fans adored her. C. Butler-Andrews wrote of Carrie Nation, "Proving that woman's moral force; Like man's, is held, as last resource, By sword or hatchet."[15] Carrie Chew Sneddon's poem added to Butler-Andrews's sentiment: "Oh, woman, armed with one little hatchet; Fighting for justice and right; And with your brave mother courage; Knowing your cause was right."[16]

This large following gave Carrie Nation the pulpit to tear down all alcohol, but she found whiskey especially despicable for its medicinal marketing. "Whiskey . . . never introduced their products by reason or arguments, they never appeal to thought, but suggestion or temptation, and as oft as the eye is lifted, as one walks up the streets of our cities there are hundreds of advertisements to meet the gaze; most every one has a false basis," Nation wrote in her memoirs. Nation and the WCTU's claims against liquor worked. Before she died of what was thought to be syphilis in 1911, Nation had converted countless women into courageous hatchet carriers eager to split open whiskey barrels for the futures of their husbands and sons. She also fueled a movement that needed her odd ways to survive.

The WCTU and other temperance lobbies maintained a captivated audience after Nation's death, winning over politicians like Minnesota congressman Andrew John Volstead. Meanwhile, World War I loomed, and the brewers and distillers were fighting each other. Brewers tried to separate themselves from distilled spirits, with the U.S. Brewers Association saying beer was more like wine because it was light and soft. When the two alcohol sects decided to part ways in their stance against Prohibition, their opponents caught the two groups in a vulnerable position, and the federal government needed the authority to manage food and fuel pricing for World War I.

With the passage of the Lever Act of 1917, also known as the Food and Fuel Control Act, the government gained control over the food and fuel industries. This authorized President Woodrow Wilson to regulate output, distribution, and prices of food and fuel. In a late amendment to the act, Congress wrote that foodstuffs were absolutely prohibited in alcohol production. The act made a distinction between hard liquor and beer, a welcomed addition for the brewers, since hard spirits became forbidden.

This striking blow to alcohol manufacturers served as a huge victory for the temperance women. In November 1917 New Mexico's first lady, Mrs. W. E. Lindsey, said, "Aside from the long list of awful tragedies following in the wake of the liquor traffic, the economic waste is too great to be tolerated at this time. With so many people of the allied nations to the door of starvation, it would be criminal ingratitude for us to continue the manufacture of whiskey."[17] This was the temperance movement's marketing message: use the whiskey grain for food to feed the poor. Even though the alcohol grains made up 2 percent of the country's total raw material, or foodstuffs, the argument was quite convincing.

By 1918, twenty-seven states adopted Prohibition, and with World War I, the temperance camp made connections between the country's war enemy, the Germans, and America's top brewers, all Germans. Pabst, Schlitz, Blatz, and Miller were "German enemies, the most treacherous."[18] The Anti-Saloon League, WCTU, and all the other Prohibitionists reveled in the momentum of a national prohibition. When the lead lawyer of the distillers was asked what he thought about the Prohibition potential, he said, "This Prohibition is going through. It is like a great prairie fire sweeping across the country and cannot be stopped!"[19]

Congress passed the War Prohibition Act in November 1918 and created a more permanent solution in the Volstead Act in October 1919. Volstead's historic legislation defined the Prohibition features of the Eighteenth Amendment, eliminating the legal sale and production of alcoholic beverages. On January 29, 1920, Secretary of State Frank L. Polk signed the proclamation declaring the ratification of the Eighteenth Amendment. The pen he used to sign the document was given to the WCTU president. "No greater piece of constructive legislation was ever added to the Constitution of the United States than that embodied in the Eighteenth Amendment. Perhaps no amendment to the Constitution was ever so thoroughly considered, from so many angles, as was the Eighteenth Amendment," said WCTU member Deborah Knox Livingston.[20]

Thousands of women didn't get the memo. The Prohibition era alcohol stories are filled with mobsters, hillbilly moonshiners, and the occasional lady hiding a flask in her garter belt. Women meant so much more to the underground booze movement. In a time when their gender essentially made America dry, whiskey women kept the country wet.

8

Women Moonshiners and Bootleggers in Prohibition

Women running whiskey companies in Ireland, Scotland, and America were devastated by Prohibition. Their largest market was taken from them. Kentucky's Agnes Brown managed the Old Prentice Distillery (now Four Roses) after her brother's death and put operations on hiatus during Prohibition, while Mary T. Willett, cofounder of the Willett Distilling Company, waited until after Prohibition to start her family's small operation. Mrs. Camilla Bell, one of the largest shareholders in Arthur Bell & Sons Scotch Whisky, would have to focus on European markets to make up for a lack of U.S. sales. But the biggest blow may have been to the U.S. citizen.

In 1919, the *Boston Globe* reported that the United States might lose $384 million a year in taxes with 60 million whiskey gallons aging in warehouses and $8 million tied up in Boston's unsold wholesale system.[1] Since doctors could still prescribe whiskey for "medicinal purposes," the tax-stamped whiskey would just flow through the appropriate channels for the medicinal market. Female-owned Waterfill & Frazier sold 176 barrels of 1914 whiskey to W. L. Weller & Sons for $10,000.

Americans needing a drink were suddenly sick all the time, but not everybody wanted to make a doctor's appointment for a dram. One legitimate distiller saw the potential in this new Prohibited market. Instead of going underground and making whiskey illegally and making minimal revenue selling existing whiskey stocks, Mary Dowling decided to pack up the family's Waterfill & Frazier Distiller and move it to Mexico.

In operation since 1810, Waterfill & Frazier maintained a successful bourbon distillery in Kentucky with about $100,000 in capital, a small column still, and a pot still. Mary and her brothers, who also ran department stores throughout Kentucky, worked with members of the Beam family to move operations to Juárez, a border town bumping up to El Paso. They partnered with the town's future mayor and successful entrepreneur, Antonio J. Bermudez, and received significant financial investment from an unknown American businessman, who no doubt wanted to smuggle Waterfill & Frazier whiskey into the United States.

With the Volstead Act underway, the Dowlings began doing business as the D. W. Distillery. Since they made alcohol on Mexican soil, the Dowlings broke no laws. If somebody purchased D. W. Distillery whiskey and walked it across the border, the Dowlings could not have been held accountable. They were just the whiskey makers.[2]

Mary Dowling was certainly clever in her way around Prohibition, but most women could not afford to pack up and move to another country. They just broke the law at home, a time-honored tradition for moonshiners.

Women stood to make more money with the legitimate tax-paying distiller competition out of the way, but they also took greater chances as the government deployed 4,500 Revenue agents throughout the United States. When Revenue agents captured the notorious ninety-two-year-old Margaret Connelly of Clarksville, Arkansas, in 1920, the sassy moonshiner blamed her boys. "We wouldn't have been ketched," Connelly said, "if my 'old man' hadn't died, and I had to depend on the boy to help me. Them there revenuers think they are pretty smart, but I could of got 'em as they came up the trail."[3] With her husband alive, Connelly stood watch with a loaded shotgun as he made the product. The elderly woman was not the first or the last to be arrested during Prohibition.

When women moonshiners were arrested at the start of Prohibition, the story was front-page news, as if the newspapermen were proud their local ladies practiced the art of distillation. On January 3, 1920, a Cleveland woman was thought to be the first female arrested after the Volstead Act. Kenosha's Mary Kajyde was not far behind when caught selling booze on November 24, 1920.[4] Prohibition-era court records indicate women consistently received lesser sentences than men. Authorities arrested a Turkish woman eighteen times for making moonshine from potatoes. Her average term ranged anywhere from thirty to ninety days. Mississippi's Sarah Strong was the state's first "white woman moonshiner," according to several newspaper accounts in 1923, and she only served a month in jail.[5] Moonshiner Mollie Turner of London, Kentucky, became the Blue Grass State's first Prohibition-era woman to serve time in March 1922, spending three months in the slammer.[6] The likely reason for these reduced sentences was that judges understood a mother's burden.

When Columbus, Ohio, police arrived at Mrs. Mary Darquinio's home, they found four curly-haired boys deserted by their father. Darquinio attempted to support herself and children through moonshining. Arrested in November 1924, her still was seized and she received a $1,000 fine, one of the largest fines given to a woman that year. Her boys went to their neighbors while Darquinio served jail time. Ohio governor Vic Donahey commuted her sentence to five days.[7]

Politicians interfering with female punishment was not unusual. In the final year of his term, President Warren G. Harding pardoned bootlegger Anna Hozer of Muskegon, Michigan, because she had eleven children with no father—an unfortunate commonality among many illicit whiskey makers.[8]

Betty Mangrum of Jingo, Tennessee, tried to take most of the blame so her teenage son would avoid jail. In her defense, she said making whiskey was the only way she could make money. "That poor old country won't afford any other means of making a living," Mangrum told a jury in 1924.[9]

Mary Crayton, a Pennsylvania woman, told the judge she made whiskey to make payments on the farm. Although the politicians often fell sucker for the occasional sob story, Chicago judge Henry M. Walker told a Polish woman whiskey maker: "You are a travesty of motherhood. You are the mother of four children, and yet you are selling moonshine which may poison other women's sons. I am going to notify the federal authorities, and I hope they will deport you."[10]

Occasionally a woman's defense was downright hilarious. A Boston woman claimed her twenty-five gallon still was used just to make whiskey for her husband, who would go out drinking all night if she didn't supply him with liquor. When the officers seemed surprised by the size of her still, the woman said of her husband: "I know his capacity."[11]

During Prohibition thousands were arrested each year for illicit distillation and bootlegging, but even more were arrested for public intoxication. From 1920 to 1925, more than 1 million people were

1. Eric Gregory, president of the Kentucky Distillers' Association, presents Bourbon Women founder Peggy Noe Stevens with a custom-made barrel-head to commemorate the organization's creation. The Bourbon Women kickoff meeting was the inspiration for this book. *Photo taken by the author.*

2. At the Bourbon Women kickoff party at the Kentucky Governor's Mansion, first lady Jane Beshear explains the female importance to bourbon history. Beshear is known for embracing her state's heritage for the greater good. Most notably, her Horses and Hope initiative increases breast cancer awareness and has led to cancer screening for female equine workers. *Photo taken by the author.*

3. *(top)* Taken at the Labrot & Graham Distillery in the late 1800s or early 1900s, this photo illustrates the importance of women to this distillery. They are clearly the focus of the photographer's eye. Labrot & Graham is now the Woodford Reserve Distillery. *Photo courtesy of the Oscar Getz Museum of Whiskey History.*

4. *(bottom)* Until the late 1800s, distillers mostly sold whiskey by the barrel. They did not bottle their own whiskey until the late 1800s, at which time women were the chosen bottlers because they were more nimble and less clumsy. This photo was taken in the late 1800s at an unknown distillery. *Photo courtesy of the Oscar Getz Museum of Whiskey History.*

5. After the passage of the Bottle-in-Bond Act of 1897, American distillers hired women to run bottling lines. This trend continues today. This early 1900s photo was taken at the Old Crow Distillery. *Photo courtesy of the Oscar Getz Museum of Whiskey History.*

6. These two Civil War soldiers are photographed with a bottle of whiskey. The liquor proved to be both important and detrimental to both sides of the war. Doctors and nurses used whiskey to clean wounds, while soldiers often showed up to battle drunk. *Photo courtesy of the Library of Congress.*

7. Elizabeth Cumming built the most important distillery for the Johnnie Walker blended whisky. With a keen business sense, Cumming increased the Cardow Distillery's output and stature. When she sold to Johnnie Walker in 1893, the loving woman made sure her son had a seat on the board to preserve her family's legacy. *Photo courtesy of Diageo Archive.*

8. During the nineteenth-century temperance crusade, women stood outside of saloons and prayed, as is depicted in this *Frank & Leslie's* 1874 illustration. The Prohibition movement changed its efforts when Carrie Nation started showing up with hatchets. *Photo courtesy of the Library of Congress.*

9. Carrie Nation became the face of the Woman's Christian Temperance Union. Nation and her gang of hatchet-wielding ladies broke whiskey barrels, bars, and bottles to promote Prohibition. *Photo courtesy of the Kansas Historical Society.*

10. In the early 1900s, women worked at lumber mills and whiskey cooperages like this. They stacked wood and made barrels used to age whiskey. *Photo courtesy of the Independent Stave Company.*

11. *(opposite top)* When the Volstead Act took effect, whiskey was poured into the streets and the Revenue Service hired agents to seek illicit still operators. But the criminal syndicates found a loophole in certain states: men could not frisk women. Thus women bootleggers could sneak booze across state lines much more easily than men. *Photo courtesy of the Library of Congress.*

12. *(opposite bottom)* Just before Prohibition became law, Mary Dowling and her family packed up the Kentucky-based Waterfill & Frazier Distillery and moved to Juarez, Mexico. The company's 1927 advertisements appeared in newspapers near the Texas border. Al Capone reportedly purchased whiskey made in Juarez. After Prohibition, the Kentucky bourbon distillers pursued legal efforts to stop the flow of Dowling's whiskey into the United States. In 1964 Congress declared bourbon to be "America's Spirit," which gave the term *bourbon* geographical protection and made Mexican bourbon illegal.

13. Gertrude "Cleo" Lythgoe was known as the Queen of the Bootleggers. She began her smuggling career as a legitimate liquor wholesaler in the Bahamas but quickly saw that the real money was in bootlegging. Lythgoe became an international sensation, with newspaper journalists writing stories on her and men sending her marriage proposals. She retired in 1926 after a brush with the law and was thought to be worth millions. *Photo courtesy of Flat Hammock Press.*

14. Although she had supported Prohibition, Pauline Sabin later led the women's crusade for repeal. She argued for state's rights and contended that Prohibition made the bootlegger stronger. Many politicians credited her with repeal. *Photo courtesy of the Oscar Getz Museum of Whiskey History.*

15. The Early Times Distillery in Louisville in the mid-twentieth century. Women workers outnumbered the men five to one. *Photo courtesy of the Oscar Getz Museum of Whiskey History.*

16. When Bessie Williamson took the Laphroaig secretary job in 1934, she probably did not fathom how greatly she would affect the Scotch whisky world. She not only saved the Laphroaig Distillery from a military takeover but also changed the American demand for Scotch from blended to single malts. She is considered the First Lady of Scotch. *Photo courtesy of Laphroaig.*

17. *(above)* The 21 Brands Distiller Corporation was an important post-Prohibition Kentucky distillery. Women contributed to the company's bottling line and helped market 21 Brands' popular products, including Ezra Brooks. *Photo courtesy of the Oscar Getz Museum of Whiskey History.*

18. *(right)* Locke's Irish Whiskey was twice owned by women during the company's storied history. They marketed liqueurs nearly one hundred years before the modern flavored-whiskey craze.

19. Marge and Bill Samuels Sr. stand in front of their newly acquired distillery in the 1950s. Marge changed whiskey packaging when she created the Maker's Mark bottle and invented the red wax that would become paramount to the brand's success. If she had not insisted on giving the Maker's Mark bottle a handcrafted look, her husband might have pursued the less expensive packaging. *Photo courtesy of Maker's Mark.*

20. Victoria MacRae-Samuels is the vice president of operations for Maker's Mark distillery. She runs the production of bourbon, selects the grains, and manages the distillation and barrel warehousing. *Photo courtesy of Maker's Mark.*

21. Lynne Tolley is the great-grand niece of Jack Daniel. She serves as a taster for the premium Jack Daniel's products, such as single barrel and Gentleman Jack. Circa 1980s. *Photo courtesy of Jack Daniel's Tennessee Whiskey.*

22. After a successful career in music, cutting three albums and touring Europe, Heather Greene fell in love with whiskey. Greene took a whiskey bartender position that led to a William Grant ambassadorship, where she promoted Glenfiddich. Today she is the whisky sommelier for the Flatiron Room in New York. *Photo taken by the author.*

23. Kate Shapira Latts is vice president of marketing for Heaven Hill Distillery, which produces Evan Williams, Larceny, and Elijah Craig bourbons. Her team developed the branding, packaging, and marketing for Larceny. Sixty years ago women were mostly bottlers in the whiskey business. Today they run every aspect of it. *Photo by the author.*

24. Helen Mulholland is the master blender for Bushmills. Her tasting panel is comprised of women only, and Mulholland says her replacement will be a woman. *Photo taken by the author.*

25. Known as the "Bad Girl of Bourbon," Joy Perrine was making whiskey cocktails before it was cool. *Photo taken by the author.*

26. Allison Patel founded Brenne French whiskey in 2012. She's one of several young women who have started new whiskey brands. Patel is also the president of Local Infusions LLC, a boutique spirits importer. *Photograph by Sebastian Yao of Fix It In Post Photography. Courtesy Allison Patel.*

27. Award-winning chef and Bourbon Women member Ouita Michel is Woodford Reserve's chef in residence. Michel has used bourbon since she discovered how well it pairs with pork. She's one of the leaders in the cooking with bourbon trend. *Photo taken by the author.*

28. As the lead bartender at the Silver Dollar in Louisville, Kentucky, Susie Hoyt runs one of the state's best bourbon programs. In spring 2013, GQ Magazine named Silver Dollar one of the best whiskey bars in the country. Half a century ago, women were not allowed to serve alcohol in Kentucky bars. *Photo taken by the author.*

29. Rachel Barrie is the master blender for Bowmore, McClelland's, Glen Garioch, and Auchentoshan Scotch whiskies. Before taking this position, Barrie was the master blender for Glenmorangie and Ardbeg. She was the first modern female blender to be hired in 1995. Since then, she has opened the doors for many young women to enter the spirits business. *Photo courtesy of Morrison Bowmore Distillers.*

30. MaryKay Skrypec Bolles is the vice president of Global R&D for Beam Inc. She develops new products for Beam Inc. and represents the latest type of female executives in the whiskey business—women leaving other industries for new opportunities with substantial companies. Skrypec is a former Gatorade exec. *Photo taken by the author.*

arrested for drunkenness, with Chicago owning the city record of 92,900 arrests in 1925.[12]

Within six years of passing Prohibition, temperance supporters realized that drinking had actually increased. Speaking at a 1924 press conference, Bishop Thomas Nicholson, president of the Anti-Saloon League, admitted that "drinking among women is rapidly increasing."[13] Journalists, policemen, and lawmakers said Prohibition only opened the door for young girls to drink harmful intoxicating liquors.

In some cases, the moonshine was deadly. In 1920 1,064 people died. Five years later, with the increase in homemade liquor, that number nearly quadrupled.

People wanted to drink, and if they could not find a reliable source, they tried making bathtub gin or their own moonshine, not knowing the potential dangers without the proper training. Chicago's "Moonshine" Mary Wazonsak was convicted of manslaughter after making and selling moonshine that killed a man.[14] At the Ireland Liquor Commission in 1925, Dr. Arthur Shadwell blamed moonshine, "the poteen of the United States. It is made by all sorts of people, and they have complete plants for making it and bottles and labels. They can supply anything that you ask for, but the liquor is all the same. The rate of profit goes up to some thousands percent, as it is very cheap. The bootleggers pretend that it is smuggled, because that is supposed to be the best."[15]

When it came to bootlegging the illicit whiskey, women were the best. "We find the woman bootlegger the hardest to catch," said Reverend C. C. Brannon of Blackwell, Oklahoma, a Prohibition enforcement officer at Indian Reservations.[16] For all the contributions women made behind the still, their Prohibition talents were in hiding from the law, sneaking liquor into the country, and doing whatever it took to make sure alcohol found the speakeasy. Prohibition director Elmer C. Potter said women were always illegally trafficking booze. "I have never known a time when there was not a very considerable proportion of women apprehended," he said.[17]

Women bootleggers ranged from the pretty faces to the shot callers. They included onetime bootleggers looking to make quick cash and rich women financing ships hauling $100,000 worth of smuggled whiskey. Women were so good that, at one point, agents believed female bootleggers outsold the men five sales to one.

Even the most rookie of bootleggers practiced tried- and-true systems to fool the police. If a Revenue officer showed up on her doorsteps, a woman bootlegger pretended to faint on his shoulders. Coming to, the lady batted her eyelashes, flirted with the lawmen, letting him know how handsome and strong he was. Should he not buy her act and want to search the premises, the woman screamed as if she were being violated.

Young, pretty females transported small quantities of whiskey in baby carriages, beneath skirts, and in their blouses. Male Revenue agents were so nervous, or perhaps gentlemanly, that they rarely checked under a dress or in her blouse. In some states, men were not allowed to search women. Ohio police officers could suspect a woman wearing a puffy dress of storing a case of whiskey between her thighs, but could not physically search her.

After searching a suspected speakeasy in Hamilton, Ohio, and individually patting down every man in the room, agents endured a woman jeering them. "A painted-up doll was sitting in a corner. . . . She had her arms folded and at our command she stood up. But then came the rub. She laughed at us . . . then defiantly declared to bring suit against anyone who touched her," an agent said in 1924.[18]

This legal loophole led to government officials demanding that Roy A. Haynes, the national Prohibition commissioner, create a plan against female bootleggers. By March 1922, more than 100 women awaited trial in New York, Washington, and Philadelphia. And when they appeared before a jury, jurors rarely meted out the same punishment as for the male lawbreakers. "If the present increase in women bootleggers continues indefinitely, they say, women soon will have a monopoly in retail sales of liquor."[19]

Within the first two years of Prohibition, smuggling syndicates realized that male agents faced difficulties in apprehending women and capitalized on the government's weakness. They employed women to run rum from Florida and deliver whiskey into the cities. Men even hired pretty women just to travel with them, because it decreased the odds of getting arrested. "With a homely girl, a man may get arrested between a certain Kentucky town and this city for carrying a pint of corn liquor," according to the West Virginia *Charleston Mail.* "With an unusually pretty girl . . . he might get away with ten gallons."[20] A woman in the car also reduced a bootlegger's chances of getting searched.

The *Boston Daily Globe* wrote: "The best way to escape trouble on the road is to have a woman along and keep her where she can be seen. . . . No self-respecting federal agent likes to hold up an automobile containing women."

In March 1922, the first woman Revenue agent, Miss Georgia Hopley, made it clear that it takes a woman to catch a woman. Women "resort to all sorts of tricks, concealing metal containers in their clothing, in false bottoms of trunks and travelling bags and even in baby buggies," Hopley told the *Boston Sunday Globe*. "On the Canadian, Mexican and Florida borders, inspectors are constantly on the lookout for women bootleggers who try to smuggle liquor into the States. Their detection and arrest is far more difficult than that of male lawbreakers."

Hopley's hiring also encouraged local police departments and county sheriff's departments to hire women to seek same gender bootleggers. Small newspapers in hotbed whiskey towns ran front-page stories with big bold typeface headlines recruiting female cops, such as the front page of the December 17, 1924, *Hamilton Evening Journal*: "Officials Face Problem of Eliminating 'Woman Bootlegger.' Need Women Officers." This recruiting effort signaled that there was a target on the woman bootlegger's back. Hopley and the other Revenue agents meant business, but the bootleggers still outsmarted the law at almost every turn.

Women bootleggers often kept a paper trail of politicians and revenue agents they paid off. When Mary Gilseth of Minneapolis was arrested, she offered authorities corrupt politicians and police officers in lieu of serving time. Gilseth showed the court more than $1,300 in bribes to a state senator and local police.[21] Sometimes that paper trail was not the best idea. In Templeton, Iowa, a rye whiskey epicenter and one of Al Capone's favorite towns, Col. George C. Parsons tracked down more than $100,000 in illicit hooch just by following a woman's bank statements, where she made weekly $500 deposits.

In Indianapolis, authorities considered Ruth Davis one of the city's top bootleggers and kept her under surveillance. They followed her to the train station, where Davis picked up several steam trunks. Police then accessed her train shipment logs and saw she made regular pickups from Louisiana trains. They suspected Davis worked with a Cajun bootlegger and bribed train officials to let the trunks pass. When agents raided her residence on June 30, 1925, they seized seventy-six quarts of whiskey valued at $2,500, $1,000 in cash, and about $5,000 in diamonds. It was considered one of Indianapolis's largest busts of the year.

Women didn't always get caught. On February 19, 1930, nearly every newspaper in the country ran a front-page article about a mysterious "Blonde Woman." After a red monoplane unloaded Canadian liquor into her truck, pilot Clinton R. Hellingenstein squealed to agents about the woman, saying she paid $28, but he did not know her name. The police never found her, but trying to find a female bootlegger in Zanesville, Ohio, one of the country's top whiskey towns during Prohibition, was like searching for a needle in a haystack. The Blonde would have been just another tough gal with a lead foot delivering whiskey to thirsty customers.[22]

Like the mysterious Blonde, authorities tenaciously pursued high-profile suspects, especially when large sums of money were involved. Customs officials kept tabs on New Hampshire bootlegger Hilda Stone, a chief lieutenant in a Greenfield, Massachusetts, rum-running gang. They arrested her four times but could never make anything stick. At a hearing, she told officials she liked running liquor for the "thrill of it." That was certainly a unique reason to traffic illegal liquor; most ladies loved the money. Miss Frances Cannistraci's "Olivet Distributing Company" business at 252 Hudson Street, New York, made $2,000 a day in 1926 bootlegging whiskey into New York. Cannistraci's bail was set at $10,000, a hefty sum for a female lawbreaker.[23] When a Milwaukee woman was arrested, she admitted to earning nearly $30,000 a year. With a fine of $200, she netted more money than most company CEOs and New York Yankee players with the exception of Babe Ruth, who made $52,000. Who wouldn't take a risk for that kind of payoff?[24]

Because women protected their hooch and money at all costs, Connecticut's *The Hartford Courant* declared the "female bootlegger. . . . more deadly than male" and authorities often shot at women first and asked questions later. After he killed bootlegger Louise Horton, the Herington, Kansas, sheriff said, "a liquor crazed woman with a pistol is a combination which cannot be treated lightly."

Among the violent types, Filumena "Florence" Lassandro, a young Italian immigrant, worked for Emil Picariello, better known as the "Emperor Pic." She helped in Pic's legitimate ice cream business, but on the illicit side she smuggled alcohol from British Columbia to Montana.

In September 1921 the Alberta Provincial Police pursued Pic's son, Steve, transporting liquor, and Constable Stephen Oldacres Lawson shot Steve. Pic and Lassandro retaliated, showing up at Lawson's home and killing the officer in front of his family. Their trial became a controversial story in Canada. Both Pic and Lassandro were Catholic in a significant Protestant area. Sympathizers believed they were mistreated because of religion, and Emil tried to convince Lassandro to take the fall for him. Lassandro allegedly confessed to police after the arrest, but later adamantly denied confessing and underwent a weeklong trial that found her guilty. Coleman, Alberta, judge William Walsh sentenced her to death December 2, 1922, and said: "The only thing that can be said in favor of the prisoner, Lassandro, is that she is a woman. I know, of course, quite well the reluctance that there is to execute the death sentence upon a woman and that, of late years at any rate, such a thing has not been done in Canada. That is, of course, a question of principle which is not for me. If she was a man, there could be no question but that the sentence should be executed."[25]

Walsh's ruling led to a public outcry throughout Canada. Lassandro's supporters wrote the governor general of the Dominion of Canada: "Florence Lassandro is of alien birth, coming from nations which cannot understand the proscription of intoxicants and the placing of such liquors under legal ban. . . . Commute the sentence of death passed upon the said Florence Lassandro to imprisonment for life or such other period as to Your Excellency may seem meet." There was also strong contingency arguing against Lassandro's clemency. According to a letter from British Columbia citizens addressed to the minister of justice, the people protested a second trial for Lassandro and urged the death sentence be carried out. Many law-abiding citizens feared showing mercy to Lassandro would open the door for other bootleggers.[26]

In her final plea for clemency, Lassandro telegrammed J. E. Brownlee, the Canadian attorney general: "While we were nearing Lawson's House, I noticed that man in house was a police—could tell that by his britches. I said to Picariello: 'Whatever you do, do not shoot.'" She told the attorney general that despite the Pic's attempt for her confession, she never admitted to pulling the trigger. "If anyone tells you that I have confessed, tell them that they are damn liars," she wrote.

But her letters were not enough to keep her alive. She was executed. Lassandro was the only woman hung in Alberta.

The fact is bootlegging was a dangerous and costly business. English-born Mrs. Gloria de Casares, wife of a wealthy Argentinean merchant, commissioned ships, such as the five-masted *General Serret*, to haul whiskey from Europe to America. When detectives seized her "whiskey ship" in London on its way to the United States on September 11, 1925, they found 10,000 cases of Scotch, and it didn't take long for her captain to fess up. Captain Whitburn admitted they were "whisky runners. . . . When we get the necessary dough, we will be on our way to the coast of America."[27]

Clearly having poor taste in friends as well, Casares's girlfriend told reporters that the Englishwoman frequently bragged about running whiskey. Casares vehemently denied the accusations, essentially saying she owned the ships but knew nothing of the whiskey. England deported her.

In a bizarre twist, two years later, Casares attempted to enter the United States without a visa. With the whiskey ship looming over Casares's record, U.S. officials allowed her fifteen days in the United States for a $500 bond. They could not risk a suspected large-scale whiskey bootlegger to roam the country. After Casares overstayed an extension, the Department of Labor issued a warrant for her arrest, and she left for England, where authorities immediately apprehended her and confined her to a hotel room, seizing her clothes and bags to make sure she did not leave without paying an undisclosed fine. "What am I to do? First I am deprived of my nationality. Now they want to deprive me of all my clothes over $25 worth. Twenty-five dollars is just about enough for a hat. Do they expect a woman to go about the world with $25 worth of clothing," Casares told the *New York Times*. A few minutes before her boat, the *Caonia*, was scheduled to leave, an unknown car arrived and paid whatever debt she owed. That was the last known sighting of a woman thought to have smuggled $100,000, possibly more, of legitimate Scotch whisky into the United States. Whether she truly knew of her alleged whiskey ships remains a mystery.

Another rich female bootlegger importing Scotch was Gertrude "Cleo" Lythgoe, a licensed liquor wholesaler from Nassau, Bahamas. Born in Bowling Green, Ohio, Lythgoe was the tenth child of an English father and Scottish mother. Tall and slender with a dark complexion and piercing gray eyes, Lythgoe passed as Native American, Russian, French, and Spanish, always keeping people guessing. Allusive and daring, she offered various nationality stories and never corrected people when they mistook her for Persian or Russian, only adding to her mystery. Some Bahaman bootleggers thought she was a spy for the Americans, while others figured she was a British liquor distributor because of her connections in Scotland.

A former stenographer in San Francisco, Lythgoe worked in New York for a Scotch whisky company. She lost a lot of money in the stock market and saw opportunity in the Prohibition, which "caused big demand for liquor, and fortunes were being made," she wrote in her memoir, *The Bahaman Queen*. "I felt this was the only door of opportunity open. . . . I couldn't lose any more and had everything to gain."

Cleo never says whom she worked for, but bootlegger Bill McCoy believed she was an agent for Haig's and McTavish's Scotch whisky. If this is true, she helped supply the United States with two of the premier Scotch brands of the time. American businessman Joseph P. Kennedy, father of the future president, arguably made quite a large sum selling Haig & Haig whisky.[28] While other bootleggers were peddling watered-down and colored-up liquor, Lythgoe catered to the premium markets, offering the best Scotch and highest grade American whiskey. She sold 2 million gallons of rye whiskey in 1923. But this success did not come without sexism.

When she first arrived in Nassau, many men would not do business with her because of her gender, and she came across club entrances with "no skirts" signs. The island's top men spread rumors that she was a Revenue agent working undercover. Nassau was not a safe place for a pretty woman, either. Once Lythgoe came home to find a strange man at the foot of her bed. "I want a kiss," he said. Lythgoe pushed him away and pretended to go for the pistol underneath the pillow. The man left, but rape was a real possibility for the Bahamas' first woman to own a wholesale liquor license. Another man, knowing the amount of cash she had, tried to get her alone to throw her overboard and steal her money.[29] It's hard to say whether these were the acts of common criminals or intimidation tactics employed by her competitors.

Because she had such great access to American and Scotch whiskies, Lythgoe's product quality was unrivaled. That did not stop her competition from badmouthing her spirits. When one man spoke ill of her whiskey, Lythgoe found him at the barbershop, shaving cream on his face, and pulled him into another room. "I just warned him," she said to a reporter. "I told him I'd put a bullet through him as sure as he sat there. He went away mighty quick."[30]

As her wholesale business grew, she realized that the best money was in the bootlegging. She partnered with Bill McCoy to supply America with legitimate Scotch whisky as well as vast amounts of rye and bourbon that Lythgoe's company acquired. McCoy recalled: "Women on a ship sometimes are considered Jonahs. It was not so with her. It was plain to my crew at once that she was right. They liked her from the start. . . . An able thoroughly competent girl was she; no twittery jane at whom one could make passes with impunity. She expected others to mind their own business as she attended to hers. She worked at that overtime and in its course she nearly ran me ragged."[31]

Cleo took the ship, *Arethusa*, to near Florida, where she searched for speedboats that could carry anywhere from 5 to 200 cases of whiskey back to the mainland. The speediest boat, the *Cigarette*, packed up to 600 cases of whiskey. The bootleggers were armed; Lythgoe carried a large pistol. If the Coast Guard had happened upon them, it would have been a bloody mess. Their real concern, though, was hijackers. Gangs made their living by hijacking bootleggers from the Detroit waterfront to just off the coast of Florida.

Aside from occasionally pulling her gun for protection, there's no record of Lythgoe engaging foes in a gunfight. And, if it happened, it would have likely been chronicled. No whiskey-related woman before or after Lythgoe received more press. For a six-year span, from 1920 to 1926, Lythgoe was a media darling, with English, American, and even Canadian reporters camping out at her hotel and wiring her whereabouts just before deadline. She claimed reporters never quoted her accurately, but they followed her and photographed Lythgoe in a fashion that would make today's celebrity paparazzi proud.

West Indies Bootlegging

The veritable queen of the bootleggers will arrive in New York shortly from Nassau, capital of the Bahamas and capital also of the West Indies bootlegging trade. She is coming here to invest some of her wealth in Fifth Avenue finery and to "do" Broadway as she has always longed to do it, but, according to her fellow intimates in Nassau, her chief desire is marriage with "the right man" and a suburban cottage, for which she would gladly forego the adventure and large income of her present post. . . . She has rejected more proposals of marriage than most royal damsels ever received.—*Chicago Tribune*, December 25, 1923

The Queen Will Arrive

Paris, Sept. 16—Another million dollars' worth of whisky, including all the popular Scotch, Irish and American brands, is soon to leave Europe for the Bahamas to be smuggled into the United States. This was admitted by Grace Lythgoe, an Englishwoman, who is head of probably the largest international whisky business in the world, and is now in Paris concluding transport and other arrangements with Bordeaux exporters.—*Kingston Gleaner*, Jamaica, September 25, 1923

Unfortunately for Lythgoe, this unsolicited press placed a bull's-eye on her back. She was frequently searched at the Bahaman port. After being strip-searched by a female officer, and knowing she broke no Bahaman laws, Lythgoe asked an American consul: "Why do those people do those awful things? Why are they so prejudiced and jealous? After all, I'm just the handmaiden of a British firm in a British colony." The man replied: "Miss Lythgoe, you've gone biblical."[32] Technically Lythgoe was right. As long as she did not transport her liquor into U.S. waters, the licensed wholesaler broke no laws and resented the press calling her a bootlegger, even though she admitted to bootlegging in her 1964 memoir and sailed on many whiskey ships before this particular pat down. Despite her transgressions, Lythgoe always played the innocence card. "I'm just a business woman with a business legally registered at Nassau. I work hard for what I earn, and am no more responsible for what happens to the liquor after I sell it than is the merchant of whom I buy it," she told a reporter in 1923.[33]

There was little she could do to control her title after British reporter H. de Winton Wigley's well-written story "Cleopatra, Queen of the Bootleggers" hit the wire and ran in hundreds of newspapers around the world. By October 1923, every newspaperman covering Prohibition wanted an interview with the woman who "stands alone and fearless—a triumph over her environment—a woman, who would grace any London drawing-room."[34]

Lythgoe became such an iconic celebrity that she received hundreds of love letters and marriage proposals from all over the world. Fans wanted to borrow money, introduce her to their sons, cook for her, and invite her to birthday parties.

Love Letters to the Queen of Bootlegging

Finland, January 10, 1923

Miss Gertrude Lythegoe, Nassau

My Dear! Will you lend a very good but poor boy little of money to help to come to America? Yours very truly, A.L.

England

I am utterly astonished that a beautiful and-charming young lady like you should disgrace herself by associating with the scum of the earth, for it is very certain that nobody who calls, themselves either, ladies or gentlemen would lower themselves so-much as to engage in rum and whisky selling, and especially when the American authorities have prohibited it. If I was the Government I would send some gunboats and blow them to smithereens when they got into American waters. . . . I only wish you lived in England. I would marry you, as a home life would be far more suitable for you than your present occupation. Signed, ONE WHO LOVES YOU

Osawatomie, Kansas, November 20, 1923

Dear Miss Lythgoe: I have read with great interest an account of your thriving business and am writing you to say that I sure admire your business ability and to apply to you for a position. . . . I am a cook . . . and am "raring to go." . . . Please don't treat this as a joke, as I mean sure enough I want to get where a man can take a long breath and not get pinched doing it. At any rate, please answer my letter to let me know that you received it, which in itself will be a great favor to me. Very respectfully yours, W. A. S[35]

This fame only made her more vulnerable. When she was arrested for check fraud in a case of mistaken identity in Miami, an attendant realized he had a bigger fish than just the hot check writer and called federal authorities, telling them he had obtained the Queen of the Bootleggers. In a case of bad timing, Cleo's former workers were arrested around the same time for liquor smuggling. In 1925, after the

Miami agent alerted authorities of her whereabouts, Lythgoe was arrested and taken to New Orleans for federal prosecution of violating Prohibition laws. The government claimed she smuggled 1,000 cases of whiskey aboard the British schooner *Gladys Thorburn*. As soon as she was arrested, Lythgoe complimented the "courteous treatment . . . at the hands of representatives of the federal government. . . . I have never come into contact with a more gentlemanly group of officers." For as sassy as she was to the customs officials, Lythgoe must have known her "vinegar" side would not win this fight. Lythgoe said that the whiskey was most certainly hers, and she thanked the authorities for finding it, because the two men stole it. "I never got a cent," she claimed.

Here was Gertrude "Cleo" Lythgoe, the world's most beautiful bootlegger with fans spanning the globe, and her defense was her whiskey was "stolen." During Prohibition, a bootlegger of her magnitude, no matter the technicalities that would have arisen with her Bahamas' license, would have at least been publicly ridiculed and served nine months in jail. But Lythgoe turned state's witness and testified against Fred Young and Buddie Larocca.[36] Maybe the two sailors were afraid of Lythgoe, or the federal officers liked being praised in the press by the Queen of the Bootleggers, or maybe Lythgoe told the truth. Whatever were the real circumstances, the world's most notorious bootlegger was free of charges.

After New Orleans, Lythgoe retired from her wholesale liquor business. "I've stood on my own feet, and I'm ashamed of nothing," she told a reporter in 1926, adding, "I don't need a man to tell me what to do. . . . I'm not getting married."[37] According to the *Wall Street Journal*, Lythgoe was worth millions. In her post-Prohibition life she remained as mysterious as in her bootlegging days. Even in her cryptic memoirs, she admitted little about what might have been deemed illicit activity. After Lythgoe left the whiskey trade, the press never found another woman quite as colorful or as beautiful as the true Queen of the Bootleggers, even if they crowned other women with her title.

According to several newspaper accounts, more than a dozen American women were called the Queen of the Bootleggers. After Mary White's trial, where federal authorities showed her $5,000 in cash as evidence, a reporter called her the Queen of the Bootleggers. White, a stout woman with a "swarthy complexion" and missing front teeth, said: "I wish to hell I was. Don't ask me any questions because I have nothing to say."[38]

When they weren't the queen, women earned other monikers. In Kansas, Esther Clark was the "hen house" bootlegger after hiding liquor in her henhouse in 1930. Out west, women bootleggers were "bustle squeezers." They sold lemon extract, grape juice with a kick, peyote, prune juice, cold tea, whiskey beer, and wine. Bustle squeezers were dishonest, passing water bags of tea and prune juice as whiskey.[39]

After Lythgoe's retirement, the Revenue agents and police started to downplay the significance of women bootleggers. Legal authorities told the public that the woman bootlegger exists mainly in fiction. Mary Sullivan, director of the woman's division of the New York Police Department, told the Associated Press on November 19, 1926: "A woman can't load and unload a truck of liquor and that is the same unless you are among the high-up."[40] Sullivan apparently had never been to Lebanon, Missouri, where the whiskey cooperage Independent Stave Company employed women to build and load barrels. In an early 1900s photo, three Independent Stave Company women are shown stacking ten-foot boards fifteen feet high. Though they were wearing dresses and their hair in buns, they clearly could do the man's work Sullivan claimed women could not.[41]

In propaganda mode, the New York branch of the Anti-Saloon League even reported only nine women bootleggers existed through the first six years of Prohibition. It's certainly understandable that the Anti-Saloon League would not have accurate arrest records for the entire country, but the boldface inaccuracy clearly shows their marketing team believed the woman bootlegger needed to be publicly dismissed. Just four years prior to these ridiculous claims, agents admitted that 100 women bootleggers awaited trial.[42] Not only were women bootleggers continuing operations but they were getting smarter and requiring much more of the agency's attention.

Stella Beloumant, the leading bootlegger in Elko, Nevada, drew an entire task force in 1926. The U.S. attorney's office, the No. 2 official for the Prohibition Administration, two dry agents, a district attorney, and a squad of sheriff's deputies executed a twenty-four-hour stakeout that rendered the seizure of 820 gallons of Beloumant's wine. That amount means she maintained the equivalent of 4,140 0.750-liter bottles of wine. Her stash equaled nearly half that the famous French wine appellation La Romanée of Burgundy produces in an entire year.[43] The agents likely spent a month or more preparing for the bust and obviously contradicted Mary Sullivan's notion that women bootleggers were fiction. The temperance movement and the associated politicians needed to control the country's view of women. It was difficult for a church-going America to comprehend mothers and grandmas strapping flasks to their inner thighs or toting revolvers to protect a truck full of hooch. Prohibitionists wanted citizens to believe good women made apple pie and tucked their children in bed at night.

But there's no way the Prohibitionists could hide the firestorm of law-abiding women fighting them in political circles.

9

Repeal Women Saving Whiskey

Contrary to what the WCTU women wanted society to believe, not all women supported Prohibition. Two years after the Eighteenth Amendment became law, the *Literary Digest* polled 2 million women, and more than two-thirds said they wanted either an act modification or repeal. Workingwomen appeared to strongly oppose the law with slightly more than 90 percent voting against total dryness. This early poll shows that Prohibition's supposedly greatest support group, the female population, doubted the law and the country's ability to enforce order.[1]

Many anti-Prohibitionists still blamed the saloon, with the *New York Morning Telegraph* writing that the saloon "did not respect the law before we had a Prohibition Amendment any more than bootleggers respect it now. Had it been a self-respecting institution, law-abiding and clean, if it had kept out of politics, it might not now be in the scrap heap."[2] Other common arguments against Prohibition pointed out that the law only increased drinking and crime. Journalist H. L. Mencken famously wrote: "Five years of Prohibition have had, at least, this one benign effect: They have completely disposed of all the favorite arguments of Prohibitionists." Mencken and like-minded influencers spawned one repeal organization after another, but none really had any teeth until a powerful rich woman opposed the law.

Pauline Morton Sabin was the daughter of Paul Morton, President Theodore Roosevelt's secretary of the navy, niece to the founder of Morton Salt, and the wife of Hamilton Sabin, president and partner of J. P. Morgan. So much more than a beautiful woman who came from and married into money, Pauline was a political fireplug. She became the first female member of the Republican National Committee and greatly influenced female voters as well as the country's elite men. At age thirty-four, Sabin, who entered politics to campaign for suffrage, founded the Women's National Republican Club in 1921 and original-ly supported Prohibition, saying a "world without liquor was a beauti-ful thing." Her mind soon changed.

In 1928, the Women's National Republican Club surveyed 1,500 women in thirty-eight states and learned that nearly 1,400 wanted repeal or modification of the Volstead Act. Sabin admitted that the corner saloon was no longer visible and taking men away from their families, but she realized "respected citizens" were breaking the laws just to get a nightcap. In her essay for the *Outlook*, "I Change My Mind on Prohibition," Sabin wrote: "In my opinion, the majority of women with young children favored prohibition because they felt that when the Eighteenth Amendment was enacted drinking to excess would never be a problem in their children's lives, that temptation would be completely eliminated. But now they are wondering and troubled about the result. They have found that their children are growing up with a total lack of respect for the Constitution and for the law."

When Sabin founded the Women's Organization for National Pro-hibition Reform in 1929, it changed the reform conversation of "it's just not working" to a moral degradation discussion of their children. Former WCTU members joined the WONPR. They believed enforcing Prohibition was worse than a wet society. In essence, Sabin used some of the same arguments that Prohibitionists used for banning alcohol, saying that the law nurtured crime and made drinking stylish. Perhaps most important, though, Sabin and the WONPR argued they were teach-ing tomorrow's leaders to not respect the law, since everybody was breaking the Prohibition mandate. Repeal women said legislation could never eradicate alcohol's temptation and that liquor traffic should be controlled by state regulations, not by a federal law. Sabin told the House Judiciary Committee on Prohibition: "They thought they could make Prohibition as strong as the Constitution. But instead they have made the Constitution as weak as Prohibition."[3]

Some Republican women called Sabin a traitor when learning about her repeal intentions, but the women who mattered most were on her side: Mrs. Archibald B. Roosevelt, the daughter-in-law of President Theodore Roosevelt; Mrs. Courtland Nicoll, the wife of an attorney and New York state senator; Mrs. E. Roland Harriman, wife of the mil-lionaire philanthropist; Mrs. Cornelius M. Bliss, wife of the former U.S. secretary of the interior; Mrs. Cummins E. Speakman, wife of a wealthy businessman; and Lolita Coffin Van Rensselaer, activist and author of the 1916 magazine essay "Protection of the Immigrant Women." Through their husbands and their own efforts, they joined Sabin in founding the WONPR and were among the most important women in the United States. If they all met for tea in a public place, it was newsworthy. But the fact that they were putting their reputations on the line and willing to stand up against Prohibition gave the WONPR more substantiated credentials than all other repeal organizations, including the Women's Moderation and the Women's Committee for Repeal of the 18th Amendment.

Sabin's band of sisters made Prohibition repeal fashionable, winning significant space in every major newspaper and gaining the support of politicians on the fence about the issue. The organization's first convention was held in Cleveland, the same city where the first female bootlegger was arrested.

1930 WONPR Convention in Cleveland, Ohio
We are convinced that National Prohibition is fundamentally wrong. (a) Because it conflicts with the basic American principle of local home rule and destroys the balance established by the framers of our government, between powers delegated to the federal authority and those reserved to the sovereign states or to the people themselves. (b) And because its attempt to impose total abstinence by national government fiat ignores the truth that no law will be respected or can be enforced unless supported by the moral sense and common conscience of the communities affected by it.

We are convinced that National Prohibition, wrong in principle, has been equally disastrous in consequences in the hypocrisy, the corruption, the tragic loss of life, and the appalling increase of crime which have attended the abortive attempt to enforce it; in the shocking effect it has had upon the youth of the nation; in the impairment of constitutional guarantees of individual rights; in the weakening of the sense of solidarity between the citizen and the government which is the only sure basis of a country's strength.[4]

In the WONPR's recruiting flier, "For Your Children's Sake," the organization asked women if they would help "Clean up the speakeasies?

Abolish the gin mills and roadhouses? Put the bootlegger out of business? Take the profit out of crime? Restore respect for the law?" Women could do all those things by working to repeal Prohibition and joining the WONPR. Just as the WCTU shocked women into joining, the WONPR converted dry women into repeal women.

By 1931, WONPR boasted 1.5 million members from all economic levels, which included working women, high society trust fund daughters, and housewives.[5] Some temperance women called these repeal ladies whores and drunken barflies. Methodist Church leader Clarence True Wilson said Sabin and her friends were a "little group of wine drinking society women who are uncomfortable under Prohibition." Georgia WCTU president Dr. Mary Harris Armor said in 1930: "As to Mrs. Sabin and her cocktail-drinking women, we will out-live them, out-fight them, out-love them, out-talk them, out-pray them, and out-vote them."[6]

Sabin and her well-informed, well-presented women frequently said they would endorse any candidate, Democrat or Republican, who openly favored repeal. When the Democratic Party announced its Prohibition repeal plank in June 1932, the Republican said the Democrats sought everything her organization wanted: Repeal the amendment and strengthen interstate commerce laws to allow states to remain dry or become wet. The Democrats decision "will do more to hearten the people of this country than anything in many a moon," Sabin said.[7]

With the Democrats fully on her side, Sabin went after Republicans, arguing that the Eighteenth Amendment prevented much-needed tax revenue during the Great Depression. Sabin's most crucial point was the fact it cost $40 million a year to enforce Prohibition, and the country lost $1 billion a year in taxes.[8] This argument appealed to politicians looking to mend a broken economy.

Congress met in a special lame-duck session to pass the Twenty-First Amendment, which repealed the Eighteenth Amendment. This historic amendment made liquor transportation or importation a state issue, one of the WONPR's sticking points. Sabin said to her followers: "I believe that when history is written it will be shown that the members of the WONPR fought a gallant fight for a righteous cause."[9]

When politicians opined about the repeal results, they were quick to thank Sabin. "This convention, and the people of the state should rejoice, as I do, at the opportunity of expressing their appreciation to

Mrs. Charles H. Sabin and her devoted army of women who have so valiantly fought towards our common goal," said New York governor Herbert Lehman at his state's convention.[10] *Time* magazine featured Sabin on its cover in July 1932, and she went on to become director of volunteer services for the American Red Cross during World War II. Many historians credit Sabin as the most important figure in repealing Prohibition. Where others failed, she succeeded by appealing to women about their children, to the men and their pocketbooks, and to her countrymen's austere belief in the power of the individual state's right to govern separately from federal lawmakers. Sabin also set precedent that pro-alcohol women could successfully lobby for reform.

After Sabin's victory, the temperance women worked overtime to sneak new Prohibition-like laws into Congress. This time, wet women were ready. The Women's Association of Allied Beverage Industries became a hindrance in the new temperance efforts.

10

The Post-Prohibition Legal Battles

As positive as repeal was for the alcohol industry, nobody could possibly fathom the chaos that followed. Legalizing alcohol and giving states control was certainly better than the Eighteenth Amendment, but it meant every state created its own laws. And within those states, counties created laws. Within those counties, cities orchestrated restrictive ordinances. In some states, there were more "dry" counties than "wet" ones. Texas featured 142 completely dry counties and 82 partly dry to just 30 wet counties. Many states initially banned Sunday liquor sales or initiated a statute requiring a black tarp over liquor bottles, while some cities banned female bartenders just in case a man was tempted by a woman pouring beer or whiskey. Rhode Island forbade liquor containers smaller than a fifth, and Georgia outlawed cocktails.

Repeal made America the most difficult country for foreign wine, beer, and liquor producers to do business with. If an alcohol company wanted to offer products in the United States, its executives had to sign import agreements in every state. And that importer could not sell directly to the consumer or retailer. Importers had to sell to the distributor.

Some states, like Pennsylvania, created monopolies to control wholesale distribution and retail sales, but most states eventually adopted a regulatory agency to license import and distributor businesses. In most states, this agency is the Alcoholic Beverage Control Board, and it is in charge of enacting each state's specific laws, such as Colorado's law that prohibits liquor businessmen from owning more than one store at a time. The Federal Alcohol Control Administration enforced the federal laws, such as watching licensed distillery operations at all times.

With so many new levels of bureaucracy, the temperance movement was reinvigorated. Temperance women may have lost the federal fight, but they could change their own cities. Woman's Christian Temperance Union chapters lobbied their respective cities to prohibit alcohol sales. For twenty years, WCTU women circled their wagons at every state election, sending their votes to the dry politicians, and campaigned to keep Prohibition in the states or counties that still enforced it, but they maintained vigilant pursuit of a federal law to effectively create a new type of Prohibition.[1]

Once again, the WCTU found politicians with like-minded beliefs eager to write bills to support the dry cause. They also found a new female organization ready to fight them at every federal measure. Formed in 1944, the Women's Association of Allied Beverage Industries became an important beverage industry interest group that maintained a steady membership of about 7,500 industry employees. They worked for brewers, distilleries, and winemakers and became the ladies' industry voice. They were badly needed in the 1950s when Congress held ten hearings about alcohol advertising.

Despite the Federal Alcohol Administration Act of 1935 regulating alcohol's advertising and claims, as well as the industry's volunteer measurements, like not marketing to children, the temperance supporters believed distillers and brewers needed government regulation on advertising.

When Republican North Dakota senator William Langer introduced an alcohol advertising bill, HR 4627, in 1956, the WCTU had already been lobbying for advertising reform in Mississippi and garnered support from social drinkers as well as the alcoholics, who blamed advertising for their addictions. Mrs. R. L. Ezelle, president of the Mississippi Woman's Christian Temperance Union, wrote: "Alcoholic beverages are responsible for millions of alcoholics; temporary intoxication causes thousands of deaths through accidents and disease, as well as other tragedies too many to enumerate. . . . Advertising is meant to sell the goods advertised and the $250 million advertising campaign of liquor and beer manufacturers is flooding this nation with the most glamorous, misleading advertising of all time, without a suggestion of the dangers in the drug alcohol."[2] Langer's bill proposed to outlaw interstate advertising of alcohol and prohibited interstate transportation of advertisements of alcoholic beverages by newspapers, radio, television, or periodicals with fines up to $1,000 and one year in prison. Under this bill, it would be illegal for Jack Daniel's to purchase a full-page ad in the *USA Today* because the national newspaper would cross state lines.

These alcohol ban proposals came during a time when many "square" parents wondered about rock and roll, a guy named Elvis Presley, and hormone-crazed teenagers driving fast muscle cars. Much like WCTU did to spin the wheels of Prohibition, they tried to appeal to every father and mother worried about their teenaged daughters and sons. They also had a colorful and popular politician in their pocket. "We found teenagers being led from beer parties into dope. . . . When every evening over radio and television come these urgings to drink glass after glass after glass," Langer told the Associated Press. Canada banned alcohol advertising, and the Maine legislature voted 90 to 17 in favor of asking Congress to ban alcoholic beverage advertising. Langer's words pulled on the heartstrings of parents of drunken teenagers. But the measure failed by one vote in the committee.

On the other hand, Americans appeared uneasy about the state of alcohol in their country. In 1956 drunken drivers were involved in 30 percent of all fatal traffic accidents, and 22 percent of adult pedestrians killed had been drinking. The science behind understanding the effects of alcohol was much better, too, with government literature explaining that two cocktails may reduce visual acuity and that it takes at least three hours for alcohol to metabolize. Dr. George W. Crane, a psychologist and newspaper columnist, told Congress that more people died from alcohol than in the Korean conflict. This type of thinking strongly resonated with Americans, and many people distrusted television advertising. Americans worried that advertising liquor on television would influence children.[3] Langer reintroduced a bill to ban alcohol advertising in 1958. This time, the potential law appeared to receive sweeping support.

In Maine, Senator Frederick G. Payne said he received "tremendous number of letters . . . regarding this bill. In my limited experience as a United States Senator, only one other matter has evoked as widespread public interest." Charlotte Cook of Rockland, Maine, wrote to Payne in support of the Langer Bill, S. 582: "To ban liquor advertising on radio and TV would do much to make these mediums a real asset in the home instead of a source of trouble and harm. Liquor does not have the same status before the law as other products since it is sold under a license. The effect of its use is only harmful to the human body, hence its use should be discouraged over radio and TV instead of encouraged. The effect of such advertising on the impressionable minds of children cannot be calculated but can be easily imagined."

Langer bill proponents took a page out of Sabin's legal analysis playbook and said that allowing liquor advertising in dry counties was a violation of the voter's choice. "It seems reasonable that when an area has voted by a majority vote to ban the sale of all alcoholic beverages, it has a right to be protected from continued advertising of that product," testified O. F. Dingler of the Texas Alcohol-Narcotic Education Inc.

Meanwhile, according to the National Editorial Association, 42 percent of weekly newspapers refused alcoholic beverage advertising. And television viewers against the advertising refused to watch programs with alcohol. "Many concerned people across the America are grateful to all publications and broadcasting stations which are willing to forgo profits for the sake of clear consciences," testified Clayton M. Wallace, executive director of the National Temperance League Inc. "Broadcasters would undoubtedly be glad to be rid of the controversial advertising."

Wallace and other temperance supporters were not just fighting the alcohol lobbies. They faced challenges from the newspaper, television, radio, advertising, and even the Lithographers National Association. Every lobby sought to protect its respective interests. Media needed the advertising revenue, but it would not have been the end of the world if they had lost alcohol advertising. They could just vamp up efforts for cigarette and automobile companies. The alcohol industry, on the other hand, viewed the Langer bills as an immediate threat and another form of Prohibition. The whiskey distillers considered the legislation unconstitutional with discriminatory clauses that "would deny the manufacturers of a single product the use of interstate channels of commerce in its advertising."[4] The Kentucky Distillers Association called the Langer bill class legislation to establish a "dangerous legislative precedent" from minority interests.

The KDA's arguments were well received in the first nine congressional hearings, but this time first-term senator Strom Thurmond greatly challenged the alcohol industry's position and caused many to worry he might cast the deciding vote for alcohol advertising reform.

Thurmond, who later co-sponsored a bill that proposed to ban celebrities from endorsing alcohol products, badgered every alcohol industry personnel in their testimony.

In the most heated exchange of the 1958 hearings, Thurmond challenged Grace Ellis, the president of the Women's Association of Allied Beverage Industries, over whether she wanted her kids to become alcoholics. But, unlike several of the men who became unraveled by the senator's "gotcha" questions, Ellis only frustrated the Republican and took a strong stand for women serving in the industry.

THURMOND: Are you married?

ELLIS: No, I am single.

THURMOND: . . . If it could be your decision as to whether your child would drink or not drink, what would be your decision?

ELLIS: I would certainly train my child not to drink until he or she had attained adult years. I would feel that I would have, by that time, trained the child, by example—which I would set and which my parents set for me—of moderation.

THURMOND: . . . Would it be your desire that your child be a drinker or a nondrinker?

ELLIS: If you mean the social use of alcohol after the child had attained adulthood, I would assume that, after my training and upbringing, the child, once he gained adult status, would do this in moderation. In other words, I say there is a social place for alcohol.

THURMOND: That is not exactly the question I asked. I asked if it would be your decision that he be a drinker or a nondrinker. Which would you choose?

ELLIS: I would say the person who uses the product in moderation.

THURMOND: You would say that you would prefer your child to be a drinker?

ELLIS: If you mean by "drinker" a person who uses the product in accordance with how he has been trained, how to treat it moderately, how to treat the product, yes.

THURMOND: Is it your opinion that advertising increases the consumption of alcoholic beverages?

ELLIS: I would say that advertising——

THURMOND: And does the advertising serve any purpose except to sell the product?

ELLIS: The purpose is to establish brand identification.

THURMOND: Do you think advertising increases the consumption or sale of any product?

ELLIS: I believe the sales figures answer that. The tax reports as quoted and entered into the record——

THURMOND: Without advertising, do you feel that the sales would increase or decrease?

ELLIS: I would say nationally advertised brands would have some problem.... Bootleg sales would increase, because people would lose means by which they could make identification. I would say young people might be triggered again in opposition to this matter of advertising on a legally made product, that bootleg alcohol would increase in sales.

THURMOND: You admit, do you not, that you do have an interest in the outcome of this matter, and you feel you might be affected by the outcome of this legislation?

ELLIS: I think it is quite apparent in the identification I have given you of myself.

After Ellis's testimony, the public was outraged that a woman had the audacity to speak so strongly to a senator and could take such a strong stand in support of alcohol advertising. Ellis's 1926 Milwaukee high school teacher wrote to Senator Thurmond to apologize, saying Ellis's testimony was "so far out of line with the facts . . . to protect the interest of the industry she works for."[5]

Ellis argued that the Langer bill falsely implied liquor advertising harms children and seeks to convert young people into drinkers. Ellis reasoned with the congressional panel. Considering she was the only female representative on the alcohol side in 1958, Ellis's opinion appealed to women and discredited the WCTU. In her most captivating analogy, Ellis said before Congress: "Let us consider the case of a most widely advertised product—soap. Does the child learn to use soap because of advertising or because he has been taught to do so by his mother?" She turned the alcohol abuse conversation into a household issue, saying that "any person who abuses the privilege of drinking is beyond the reaches of advertising. The abuser has a compulsion problem."

Ellis tried to speak for her entire gender: "Most women feel that they can get their children to wash behind their ears without police inspection. Most women feel perfectly capable of getting their husband to put on a coat when company comes without having a constable in to assist them. Now that same group of women want to pass a law and the same type of thing that brought about Prohibition—to prevent advertising, certain advertising from coming into my home. I can assure these women, millions and millions of women like me, do not need their help or assistance. If I think something is evil, I do not need a policeman to keep it out of my home."

Ellis may have not been the most powerful of the voices against banning alcohol advertising, but she certainly quieted many dry politicians, and WAABI defended the industry long after the dry movement's tenth attempt to ban alcohol advertising failed. To prevent more advertising ban attempts, WAABI and other alcohol organizations created self-imposed guidelines, such as not including female drinkers in advertisements or marketing to children. They preached moderation and drinking responsibly, but also fought government-imposed sanctions, such as whiskey taxes, at every turn. To this day, the Distilled Spirits Council of the United States, known simply as DISCUS, enforces an industrywide code of responsible practices to make sure the industry avoids similar congressional hearings.

Thanks to the days of prostituting whiskey slingers, many post-Prohibition states and cities barred women from serving alcohol. Most ordinances were on the books before Prohibition, and nobody refuted them because of the unsavory connection between women and bars. During Prohibition, investigators determined one of the main draws to speakeasies was a beautiful woman in feathers and silk. Speakeasy owner Mary Louise Cecilia, who went by Texas Guinan and was nicknamed Queen of the Night Clubs, greeted gangsters at the door with a friendly, "Hello, suckers!" Flapper historian Kelly Boyer Sagert wrote of Texas Guinan: "Police raided her clubs and padlocked them so frequently that she began wearing a necklace made of padlocks."[6] Another famous flapper, Hinda Wassau, the "Blonde Bombshell," became the first upscale striptease success, shaking her stuff to adoring guests.[7] This new breed of women sang, danced, made cocktails, and wore as little clothing as possible. For many women, the likes of Guinan and Wassau represented feminine freedom. "We women had been emancipated and weren't sure what we were supposed to do with all the freedom and equal rights, so we were going to hell laughing and singing," *New Yorker* columnist Louis Long told Harrison Kinney for his biography on James Thurber.[8]

But not everybody agreed. After Prohibition's repeal, many lawmakers considered it chivalrous not to allow women behind the bar or even serve them at a tavern. A 1938 Kentucky law stated that women could be served intoxicating liquors at tables only. "No distilled spirits or wine shall be sold, given away or served, on premises . . . to females except at tables where food may be served," the Kentucky law stated. This same state, where some women owned shares in whiskey distilleries, also did not allow women employees a license for the sale of alcoholic beverages. Kentucky prohibited "any female as a barmaid or for any duties with the respect to the sale of alcoholic beverages except to wait upon tables or serve as cashier or usher." These sexist laws existed all over the country. In Michigan, a woman could not tend bar in a town of 50,000 or more residents unless they were the bar owner's wife or daughter. In cities, where female bartenders were legal, male bartenders often saw them as a threat. Bartender unions in New York, Illinois, Massachusetts, Rhode Island, and California lobbied for ordinances excluding women from behind the bar. In the late 1930s, San Francisco Local 41 marketed a simple message: "Union Men! Do not patronize taverns that have WOMEN behind the bar. These places are all UNFAIR to organized labor. Demand the Union Button from the bartender that serves you."[9]

During World War II, male unions changed their tune, saying women could replace the bartenders. They retracted their barmaid invitation when the men returned from war.

If women tended bar in cities with laws banning them, they were arrested, fined, and often jailed. In 1948 the Supreme Court in *Goesaert v. Cleary* upheld the Michigan law that only allowed female family members of the bar owner to work at the tavern. This set landmark case precedent for any woman challenging their respective city or state laws. Four Sacramento, California, women were arrested and charged with violating state laws when posing as bartenders in 1953. In a time when women were lobbying for equal rights in many industries, these four women claimed that the state law was unconstitutional. The judge did not agree. He upheld their arrests without a comment on the law's validity.

Even women who owned bars were at risk of going to jail. When Philadelphia bar owner Kate Dineberg could no longer afford to pay two male bartenders, she started pouring beer herself. In 1962 the Pennsylvania Liquor Control Board claimed that she violated the state's Barmaid Act, a law forbidding females to serve alcohol behind the bar. The judge reversed a ten-day suspension of her business and said she was no threat to "public morals," but Dineberg had to pay for a defense attorney and take away from her business just because she had served her legal-aged clients.

No Place for a Woman

A bartender assumes considerable responsibility, which often involves brute force when he dons an apron and steps into his job. The place is hardly one for a woman—unless she is assuming full responsibility for the situation as owner of the saloon. Mayor Clyde Wiserman made a thoughtful move in announcing enforcement of a long-standing ordinance provision against any but owners tending bar if they are females. The ruling may well raise the question of bar maids and waitresses in the future. It should be understood, however, that the bartender, theoretically, is lord of all he surveys behind his broad and shining expanse. There's a difference.—*Alton Evening Telegraph* editorial, August 17, 1965

By 1964, twenty-six states had prohibited women from bartending. Men and women, as well as unions and leagues, fought the respective laws. John Iocovozzi, a Georgia bar owner, threatened to sue the state under the recently passed Civil Rights Act to give female bartenders equal rights. Several qualified women applied to John Iocovozzi's bar, but he could not hire under the state's law. Georgia, which did not even allow mixed drinks until 1964, ignored his claim that it was a civil rights issue.

In Appleton, Wisconsin, the Outagamie County Tavern League fought the Appleton City Council over a twenty-five-year-old ordinance because it wanted women to have the same rights and restrictions as men. Unless citizens were able to convince their city council members or state legislature to change the law, they did not receive favorable rulings, since the Michigan law was upheld by the Supreme Court. One judge said banning women from bartending was "chivalry toward women."

This same attitude existed toward serving female guests. During World War II, women without dates were banned from many bars. In 1943 New York's Little George's on Sixth and Broadway banned women from its bar, saying unescorted women targeted soldiers and their wallets. The owner considered the rule patriotic. "If I can't operate a tavern in suit Uncle Sam, then I won't operate one," said George N. McKeown. "I'm trying to raise social standards of saloonkeepers." In Louisville, Kentucky, Quino's Café refused to serve women. "Men like to sit around and talk among themselves—besides, we have plenty of business without women," said owner B. M. Heintzman. "Personally, I don't like to see ladies in the bars."[10]

Despite banned women laws being upheld by the U.S. court system, a 1972 Equal Rights Amendment would have eliminated laws that prohibited professions from banning workers based on gender. But it lacked three-fourths of state approval for ratification to become law. By 1977, 77 percent of Americans were living in states that had ratified the amendment, and more than forty-five organizations boycotted cities, such as Chicago and Atlanta, in states that did not ratify it.[11] Women also marched Washington, demanding equal rights, and refused to hold conventions for their organizations in non–equal rights states. Groups such as the Concerned Women for America protested the Equal Rights Amendment on the basis of protecting family values, and the amendment died in 1982. Still women made their voices heard, and cities and states dropped their bans on women bartenders.

A woman's right to serve alcohol and to be served was just a small part of the women's equal rights movements of the 1960s and 1970s, but every female bartender today owes a debt of gratitude for the battles that women fought fifty years ago. Even after they were allowed to tend bar, they endured sexual harassment and the kind of treatment that just would not be tolerated by today's standards.

When Joy Perrine first started tending bar in the early 1960s in St. Croix, she faced awful ridicule and lecherous and offensive comments from customers. As a twenty-year-old woman who came to the island to experience an artist's life and only worked bar to earn a paycheck, Joy left work in tears every day. "My boss finally told me to stand up for myself," Perrine said. "You have to stand your ground and give it right back." She moved to Louisville in 1978, six years after the state lifted its ban on female bartenders, and began working with a young up-and-coming chef named Dean Corbett.

More than thirty years later, Perrine authored *Kentucky Bourbon Cocktails* and became known as the "Bad Girl of Bourbon." She was mixing bourbon cocktails long before it was cool. In fact, Joy infused fruits with bourbons in the 1970s, thirty years before the process became in vogue for cocktail making,[12] and she pioneered the movement to use syrups other than the traditional simple syrups.[13]

Jefferson's Reserve bourbon and rye whiskey cofounder Chet Zoeller said that Perrine was one of the most important bourbon figures in the past quarter century. "She was not afraid to take what has traditionally been a very conservative, stand-alone spirit and mix it in a variety of juices, fruits, and other ingredients to create drinks that appeal to many different palettes," Zoeller says. And it is darn near heartbreaking to think that lawmakers from the 1940s to the 1970s deemed it "chivalrous" to keep talented women like Joy Perrine away from the bar.

Of course, these same lawmakers probably would have liked to put an end to women bootleggers, if they could catch them.

11

Post-Prohibition Women Bootleggers

The end of Prohibition changed nothing for criminal-minded women evading taxes and living their illicit American dream. Why go legit after Prohibition showed them how to make a successful living without getting caught? Bootleggers used all the skills they learned during Prohibition, including violence and court sympathy.

Women received lighter sentences than men, using the tried-and-true "I did it for my kids" excuse. When Decatur, Georgia, police arrested a woman, they learned her son suffered from leukemia and she bootlegged whiskey to finance the treatment. The officers decided they did not have sufficient evidence to convict, so they let her go. Minnie Emmons, a renowned Oklahoma bootlegger, was caught in 1955 with illegal liquor. When they apprehended her for her seventh arrest, they learned the forty-three-year-old mother was pregnant. Instead of pressing charges, the county attorney opted not to jeopardizing motherhood. "I know when I'm licked," the Oklahoma attorney said.[1]

After Prohibition, bootlegging meant something different in most parts of America. People still transported moonshine across county and state lines, but much of the bootlegging just meant they were selling legitimate product in dry counties. They purchased a case of whiskey legally in a wet county and sold it in a dry county. Local police would get tips that women were selling from their homes and search their premises, often without a warrant.

In 1953, sixty-year-old Callie Dixon received a six-month sentence after Adeline, Texas, cops found eight cases of malt liquor, two cases of canned beer, sixteen half-pint whiskey bottles, and gin. When her attorney made a motion to dismiss, showing the products were legitimate with duty paid, the judge dismissed the plea on account of the

1902 county dry law that allowed police to search her premises based on the bootlegging complaint.[2]

The most common arrest for a woman bootlegger was selling to minors. When Lena Fucaloro boozed up a boy and several of his friends in Des Moines, the father took the drunken boy to the cops to rat out the bootlegger. She was immediately arrested.[3]

In Cleveland, a city notorious for law-breaking ladies, Ludmila M. Fretch, a.k.a. Lillian Stancel Poles, a.k.a. Lillian Marie Poles, ran the city's largest illegal liquor racket in the 1960s. She spent every morning hitting the street corners supplying her bootleggers with hooch. On June 19, 1963, agents in the Northern District of Ohio suspected she was selling whiskey at 6112 Kinsman Avenue. Ludmila had been arrested several times over thirty years, so local and federal officers likely kept a close eye on her activities. They sent an undercover buyer to her apartment building and purchased liquor with marked bills. Authorities later raided her premises and found twenty gallons of distilled spirits in gallon jugs, pint bottles, and other containers, all without tax stamps. Ludmila was arrested and made bail the same day for $500, the modern equivalent to $3,000.

In her bond paperwork, Ludmila claimed her net worth was $12,000 and most of that was tied up in property. She pled not guilty initially, but later changed her plea to guilty "of the offense of having unlawfully possessed distilled spirits in containers which did not have affixed thereto tax stamps." U.S. District Judge James C. Connell, who was appointed by President Dwight D. Eisenhower in 1954, placed the bootlegger on four years' probation. "That means that anytime within that time that you get caught in anything like this again you will sentence yourself to jail. Not us, you," the judge said. "You have no business bootlegging, and I mean no business. Your husband works, he makes this kind of money, it is just too bad you own that property in the neighborhood where people will buy the stuff. You are found with three $1 bills that belonged to the State Agents an hour before, and the next time it happens, lady, you will sentence yourself."

Since Ludmila managed the property for tenants in the area where she was caught, she wanted to know if she could still manage it. The judge admitted she could, but said, "The temptation, I think, will be too strong for you. You ought to let somebody else do that because as sure as you go back you get yourself mixed up with some more illegal whiskey."[4]

Ludmila was never arrested again, but it's unknown as to whether she gave up bootlegging. The good ones just learned from their arrests and changed their tactics to keep from being caught again.

Maggie Bailey of Harlan County, Kentucky, may have been the state's largest bootlegger and was extremely careful. She asked a buyer's parents' names before exchanging liquor for cash. If she did not know the parents or have a mutual friend, no booze was sold. Standing five-foot-four and usually wearing a print dress, Bailey was a legendary figure who sold illegal liquor from the time she was sixteen in 1921 to the year "she got saved" in 1996. Bailey never made moonshine, but she purchased it from area 'shiners to sell out of her rented shack in Clovertown, a small rural town. Bailey never sold to children with one exception.

When a curly-headed neighbor boy knocked on her door for a half-pint of moonshine, according to *Illegal Odyssey: 200 Years of Kentucky Moonshine*, Maggie asked why he needed it. The boy replied, "Our little sister's laying a corpse and Poppie wants to make camphor to put on my little sister's face to keep it from turning black so we can have a funeral." She obliged, and the boy later became Judge Edward G. Hill, who told local law officials not to place Maggie in his court.

There was a good chance the sheriffs in Harlan County were supplying Maggie with her early moonshine anyway, so it is doubtful they would arrest her. Former Stitzel Weller executive Norman Hayden remembers traveling through Harlan County and wanting to taste some of the area's moonshine. He asked the sheriff where to get the good stuff, and the officer walked him to the back of his law enforcement vehicle, popped the trunk, and said, "Taste some of mine."[5]

Federal agents even admitted it was nearly impossible to bring a case against Maggie, mostly because everybody loved her. She cooked green beans and cornbread for any stranger and gave money to the poor. Maggie genuinely cared about everybody's well-being. She was the Robin Hood of American female bootleggers in much the same way Kate Kearney, the Irish poteen maker, fed the poor during the Great Famine. She put clothes on the backs of the children whose parents had no jobs. She gave coal to families who could not afford to heat their homes and donated thousands to community churches regardless of denomination. Many believe that's why she was so difficult to convict in a local or county court. "I don't care what the evidence was, the juries would not convict her," Harlan lawyer Eugene Goss told the *Harlan Daily Enterprise*.

When she and her husband stole a cop car in Tennessee on their honeymoon, half of Harlan County showed up to bail her out. And when the law did come sniffing around, somebody always offered to take the fall for her.

After Prohibition, Maggie attempted a legitimate license and sold tax-paid whiskey, but she said most customers still wanted the white moonshine. Plus, the illicit product was cheaper, and "I could double my money, that's why my moonshine business was better than my legal whiskey business. I had big business and made more money selling moonshine than I ever did selling legal stuff." For as stealthy as she was, Maggie did get caught.

In 1941, she sold to an undercover federal agent and was sentenced to two years in the Alderson, West Virginia, correctional facility. More than twenty years later, state police discovered booze at "Mag's Place" and $500,000 in cash and securities. But her brother-in-law Tyree Davidson took the fall. Following this arrest, the Internal Revenue Service realized Maggie Bailey never paid taxes. She also refused to keep her money in the bank after losing it in the Great Depression, so most of her cash sat securely inside foot lockers. The IRS placed $1.37 million in liens against her property, while the Kentucky Department of Treasury issued $3,708 in liens for back taxes.

The IRS sued Maggie for $170,391 in taxes and penalties between 1942 and 1963. In the 1970 trial, U.S. Tax Court Judge Norman O. Tietjens said Maggie "by reputation was the largest bootlegger in Harlan County." He admitted Maggie did not operate her business like most businesses, avoiding banks, industrial installations, construction, and making no financial arrangements with banks. The fact she kept no records of sales worked in her favor. The judge threw out the $170,391 amount, but upheld the claim she owed $18,000 in delinquency and late-filing penalties as well as $3,000 in penalties for the period between 1945 and 1954. All and all, it was a victory for Maggie, but after the trial, the authorities kept a close eye on her.

All Harlan County accounts of her life say she didn't give up selling until the 1990s when she "got saved" in the church. Despite the authorities constantly harassing her, Maggie continued to make a profit and usually evaded the police. Her secret to success was good hiding places. Maggie kept bottles of Maker's Mark, Jack Daniel's, Canadian Club, and other popular brands behind a coal bin. State police would raid the house, but they couldn't find any alcohol. Said one of her former lawyers, Otis Doan: "She had a secret door that was behind that coal bin and when you opened it up, you kind of stooped over and you went in there and there was a room full of liquor. Maggie was smart and she was nice to everybody, spoke to everybody. . . . Everybody was welcome at Maggie's house. When the police officer would come to raid, she'd offer to cook him something to eat while he was there."

Once in the 1970s, though, Maggie went inside the coal bin for a new customer and through a slight window, she saw state police pull into the driveway. Maggie latched the door shut from the inside. When she pulled the latch, however, it took away her outside view and Maggie would have to guess when to walk out. She sat there for a couple of hours and thought by that time they had left. "When she opened the coal bin door and walked out, she walked right out into the face of the state police and they found one of her big hiding places. She'd tell that story and just laugh," Doan told me.

When passing through the state, dignitaries drove to Harlan County just to meet her. On her 101st birthday, President George Bush, Kentucky coach Tubby Smith, Rich Smith, Senator Jim Bunning, and State Senator Daniel Mondiargo sent her birthday greetings. She was the cornerstone of a community and remains an important person to the local culture.

In the hills, many women like Maggie made their living making moonshine. A 1980s federal whiskey measure increased taxes 19 percent and created an uptick in illicit stills. But the operations were nothing compared with the old days. In 1935, two years after Prohibition, federal agents raided 15,712 stills. Twenty years later they seized 12,509 stills and only 8 in 1985. The fact is that the market for illicit whiskey was in the mountain rural areas, and legitimate whiskey was cheaper and better.[6]

The most famous woman moonshiner in the 1960s was Melissa Lester of Bartley, West Virginia. "I used to have the biggest submarine still in the country," Lester said. She started making moonshine after only receiving $57 a month from Social Security. "Heck, my kids would have starved. I had to do something, so I made mining timbers and moonshine whiskey," she said. She made whiskey from cracked corn, raisins, and other people's whiskey. "I made good whiskey," she said. But the truth is that not everybody made decent moonshine.[7]

After the 1950s, the main reason that local law enforcement agencies tracked illicit whiskey was for the health of their citizens. Tax revenue became a lesser priority compared with people going blind or dying from bad moonshine. In the 1970s federal and state agencies in high moonshine areas increased patrols near creek beds to find water sources for stills. It is at these still sites where most of the deathly contamination occurs. "You wouldn't believe the filth I've seen around stills," Glenn Burner, a federal agent in West Virginia, told the Associated Press in 1976. "Rats are a particular problem because they are attracted by the rotting mash." Bad moonshine was even a problem for the illicit whiskey makers. When they were arrested, moonshiners frequently asked the officers to inform the judges that they made good clean stuff. The last thing they wanted was the reputation for making blinding moonshine.

The moonshiner stings of the 1970s and 1980s eradicated most of the good ones, but occasionally a moonshiner, like Popcorn Sutton, came around and made whiskey so good that consumers were willing to pay cognac-like prices and risk getting arrested. But Sutton was a rare talent who earned the respect of legitimate master distillers like Wild Turkey's Jimmy Russell.[8] After World War II, the future of whiskey rested in the hands of legitimate distillers, marketers, and brand executives. Although it was primarily a boys' club, women changed the flavor and packaging of Scotch whisky and American bourbon.

12

Whiskey's Progressive Side

The first half of the twentieth century made business difficult for whiskey distilleries. Even before Prohibition, the government interfered with production to ensure grains and alcohols were used for the World War I effort. By the time temperance women won the argument on Capitol Hill, so many distillers struggled to make ends meet that Prohibition mattered little to near-bankrupt businesses. After repeal, much excitement and investment circled around the whiskey business, and distilleries greatly valued female labor, especially on the bottling line.

Since Congress passed the Bottled-in-Bond Act of 1897, which ensured BIB-labeled whiskeys were distilled, aged a minimum of four years in bonded warehouses, and bottled at 100 proof at one distillery, whiskey brands transitioned from selling barrels to bottles.[1] This also created new opportunities for women, because they were considered better bottlers than men, a precedent set in the European wine vineyards. "A great deal of work in the vineyards of France and Switzerland is done by women. Their fingers are smaller and more nimble," wrote Virginia Penney in the 1868 book *Five Hundred Employments Adapted to Women*. In a late 1800s photo at the Labrot & Graham Distillery, proud women stand behind bottles and whiskey cases. Their wage is unknown, and their names are lost with time, but these women represent a progressive side to the distillery business. Fifty years before most industries even considered hiring women, whiskey companies empowered women when it was not socially acceptable. This was true in all whiskey-making countries.

In Canada after Prohibition, nearly every distillery in the country used women on the bottling line. Women at G&W Distillers operated a canning production facility that closely resembled an automobile assembly line. At the Seagram plant in southern Ontario, women maintained a fast pace and measured their success by how quickly they could tie a ribbon around a bottle. In some cases, men reported to women, who had full managerial duties. At the plant that made Crown Royal Canadian Whisky, a forelady assigned jobs, managed the lines, and made sure her bottling ladies completed the tasks on all the Seagram brands. Seagram bottling line worker Trudy Schneider said the duties varied by the day: sometimes labels went on the bottleneck and sometimes the women were placing a seal or tying ribbons.

In the United States, women ran the bottling lines at Jack Daniel's, George T. Stagg, National Distilleries, Stitzel Weller, Old Forester, Labrot & Graham, and many others. If a consumer purchased a bottle of bourbon or Canadian whisky in 1940, the chances of it being bottled, labeled, and corked by a woman were extremely high. However, that's not the only contribution women made to whiskey. Marguerite Wright of Stitzel Weller and J. Gordon Baqule of Brown-Forman started entering once boys-only meetings as marketing directors, while Mary T. Willett was a partner at the new Willett Distilling Company. Willett was a small distillery one mile south of the Old Kentucky Home in Bardstown, Kentucky, with the capacity of 300 bushels a day and two 5,000-barrel warehouses. Mary and her brothers filled their first barrel of whiskey on March 12, 1937.

Mary Dowling maintained her family's Waterfill & Frazier distillery in Mexico under the D.W. Distillery label. The Mexican whiskey became something of a thorn in the side of new brands like Willett's. From the late 1930s to early 1960s, no laws prevented Dowling's company from flooding the market with Mexican bourbon at a much lower price than the American companies could produce it. *Bourbon* did not become a geographically protected term until 1964. Furthermore, strenuous Texas dry laws made the closer-to-home bootlegged Juarez whiskey extremely popular in the Lone Star state.

According to a 1937 *El Paso Herald-Post* article, Mary Dowling's distillery stored 8,000 barrels, which was triple the inventory of the original Waterfill & Frazier distillery in Kentucky. Thanks to their full production during Prohibition, D.W. maintained an advantage over American distilleries and was able to sell well-aged premium whiskey. The new U.S. brands were forced to sell unaged or very young whiskey at a much higher price than the Mexican products. Dowling made Mexican bourbon to compete with people in her home state, Kentucky. If she went to Kentucky Derby parties or golf outings, she probably did not talk to many wives of the distillers. They likely viewed her as a pariah, and their negative sentiments would only fester over the next couple of decades. But American whiskey makers could not take legal action against Mary for using the term *bourbon* in her Mexican-made products. After Germany invaded Poland in September 1939, the distillers had bigger priorities.

During World War II, alcohol production became an important factor for both sides of the war. Germany forced French winemakers to continue operations and made significant revenue from France's five famous winemaking regions.[2] In Scotland, whisky production came to a halt with all the country's barley being saved for food supplies. At the Laphroaig Distillery in Islay, the distillery became a major armory. From 1939 to 1945, Allied troops billeted at the Bushmills distillery in Ireland. In the United States, distilleries made industrial alcohol to create rubber, parachutes, jeeps, antifreeze, rayon, hand grenades, Howitzer shells, and aviation fuel. Less than ten years after Prohibition, U.S. whiskey manufacturers were primarily used for the war effort.

With men fighting, women performed every job the man did in the distillery. Distillery managers must have been confident in the shift to a mostly female workforce. Women had been working at the distillery for several decades now, so what was adding a few more jobs to their title?

Women working in factories were much newer to other American industries. The iconic "We Can Do It!" poster of Rosie the Riveter flexing her biceps in a factory became the symbol for every woman doing a man's job.

"Although we were unhappy about this war, we shared enthusiasm to support the effort because we were attacked [in Pearl Harbor]," said Frieda Loretta Calvano of New York, who worked for DuPont packing gunpowder into bomb detonators.[3] For the first time in American history, women were pipefitters, riveters, inspectors, and radio installers. They were still mothers, and many were becoming widows, but they pressed on, helping military production facilities create 300,000 aircraft, 12,000 ships, 86,000 tanks, and 64,000 landing craft as well as millions of artillery shells and weaponry.[4] The press was fascinated with women working at hard labor jobs, crowning Vera Anderson, a welder from Mississippi, "America's no. 1 torch girl." Women were also in positions of power.

Secretary of Labor Frances Perkins greatly influenced laws, such as the Wagner Act, which protected workers' rights to organize and would help women after the war. In 1942 Wisconsin, Iris Olson was named the first female labor executive in state history. Women even operated a professional baseball league to entertain Major League Baseball fans while the stars were at war.[5]

Female workers increased 141 percent and stay-at-home moms decreased 20 percent.[6] By 1944, 19 million women were working. They were the heroes of the American home front, but their service took a backseat to the thousands of veterans deserving their jobs back.

Women were ousted from their industrial positions and baseball, stripped of their individualism, and expected to return to their homes. The war was over; their use to society was minimalized by old principles. Women went back to the accepted jobs in nursing and clerical duties, as 75 percent of the women working in the aircraft and shipping industries lost their jobs. They were good enough to keep industry alive during the war, but were laughed at when requesting permanent positions. One War Department brochure said: "A woman is a substitute, like plastic instead of metal." Women fought back.

From Alaska to Great Britain, women organized to fight for their rights to work in a man-first society that desperately needed female labor during the war.

Where other industries failed to realize a woman's place after World War II, whiskey distilleries valued women. Norman Hayden started working at the Stitzel Weller Distillery in 1945 and said distilleries recruited women for bottling lines because they were just better at the job than men. "They could adjust much easier, because of the time involved sitting for extended periods of time, affixing labels," Hayden told me. Distilleries also recruited college-educated women for non-bottling-line jobs. "They were encouraging us to apply for jobs" after graduating college, said Jean Whitaker, a former chemist at the George T. Stagg distillery in 1945.

While other industries were cutting women loose, whiskey plants were giving them raises. Bottling line women were even protected when in the late 1940s the U.S. halted whiskey production to save grains to help feed Europe post World War II. The AFL Distillery Workers Union estimated 30,000 to 100,000 distillery workers lost their jobs during this food rationing, but made sure the bottlers and salesmen kept their positions. A woman bottler was one of the safest and best-paying factory jobs in the country.

According to the U.S. Bureau of Labor Statistics, women bottling line attendants earned $1.40 an hour in 1952, nearly double the amount of the national minimum wage.[7] Bottlers made more money than many U.S. households and bucked the 1952 Census's theory that the "relatively low incomes of the families headed by women can be explained in large measure by the fact the chief bread-winner in these families tends to be a person who did not expect to assume the responsibility of providing for a family and may not have been well prepared for this task when faced with it."

A full-time woman bottling attendant made about $3,000 a year, just $900 below the median income for all American families, and nearly equal to the man's average income. "The money influenced me to apply for the bottling line. . . . The first job I had down there was what we called pre-wrap on the holiday season," said Jewell Sorg, who worked for George T. Stagg, the current Buffalo Trace Distillery from 1961 until the 1990s. "After two weeks, I went home and told my husband, 'If that's what I've got to do the rest of my life to make a living we're going to have to do something else.'" Like many young women in the 1960s, Jewell did not accept the lowest position on the totem pole. After her temporary duties on the bottling line, she managed the tasting panel, where she mixed whiskey for tasters to consider and criticize. These types of opportunities were all over the distillery. "Anybody who was willing to put forth some effort and had basic office skills could get employment fairly easy at the distillery," Sorg told me. In fact, the only thing that kept women from advancing was often the cultural issues of the time.

In the 1950s, one woman, who wished to remain anonymous, was in line to become the master distiller for a major brand. But her boss said she was overlooked because women could not wear slacks. When the woman was tending to the vats, management worried the workers would stand under the stairs and look up her dress. There were also old wives' tales quietly passed down from distiller to distiller that kept women from advancing in distiller positions. A common concern was that menstruating women would destroy the yeast.

Women were also frequently dismissed from the warehousing duties because whiskey-filled barrels were thought to be too heavy for them to move. When women did work in warehouses, men became distracted. "You had fellas that were a little over zealous. . . . Hormones go to work. And that was always a problem, but you had to lay the law down and let men know over-flirting meant immediate dismissal," Hayden told me. "Many men ended up marrying women that they had worked with, and the husband would continue to work and some distilleries would let husband and wife work together. It worked quite well."

These whiskey companies gave women opportunities in small towns, where the only other job opportunity was working as a secretary for the local law firm or government office.

In Frankfort, Kentucky, Sorg rose through the George T. Stagg operations ranks, managing the transference of whiskey from the barrel all the way to the bottle. She even worked with ATF agents, who were stationed at distilleries up until 1982, and supervised leak hunters who scurried through the warehouses in search of leaking barrels. "I only had a problem with one fella," Jewell told me, "and that was a very small problem. He didn't agree with an order I gave, and he gave me some backtalk. I said, 'Well, let's go to the front office then. And we'll get this hashed out.' He turned around and went back to work." The man never gave Jewell backtalk again. "I tried to be fair with people, as I'd want to be treated at a job," she said.

As women were fighting for their rights, women like Jewell represented an important workforce for the distillery business, which steadily employed women in areas other than clerical work. Women filled bottles with bourbon, made barrels, and marketed products. They were earning respect in an industry that did not seek attention or realize that hiring women was a progressive move. That's just how it had always been. During this time frame, a woman invented a bottle that would change the bourbon whiskey category.

After Bill Samuels Sr. finished his military service, the sixth generation whiskey distiller talked about starting a new brand. He had sold his father's distillery, the T. W. Samuels, and been pondering a new venture. But in the 1950s, entering the bourbon whiskey category would have been an ill-advised business decision. Between government interference and a sagging U.S. market, it made little business sense to start a new Kentucky distillery. Would temperance women gain political capital again? If the United States enters another war, will it commandeer grains used for whiskey production? With Scotch whisky and cognac becoming esteemed spirits, how will bourbon fair in the store? These were all questions that heavily weighed on Samuels Sr. for several years until his wife, Marge Samuels, told him to "get off his ass" and take action. Although Samuels Sr. was retired, he was still president of the school board, served on the state chamber of commerce, and was helping build the Bardstown Country Club. But there was something missing in his life that only his best friend could see: the man needed to make whiskey.

If he pursued this dream, Marge had two conditions: Samuels Sr. could not produce the same, harsh-biting whiskey profile his father had at the T. W. Samuels Distillery. She wanted something smoother, and Marge wanted to create the bottle.

In the 1950s, every whiskey bottle looked the same: about twelve to sixteen inches tall, an elongated or bulbous shape with a slender neck and complex labels that incorporated people, trees, birds, and even dogs. When consumers shopped for bourbon, they walked down an aisle of products with nearly the exact same bottles and labels. One or two may have been different, but the whiskey packaging world was in dire need of a boost when Marge started experimenting with the Maker's Mark bottle. A studious woman with a degree in chemistry from the University of Louisville, Marge had a terrific sense of design and style. She studied calligraphy and created posters for her kids.

During the school year of 1956, Bill Samuels Jr. was the associate photography editor for his yearbook. He set up a photo lab in the basement under the steps. When Marge became the de facto research and development director for bottling, she tossed her son's photography equipment and set up a half-size drafting table. Marge molded papier-mâché into the shape of a bottle and a handcrafted tattered label for the first drafts. She desired a bottle that looked more like the unique French cognac bottles that displayed a sense of artistry unfound in the American whiskey bottles. These cognac bottles used wax to seal the cork instead of industrial tape.

Marge believed the cognac's wax complemented the idea of the crafted product, but she wanted the wax to jump out and grab attention instead of just serving a functional purpose. Marge had this vision of letting the wax drip down the bottleneck, like a candle, in contrast to cognac's smoothing just below the cork. This new waxing strategy had never been attempted, at least intentionally, and Marge wanted a wax to become the new, still unnamed, whiskey's trademark look.

She took the deep fryer from the kitchen into her bottling lab in the basement. "We went seven months without French fries or fried fish," remembers Bill Samuels Jr. Heating the materials in the fryer, Marge tried different viscosities, making the wax thinner or thicker, and various color pigments from a dark and dirty brown to a gray-black wax before settling on an eye-popping red. She added a plasticizer to generate the visual effect she wanted. Marge dipped the curvy bottle into her red wax invention, letting the hot wax drip down the bottleneck forming tendrils, and placed her handmade label on the bottle of whiskey she named "Maker's Mark." As a collector of fine pewter, Marge always searched for the "mark of the maker," so naming the new whiskey was easy for her.

When Maker's Mark launched in 1959, its sexy bottle was the woman in a red dress next to ladies in jeans and T-shirts—the bottle just stood out.

But there was a little in-home controversy after the red wax. Shortly after Marge created the wax recipe, the government disallowed several ingredients. "What happened was the government started regulating the materials that you could have in the wax. . . . That caused Dad great grief," Samuels Jr. told me.

They also faced issues with the handmade paper label. As other spirits companies were streamlining bottling with more industrial practices, Marge demanded her bottles maintain a hand-torn label. Samuels Sr. said, "Screw this," because there was no way they could keep up with demand with the slowness of hand-tearing and placing the labels. Although she would not budge on the red wax, Marge caved on hand-tearing labels. It just made economic sense to move toward a semiautomatic labeling machine operated by a foot crank. They had to keep a full-time glass inspector on the payroll because the bottles were so unusual and hard to make that many came in defected with irregular bottlenecks. "You could say mom's contribution had caused dad acid reflux. . . . Every time we'd receive an order of glass we'd go through every one of them, because leaning necks didn't look right," Samuels Jr. said. Bottles came in chipped and broken.

"For the first twenty years, {the bottles} were a pain in the ass, because we could never keep a supplier," Samuels Jr. told me.

There was one other thing that gave Samuels Sr. "heartburn," and that was fixing up the distillery, another one of Marge's ideas. When they purchased the Burks Spring Distillery in 1953, they found a fine piece of property northeast of Loretto, Kentucky, on Hardin's Creek. Founded by Charles Burks in 1805, it was originally a gristmill and distillery that eventually made rye whiskey called Belle of Loretto and a sour-mash whiskey called Old Happy Hollow. At the peak of its pre-Prohibition capacity, Burks produced about 3,400 barrels a year. It was a nice distillery, but didn't really warrant any significant historical attention. Marge Samuels didn't see it that way.

In the 1950s, historic preservation included presidential homes and Civil War battle sites, not old distilleries. But Marge believed the old Victorian look of the former Burks Spring Distillery would appeal to historic-minded visitors. Instead of tearing down the old buildings and creating new ones, Marge thought it would be nice to restore them to their original form. Much like her bottle design with its dripping wax and hand- torn label, her vision for the distillery was expensive and time-consuming. And it was not necessarily accepted by Samuels Sr. They kept most of the materials from the old buildings and used them in reconstruction. She interviewed residents who lived nearby to learn about why the distillery was important to the community.

This seemed unnecessary at the time, but Marge realized the importance of history to an upstart whiskey. When the Samuels applied for a National Historic Landmark through the National Park Service, Maker's Mark, under the "Burks' Distillery," became the country's first distillery to be a historic landmark in 1980. This was all thanks to Marge's restoration vision. "She saved the place," her son said.

And some might say she helped save bourbon. Although her son is often credited for Maker's Mark's unprecedented rise in the liquor industry, there's no denying Marge's bottle design and patented red wax started the Maker's Mark conversation. Since her experimentation in the kitchen fryer, Marge's red wax has been trademarked and copied by more than 100 spirit brands, from the smaller Kopper Kettle Virginia Whiskey to category leader Jose Cuervo tequila. Lawyers for opposing sides often say, "You can't trademark a wax because cognac makers have been doing it for centuries." But Marge's careful crafting and planning of the red wax and her attention to the creation of tendrils made the red wax dripping seal "due protection" under U.S. trademark laws.

On May 9, 2012, the Sixth Circuit Court of Appeals ruled: "After a six-day bench trial, the district court found that Maker's Mark's red dripping wax seal is a valid trademark and that Cuervo had infringed that trademark. Based on those findings, the district court enjoined Cuervo permanently 'from using red dripping wax on the cap of a bottle in the sale, offering for sale, distribution or advertising of Cuervo tequila products at any locality within the United States.'"

Not only did Marge's idea for a new bottle change liquor packaging and set a landmark trademark law, her history-saving and visitor-friendly vision for the distillery planted the first seed in the increasingly popular Kentucky Bourbon Trail, one of the state's most important tourism features attracting people from all over the world. In 2011, the Maker's Mark distillery hosted more than 100,000 visitors. Marge Samuels saw this potential six decades before anybody had even heard of Maker's Mark.

As he looks back on his mother's contributions, for as accepting as the whiskey business has been to women, Samuels Jr. can't help but wonder what if society had afforded his mother the same opportunity the men received. "I think generally women have been way underutilized," he said. Despite this, and without making it a priority, Maker's Mark has always hired women for male-dominated positions and even named Victoria MacRae-Samuels vice president of operations. Victoria was not the highest-ranking whiskey woman of the past sixty years. That title belongs to one of Scotland's most cherished ladies.

13

The Lady of Laphroaig

After graduating from Glasgow University, Elizabeth Leitch "Bessie" Williamson wanted to fly for the first time, but didn't want to trek around the world. Williamson flew over lochs, bays, rivers and the Sound of Islay to land in the temperate island of Islay, one of the premiere vacation destinations in the 1930s. She stepped off the plane onto the small island of 4,000 people that shipped £8 million worth of untaxed bulk whisky to the Scottish mainland for blending. Williamson enjoyed the beach and boated to the smaller island of Texa, a 700-meter island with the sea splashing against schist and hornblende rocks. At some point during her 1934 respite, Williamson picked up a local newspaper and saw an advertisement for a shorthand typist at the local Laphroaig distillery. She applied and received an offer.[1]

When she took the position, Williamson planned to stay for just three months and must have viewed the job as an extended vacation on the beautiful island. But after owner Ian Hunter witnessed her work ethic, he offered her a full-time position. From that day on, Williamson became the essence of Laphroaig.

Prohibition had just ended, and all Scotch whiskies hoped to regain lost consumers. Whether bootlegged or hidden in American homes, Laphroaig remained available in the U.S. market during Prohibition and stood poised to capture market share with its excellent whiskies, such as the Islay Mist blend and Laphroaig Single Malt. Laphroaig also sold bulk juice to be blended for Long John, Highland Queen, Queen Anne, Dewars, Johnnie Walker, King George IV, Grant's Steadfast, Haig, and many other whisky brands.

Despite past female leadership, Laphroaig mostly employed men. But Hunter saw something in Williamson. Whether it was her incredible passion for people or unwavering business acumen, Hunter trusted her with the distillery when he traveled, giving her the keys to the company and expecting her to maintain shipments to partners and build relationships with distributors. This magnitude of female responsibility was unusual in the 1930s. Considering Laphroaig's current status as an iconic Islay single malt, in retrospect, Hunter's trust in Williamson would have been the equivalent to Henry Ford letting his secretary run Ford Motors while he traveled. This initial belief in her was only the beginning. When Hunter suffered a stroke in 1938, he asked Williamson to take over his U.S. affairs. She soon became the distillery manager.

Some have speculated about Williamson's relationship with Ian and wondered if it led to her becoming Scotland's only female distillery manager. A secretary turned manager would leave many to wonder. In Ian's correspondence with the Honorable Geoffrey Cunliffe of the Board of Trade in London, he wrote of Williamson joining him with the great billiards teacher, Riso Levi. Cunliffe replied: "Wish we were back in Islay again and look forward to seeing you in London. Love to you and Williamson from us all. Yours, G." Instead of a romantic relationship, though, Ian and Williamson's affection was purely platonic. This relationship speculation was gossip and nothing more.[2]

The fact is that, after Ian, who perfected the flavor profile of the whisky, Williamson was the most qualified person to run Laphroaig. Her experience in handling Ian's business affairs groomed her for corporate leadership, and she had a knack for the whisky business.

During World War II, many of the Laphroaig men were drafted for service. When the Scottish government requested the Laphroaig facilities for the war effort, a Laphroaig representative wrote to the Ministry of Supply: "We would suggest that our secretary, Miss E. L. Williamson, should take charge of the management, as she has been in our employment for over 10 [sic] years, and is quite capable of discharging the duties pertaining thereto, and is fully conversant with the supervision of our property."

Williamson took over Ian's full-time duties just before World War II began. Within months of Laphroaig receiving trademarks in New Zealand and Canada, Williamson added military liaison to her managerial duties. The government ceased whisky production, using grains to feed soldiers, and wanted to use Laphroaig for military purposes. If the wrong person managed Laphroaig, the government probably would have taken over the distillery without any care to the facility. Soldiers would have guzzled whisky straight from the barrel, and quartermasters would have stripped distillery equipment to melt and build military machinery. This happened to distillers in the U.S. Civil War and throughout Ireland's skirmishes. Militaries borrowing distillery facilities rarely work in favor of the distilleries. But Williamson showed moxie, refusing to acquiesce to every military demand.

When in July 1940 the Scottish Royal Artillery pursued forty-year-old Ian MacLean for a "gunner" position, Williamson wrote to the Military Service Hardship Committee: "We beg to apply for a period of exemption. He has been employed as warehouse keeper here for the past six years, having been trained to this work from boyhood. Our warehouses contain a stock of Malt Whisky, about 8,000 casks, the dutiable value of which is in the region of some £3 million. He has rendered himself indispensable by virtue of his intimate knowledge of the special conditions under which the security of this valuable stock is maintained, He is familiar with the Government regulations in regard to handling and dispatch of casks from Bond. Even if a thoroughly skilled cooper of over military age were obtainable at present, he would require to serve with the present man for a considerable period before he would be competent to undertake the responsibility which falls to this man's duties." Because every able-bodied man was needed to fight, hardships were rarely granted. But Williamson knew exactly how to communicate to the military committee. By emphasizing the £3 million and the importance of MacLean's unique ability, Williamson managed to receive a "Release for Urgent Work of National Importance" for her warehouse manager and likely saved his life.

Williamson dealt with the military on a regular basis. The first company of the Royal Engineers billeted in the distillery malt barns, sleeping on the upper floors and dining downstairs. Some military men transitioned through Laphroaig in a leave capacity, watching movies in the homemade theater while recuperating from battle. Those soldiers permanently stationed at Laphroaig enhanced the nearby Glenegedale Airport and accepted aircraft while protecting western approaches and government secrets. Field kitchens were built in the distillery houses, and the latrines known as "Lavender Square" were built around a warehouse of aging whisky. This first unit departed sometime in 1940.

More than 200 soldiers replaced the first company, and Islay became a restricted area, protected by antiaircraft weaponry. Allied forces viewed the distillery as an important location and wanted more space for military use.

When the deputy controller of factory and storage premises demanded the requisition of 23,200 square feet, comprising the malt barns and dried grains loft, Williamson negotiated a smaller need. "We quite understand the necessity for this," she wrote, "but would like to have the full use of our dried grains loft, as this is the only place where we can store our farm feeding stuffs and farm seeds." As Germany bombed Allied forces in November 1943, Williamson showed incredible fortitude to keep the Laphroaig's interests in mind. Government officials were not accustomed to working with women of power and could have reminded her that war efforts take priority over "full use of dried grain lofts." They probably had never encountered a woman like Williamson, a strong-willed, likeable lady who would not bend.

In the case of facilities, the Ministry of Works withdrew its grain loft request and inquired about the malt barns' storage capacity. The Ministry wanted 450 tons of storage capacity for an undisclosed reason. Williamson informed the government official that the malt barns held 400 tons and the military was welcome to pay for the reconstruction to carry the maximum load. In some countries, it might have been considered treasonous to suggest that the government enhance the Laphroaig facility during a time of war, but Williamson clearly knew how to manipulate the system.

For two years, Laphroaig became a major ammunitions hub. Boats pulled into the Sound of Islay, and Laphroaig workers and sailors loaded bullets, artillery shells, and large bombs. Williamson signed off on every shipment. On May 20, 1944, Williamson approved this shipment to Allied forces via the SS *Moor*: 32,078 no. 42 containers of small arms rounds, 4,634 shot cases, 312 high explosive shells, 1,670 cartons of cartridge cases, and 1,067 bomb carrier cases.[3] Had the Germans known Laphroaig stored munitions, it most certainly would have been an air raid target.

The Germans blitzed Scotland's key industry areas, randomly hitting Clyde, Edinburgh, Aberdeen, Glasgow, and Dundee. They even destroyed the Bushmills office in Dublin. Islay was safe during the war with no immediate threat. But if they had known about Laphroaig's massive 400-ton-plus ammunition depot, Hitler's air force would have prioritized the target in Scotland bombings. Laphroaig packed enough ammunition on May 20, 1944, that Williamson could have supplied a brigade, maybe even an entire division. The 312 high-explosive shells, listed as "HE shells" in the company's paperwork, would have been enough ordnance to wipe out the entire southern portion of Islay if bombed. This must have brought Williamson considerable stress, especially since her signature was on every official document. Williamson, a Glasgow University graduate turned secretary turned distillery manager, became an important Islay war operative.

While hiding the explosive rounds in the Laphroaig malt barn, Williamson continued handling regular affairs, renewing the Laphroaig trademarks, surviving accounting audits, and maintaining payroll. She also made sure nobody stole her whisky. There had to be several thirsty sailors and soldiers eager for a dram. Protecting the whisky while soldiers were at port must have been a priority and probably added to the reasons she lobbied for MacLean not to be drafted. MacLean kept a close eye on the £3 million inventory.

As the Allied forces advanced from Paris to the Rhine River, with victory well within their grasp, the Ministry of Works in Glasgow handed control back to Laphroaig, and Williamson could recommence whisky production. She no longer needed to risk her life or her employees' lives to store ammunition and artillery. The Ministry employee addressed Williamson as "secretary" instead of her rightful title as manager. Whether this was an error or intended as an insult, Williamson most certainly gained the trust of her employees and respect from all of Islay. She fought for her employees, negotiated with the government, and never buckled under the pressure of war or whisky management. In 1954 Ian Hunter died and left the company to the most qualified person on his payroll, Bessie Williamson.

Under Williamson's managerial tenure, she developed relationships with other distillers, making Laphroaig one of the most highly sought after whiskies for blending. When she visited the Dailuine-Talisker Distilleries, Williamson gave manager Allen Scot a bottle of Laphroaig. He wrote, "I am deeply grateful to you for the unexpected gift. . . . I am no connoisseur nor whisky expert but my opinion is that it is a good whisky with a flavor entirely different from our Speyside product being much heavier which may be the true characteristic of Islay malt."

Laphroaig whisky was bold and smoky, and Williamson believed consumer palates were leaning toward this style. Many 1950s newspaper articles discussed the merits of blended Scotch's peaty notes. Instead of wasting this distinctive character in blended products, Williamson envisioned making Islay single malt whisky more than a smoky note in blends; she wanted to market the Laphroaig Single Malt products.

Perhaps Williamson realized this positive peat press probably came from Laphroaig's whisky sent for blending. Why not take a shot at renewing marketing efforts with Laphroaig Single Malt whisky?

As soon as she became Laphroaig's owner, her single malt mission helped all Islay whisky and planted the seeds for today's burgeoning Islay brands, such as Bowmore, Lagavulin, and Ardbeg. Williamson marketed the island first and Laphroaig second. In an early 1960s Scottish television interview, Williamson said: "The secret of Islay whiskies is the peaty water and the peat, which we can get on the island that makes the Islay whiskey what it is. . . . Islay whisky is famous as an essence for blending purposes. We keep the whisky here anything from five to ten years, and then it's sent to blending houses in Glasgow. . . . There's an increasing market for the Islay whiskies. We can't supply the demand that we have for our whisky."

Her message of "we can't supply the demand" has become the world of whiskey's best marketing tactic. More than fifty years after Williamson used it, Maker's Mark and Pappy Van Winkle bourbons have built their brands around the "we can't supply demand" strategy. It's simple human nature: People want what they can't have, and Williamson essentially told the public, "You better buy Islay single malts before we run out."

Seeing her enthusiasm for marketing and knowing of her previous U.S. experience, the Scotch Whisky Association named Williamson its American spokesperson from 1961 to 1964. She toured the United States, from bar to bar and liquor store to liquor store, spreading the word about all Scotch whisky. "She can discuss malted barley and peat water in such a learned manner that it makes a listener wish for noon or quitting time," wrote *Chicago Tribune*'s George Schreiber of "Britain's only female distiller." Even though the United States had women working in distilleries and even female owners, reporters were fascinated by a woman running a Scotch whisky company. They often put Williamson on the offensive about her gender. "Yes, it is odd for a woman to be a distiller of whisky, but you don't have to be an odd woman to be a distiller," Williamson told an Associated Press reporter in 1962.[4]

When she retired from her role as an industry spokesperson, the American market started switching its interest from blended Scotch to single malts. This 1965 Associated Press article indicates Williamson's single malt focus worked: "The Scotch most people drink is a blend of malt and grain whiskies. But the straight malt whiskies, a heavier drink with a more pronounced flavor than the blendeds, are gaining ground. The malts have names of poetry: Glenlivet, Laphroaig, Glenfiddich, Strathisa, Glenmorangie, Aultmore, Talisker." Today single malt Scotch whisky enjoys the premium status, while blends are often relegated to the bottom shelf. One could not give credit solely to Bessie Williamson, but the single malt success was most certainly her vision when she took over Laphroaig. And it is most certainly not a coincidence that single malt Scotch whisky became premium liquor during her time as an industry spokesperson.

While touring America, Williamson met the handsome Canadian baritone Wishart Campbell. He was known as "the Gold Voice of Air" and one of Canada's most beloved musicians. When they married in 1961, it was a quiet union of two iconic people in their respective industries. But many Laphroaig employees did not like Wishart. "He was not a nice man," Eddie Morris, who worked in Williamson's greenhouse, told me. "He was terrible to her. I'll never forget this: He turned to her and said, 'You get back up to the kitchen where you belong.'"

No matter what was happening at home, Williamson still managed the distillery in stellar fashion. The year she wed, Laphroaig installed a new warehouse, and Williamson hoped to renovate the property. But she lacked the funds to properly conduct repairs. If she wanted to increase Laphroaig production, she needed outside help. So she sold one-third of her shares to Long John Distillers and sold another large chunk of shares in 1967. By bringing in outside investment, Williamson, now addressed as Mrs. Wishart Campbell, planned to convert the old still house into an oil-fired boiler, while adding a third spirit still and two new wash stills. The new boiler weighed seventeen tons and presented transport problems. Likely reminding the military what she had done for Scotland during World War II, Williamson used an Army Landing Craft for transporting the massive boiler to Islay.

This new distillery equipment catapulted Laphroaig ahead of Long John Distilleries and other Scotch brands: Strathclyde, Tormore, Glenugie, and Kinclaith. But it also represented a significant sacrifice on Williamson's part. As she gave up shares, she lost the power to manage as she wanted.

Perhaps that is what she wanted anyway. Her real passion seemed to be helping others. Williamson helped the sick and the poor, and most of all she helped her own. She kept employees past their prime and refused to lay people off based on their individual circumstances. Williamson financially supplemented her employees if they drank up all their money on payday, and she hired older workers because no pension scheme could help them in retirement.[5] She held Christmas parties for orphaned children and garden fairs for elderly ladies. "She was the nicest woman I've ever met in my life," Morris said. But the kindness chapter of her life is often forgotten, said current Laphroaig master distiller John Campbell. "She was such a huge part of the community," said Campbell, who is not related to Williamson's late husband.

For Williamson's philanthropic efforts, the queen of England was "graciously pleased" to sanction Williamson's promotion in the "Most Venerable Order of the Hospital of St. John of Jerusalem" on January 15, 1963. Williamson embodied the Order's mission of preventing and relieving sickness and injury. After the queen graced her neck with the medal, Williamson gave the oath: "I do solemnly declare that I will be faithful and obedient to The Order of St. John and its Sovereign Head as far as it is consistent with my duty to my sovereign and to my country; that I will do everything in my power to uphold its dignity and support its charitable works; and that I will endeavor always to uphold the aims of this Christian order and to conduct myself as a person of honor."

Williamson's kindness and Order of St. John status did not meld well with the realities of a 1960s corporation. Williamson looked beyond numbers and hired workers for nonbusiness reasons. From a corporate standpoint, Laphroaig could have been much more profitable if Williamson did not keep older workers and didn't hire unqualified men just so they could feed their families. Her "people first" mentality would clash with Long John's profit-driven ideals.

When Long John distiller John McDougall, who managed Tormore Distillery, was transferred to Islay, he noticed right away that Williamson still ran the show even though she no longer owned the majority of the company. "She was very much the matriarch of Laphroaig, and what Long John desperately wanted to do was get their systems, their controls, and their administration procedures in place at Laphroaig to replace the old culture of 'We do it this way because we've always done it this way.' I found out that this was the prevailing attitude very soon after taking up my position," McDougall wrote in his memoir, *Wort, Worms & Washbacks*.

Williamson sold the remainder of her shares in 1972, and she walked away knowing she had given the company everything she had for nearly forty years and left it in the hands of Long John. When she died in 1982, Islay mourned a woman who put Laphroaig whisky on the map and gave more to others than she ever took for herself. "She'll never be forgotten," Morris told me.

Williamson's legacy is taking care of the people, clothing the homeless, feeding the hungry, and employing the unemployed. Nothing can rival her philanthropic heart, but Williamson saved Laphroaig from complete military takeover and elevated single malt's status in America. Every bottle of Laphroaig stands as a tribute to Bessie Williamson, and all single malt lovers owe her a toast. Without Williamson, who knows, blended whisky might still be the Scotch of choice.

14

Modern Women

In the 1980s, businesswomen were becoming more accepted in the workplace. In 1984 women received 49 percent of the bachelor's and master's degrees.[1] Great Britain's prime minister Margaret Thatcher showed the world that a woman could lead a country, Sandra Day O'Connor joined the U.S. Supreme Court, and Democrat Geraldine Ferraro was the first female vice presidential candidate from a major party. In popular culture women were empowered, from the young and vibrant characters in *Laverne & Shirley* who operated a beer bottling line set in the 1950s, to the widows in the *Golden Girls*, who showed how women can enjoy themselves after their husbands die.

Women still earned significantly less than men and faced sexism; nonetheless, they were in a much better place than the 1950s from political and pop culture standpoints. From the whiskey side, however, the 1970s and 1980s were lost decades. Ladies continued to operate the bottling lines, worked in marketing, and occasionally broke through the male-dominated roles, but the growing spirits companies only maintained status quo. Perhaps the rest of the world simply caught up to the whiskey companies regularly employing women. The 1990s would become the Renaissance era for whiskey women.

Young women graduated from college in whiskey regions, searched for jobs in chemistry or marketing, and landed positions at distilleries. They did not necessarily seek these opportunities; sometimes the careers found them. Some women were born into the whiskey business and joined the family destiny despite trying to avoid it. However they entered the business, the 1990s was the most prominent growth decade for women in whiskey at all levels. These women changed everything about the industry, from the flavor profiles to the packaging.

Scotland's first modern female master blender was Rachel Barrie, who earned the title in 1995, but she discovered whisky much earlier. Barrie grew up in Aberdeenshire, Scotland, an important countryside distilling district. Her grandparents were farmers, not whisky makers, but everybody understood the importance of the spirit to the area's culture. In the 1970s and 1980s, Barrie remembers her grandmother mixing the local whisky from the Glen Gerioch Distillery with cream and double cream. "My first taste of whisky was at seven in a hot toddy for an earache," she remembers.

More than ten years after her first medicinal use of whisky, Barrie joined the Scotch Malt Whisky Society as an amateur in 1991. Studying chemistry at Edinburgh University, she became fascinated with whisky creation. How did it receive its color? Where did the smoky notes originate? How could a piece of wood actually enhance a liquid's flavor? She approached whisky as a scientist, thoroughly examining each process that enhances flavor. Upon graduating, she took a job at the Scotch Whisky Research Institute to study the maturation of Scotch whisky in casks. For years whisky makers dumped juice into barrels and aged it for however many years their ancestors did. Under the tutelage of the scientists at the Scotch Whisky Research Institute, Barrie took these olden processes and placed them under a magnifying glass. "There was very little known about maturation," Barrie told me. "We were using all the same materials that had been used for certainly the past couple of centuries, but of course maturation is a fairly new phenomenon. In the 1500s and 1600s, there was no maturation. It was just the aqua vitae. Maturation makes up 60 to 70 percent of the flavor. I tried to understand how much of the flavor comes from the cask and how much from maturation." She helped develop the modern sensory science techniques for optimizing the taste in Scotch whisky. "In some ways, you could say the job quite fit a female in the balance between senses and analysis," Barrie said.

She found more than 100 aromas in some whiskies, the equivalent to a Steinway grand piano. Barrie analyzed, documented and validated cask-aging methods for Scotch whisky for five years until one of the preeminent Scotch whisky brands caught wind of her research and hired her as the first modern Scotch whisky female blender in 1995.

At the Glenmorangie distillery, Barrie and Dr. Bill Lumsden, head of distilling and whisky creation, put scientific methods to work and changed the whisky industry. The Whisky Creation Team experimented with different ratios of chocolate malted barley to normally malted barley and different cask methods. Barrie blended thirty-year-old whisky, young whisky, used rum barrels, bourbon barrels, sherry barrels, changed the malting strategies, and did things that nobody had ever attempted in creating some of the best whiskies ever known to man. The Glenmorangie Sanalta PX spent ten years maturing in American white oak casks and then was transferred into Spanish ex-Pedro Ximenez (PX) casks, known as the king of the sherry barrels, for its final two years, while the Glenmorangie Signet embodied the new techniques of chocolate barley malt and specialized American oak casks. Both whiskies stunned anybody who tasted them. Barrie not only stepped outside the box; she built a new box. Before her, many whisky makers were just leaving the juice in one barrel for the standard six or more years. About the innovative Signet, Barrie said: "We started the process by using tumble roasted chocolate malted barley and continued innovating with every element thereafter. We experimented with various ratios of roasted chocolate malted barley to normally malted barley, various casking strategies, and length of maturation. Then constant sampling, refinement, and further stock selections to create the final taste I had originally imagined at the start—a rich, robust, and distinctive nutty aromatic coffee aroma and taste, like no other malt whisky before."[2] After her experimentation and proving there is something special about finishing in different cask types, everybody started using these techniques. But changing the whisky development may not have been her greatest accomplishment.

Glenmorangie Signet "Distiller" Tasting Notes

Aroma: A strong Aruba espresso fused with a trace of plum pudding, rich with sherry, and candied orange peel.

Taste: A contrast of rich sweetness with an explosive crackle of sizzling spices and bitter mocha.

Finish: A fresh spring-like breeze of mint with a bright citrus lemony-green quality.[3]

In 1997, Glenmorangie purchased Ardbeg distillery, and Barrie was charged with examining the existing Ardbeg whisky stocks. Since the

Ardbeg is in the Islay, the heavier peat process gave her a smokier whisky to work with than her Highland creations at Glenmorangie. She met with her crew once a month to discuss the development and innovation of the whiskies. Her team's Ardbeg whisky was considered among the best whiskies made over the past twenty years. Ardbeg Supernova received 97 out of 100 points in Jim Murray's *Whisky Bible* in 2010, and the distiller's flagship expressions—ten years old and Ardbeg Uigeadail—earned World Whisky of the Year in 2008 and 2009. The entire job was "pure research," Barrie told me, with the occasional media opportunity. For sixteen years, she kept whisky enthusiasts guessing "What's next?" For Barrie, in the fall of 2011, the answer came in the form of another whisky, one a little closer to home.

Instead of Glenmorangie or Ardbeg, however, she took her talents to Glasgow-based Morrison Bowmore, Scotland's biggest small distiller. Morrison Bowmore owns three distilleries, including Glen Garioch, which made the first whisky Barrie tasted. Named master blender in January 2012, Barrie joined a Bowmore label, which produces some of the world's most collectable whisky. She also blends McClelland's, Glen Garioch, and Auchentoshan single malts, giving her a wide range of flavor profiles. Operations director Andrew Rankin told me, "Rachel is one of the most experienced master blenders in our industry." At her new position with the same title, Barrie is still trying to unwrap the mysteries of the whisky. "Bowmore is the most enigmatic whisky I've ever come across. It's got everything from fruit to salt and covers the widest spectrum of the aromas," Barrie said.

Bowmore Islay Single Malt Scotch whisky begins with Legend, a smoky whisky with ripe notes of citrus and honey, and is followed by the twelve-year-old Single Malt Whisky, which brings beautiful peaty smoke and honey note to the tongue. The fifteen-year-old Darkest delivers a sophisticated nose of raisins and chocolate with underlying smoke. The eighteen-year-old and twenty-five-year-old are among the most purchased expensive Islay whiskies on the market, delivering the delicate balance of peat smoke, fruit, and toffee. There are also the limited edition whiskies: from the Black Bowmore 1964, perhaps the most complex whisky made in the twentieth century fetching $5,000 a bottle, to the 1964 Fino, only seventy-two bottles produced and all selling at $13,500. From the outside looking in, a whisky lover must ask: How can Rachel Barrie possibly improve upon these stellar whiskies? "I'm looking for a Bowmore that will have a slightly more sultry smokiness than it's ever had, and a Bowmore that will have the amplified salt," she told me.

Bowmore certainly did not hire one of the industry's most inquisitive minds just to maintain the brand as it was. Bowmore brands are in discovery mode, as Rachel Barrie seeks to uncover every aroma and to understand why whisky might smell differently on a warm day than on a cold winter evening. Is the change in the person or in the whisky? "How much of that is the dynamic atmosphere . . . water molecules in the air and barometric pressure? How much of that is affecting my glass, and how much is affecting my nose? I haven't quite understood that," said the chemist. "There is something about moments of revelation in whisky."

Helen Mulholland is another blender who seeks the answers in whiskey. As a student in the early 1990s, she took a job in the Bushmills Irish Whiskey lab for six months. Once her internship ended, she returned to school and pursued a master's degree in chemistry. There was only one place she wanted to work—Bushmills. She rose through the ranks on the tasting line, impressing the Bushmills staff with her impeccable nose and ability to spot every characteristic in the whiskey. In 2005 she was named Ireland's first modern master blender. Her blending talents and her ability to find nuances in used rum and bourbon barrels are stellar. Her nose and taste buds are so good that she can taste blind and tell you the day the whiskey was distilled. "Whiskey is my life. My life entirely revolves around the Bushmills distillery. The whiskies are like my children: I see them born. I see the malt coming in the water from the reservoir. I see how they become spirit. I get to pick the cask that they sleep in until they become mature," Mulholland told me.

During her career, Mulholland has maintained the historic Bushmills label and created some of the most exciting Irish whiskeys in history. Before she was the master blender, Mulholland worked in the lab when the Bushmills team made a discovery—crystalize malt. This process slow roasted germinated barley while it was still moist, forcing it to crystalize and thus enhancing the natural sweetness. "Oh, I still remember that beautiful smell of the crystalize malt," she said.

With the Bushmills's 400th anniversary approaching, Mulholland decided to use the crystal malt stocks aging in warehouses for a special limited edition whiskey. The crystal malt whiskey had aged in a combination of used bourbon barrels and Spanish Oloroso sherry casks, pulling in sweet and savory notes from both casks. Mulholland tasted each one and blended the various vintages, searching for the coffee and toffee notes and orange peel and vanilla and the honey, until she found the perfect combination. She mixed the crystal malt with Bushmills regular whiskey and grain whiskey to create Bushmills 1608, which earned the World Whisky Awards' "Best Irish Blended Whiskey" in 2008. "The 1608 was my first new product to develop," she said. "I wanted to do something completely different to the Bushmills range … still have the same characteristics, but to be a very different product to the lovely, big, powerful malts that we produce."

To make the 1608 Bushmills, Mulholland said: "We looked for a chocolate vanilla creaminess to the whiskey. It probably wouldn't have been the same blend if somebody else had done it. I like the creaminess and chocolate coming through." Although this whiskey might be the best Irish whiskey of the twenty-first century, Mulholland's greatest contribution may have been helping Bushmills announce its new packaging.

Whiskey enthusiasts rarely like change. Before announcing the new packaging, Bushmills needed to get in front of the launch to make sure diehard customers would understand the redesign. The public relations firm, Smarts, unveiled the new look for the ten-, sixteen-, and twenty-one-year-old single malt whiskies, using the eloquent speaker and pitchwoman Helen Mulholland to discuss the brand's heritage and authenticity. "We're immensely proud of our single malts, and it's great to see their quality recognized around the world this year. The new packaging builds on that sense of pride and helps us tell a unique story about the 400 years of local malt distilling expertise which has led Bushmills to be voted the world's best single malt Irish whiskies," Mulholland said at the launch. "Our single malts have a great taste, and there's something for everyone in the range—even for those who have never thought about drinking a single malt before. They're triple distilled for extra smoothness, and unlike Scotch malts they have no smokiness, allowing you to get straight to the unparalleled taste of malt. We're delighted that the new single malt packaging continues to match the undoubted quality of our whiskey."

The result of Mulholland's enthusiasm and ability to tell the Bushmills story resulted in more than 200 stories about the new packaging and a 20 percent increase in Bushmills malts sales after the new launch. Smarts estimated Helen reached a worldwide audience of 83 million. "Helen is superb and does not get enough credit," Colum Egan, master distiller for Bushmills, told me. "She has such passion, a natural flare for whiskey." Egan said Mulholland maintains the risk assessment portion of the business and mentors an entire team of women on the tasting panel. "There aren't many Helens kicking about, to be honest. We're very lucky she's here. If you can find me someone better than Helen, I'll give you a medal."

The 2000s saw an amazing rise in women becoming master blenders or working under master blenders. Once they got their shot in the tasting panel rooms and were able to identify properties in the whiskies men could not detect, several of the world's top whiskey brands started hiring women in the sensory panels. A former Glenmorangie brand ambassador, Angela D'Orazio, became the master blender for the Swedish whiskey Mackmyra in 2004. D'Orazio makes a whiskey that's fresh and lets the malt come through without too many woody notes. She often faces the "Oh, you're a woman blender" comment. But D'Orazio believes that a "more gender-balanced whiskey world would benefit all, from the board of directors to the distilleries, brands, consumers, whiskey bars, and festivals."[4]

After Dewar's Scotch whisky master blender Tom Aitken retired in 2006, Stephanie McLeod replaced him after working in the quality control department and brand's sensory panels. She became Dewar's seventh master blender and the first woman to hold the company's title.

In 2007, Diageo hired Carline Martin as one of several blenders working on Johnnie Walker and the only master blender for Bell's Scotch whisky. When she was operating the only distillery in Wales, Gillian Howell, a chemistry graduate from Cardiff University, was named one of the most inspirational women in business by *Management Today*. Howell helped put Penderyn single malt whiskies on the international map. But she left the company in early 2012 to work with Dr. Bill Lumsden at Glenmorangie.

Lumsden's eye for whisky talent is gender blind. "I have never recruited members of staff simply because they were women; rather, a number of people I have employed who have fitted the job description I was looking for have happened to be female, so I am not necessarily in agreement with the view that men or women make better employees," Lumsden told me. "A number of the ladies I have employed over the years have had very good noses and palates. But without statistically analyzing a lot of data, I would not like to say whether or not women in general have better palates than men."

When Kristy Lark was growing up, the last thing she wanted to do was work in the family distillery in Tasmania, Australia. At sixteen she worked weekends and holidays at the cellar. In 1996 no way was she planning to join the Lark Distillery team. "Whiskey was something my parents made," Lark said.

She went to air traffic controller school, but monitoring the landing of planes in an incredibly stressful environment lost its appeal. In 2004 Lark figured there was something to her parents' business. She decided to join the family toil, starting off as the grunt in the distillery, performing wash runs, bottling, labeling, and all the small jobs, working her way up the spirits ladder until she was knee-deep in vats of mash. "My decision to go into the family trade is something I have never looked back on," she said.

Her whiskey is certainly distinctive in that it comes from Tasmania and not America, Scotland, or Ireland. From a branding perspective, Lark whiskey faces an uphill battle of standing out on the liquor shelf, but its quality stands out with the Tasmanian peat, which gives a slightly sweet flavor with aromatic pungency. "Lark is a Tasmanian single malt whiskey, proudly unique in character and style, crafted in small batches exclusively from pure Tasmanian ingredients, matured in small barrels," Lark told me. "Given that our distillation method is so hands on, as a distiller I have been able to smell and taste each run and decide when to do important cuts. We have never decided on set cut points like other large distilleries, and as such each of the distillation runs can vary slightly from the previous. I find this very exciting that I can have such an impact on the final taste of the whiskey we make."

Like Kristy Lark, Kate Shapira Latts was born into the whiskey business. The daughter of Max Shapira, the president of Heaven Hill Distillery in Kentucky, the largest U.S. independent family-owned and operated spirits company, Shapira Latts remembers a family house with no regular water glasses. "Our water glasses were old style Heaven Hill highball and lowball glasses."

Shapira Latts knew she wanted to enter business. Her mother thought the teenager would become the president of a cosmetics company. In college Shapira Latts found a talent for foreign languages and speaks fluent Spanish and French. After graduating with an MBA from the University of Louisville, she worked for Proctor & Gamble launching classic consumer packaged goods worldwide. In 2001 she returned to the family business, becoming the director of marketing strategy. Her return came during the resurgence of bourbon. One of her first Heaven Hill tasks was creating strategic marketing efforts for the Evan Williams brand, the company's flagship whiskey, which is "hugely important for our company." Her marketing team helped make Evan Williams one of the more appealing whiskeys to a diversified market.

Now Shapira Latts oversees the marketing for Heaven Hill's entire portfolio, which includes a wide range of tequilas, rums, and liqueurs. She's spent much of her career outside of whiskey, building the company's market share in other categories with brands like Burnett gin, Pama liqueur, and Hpnotiq. The whiskey portfolio works like a well-oiled machine, and Shapira Latts typically comes in when there's a new product launch or a major strategic decision. In 2012 her team developed the name, concept, brand positioning, packaging, and marketing plan for a new brand of bourbon called Larceny.

In a time when whiskey history was becoming increasingly important in pop culture, Heaven Hill built a story around Larceny. Shapira Latts's team named it Larceny after a crooked treasury agent who stole bourbon to make his own whiskey. Larceny's clever story has been paramount to its success.

It is the somewhat controversial history of John E. Fitzgerald and his eponymous bourbon brand that provides the story, and name, to Larceny Bourbon. . . . It is actually the story of the Old Fitzgerald brand, made famous by the late Julian "Pappy" Van Winkle Sr., which forms the historical basis for Larceny bourbon. According to industry lore, John E. Fitzgerald had founded his distillery in Frankfort, Ky., shortly after the Civil War ended, making his bourbon available only to steamship lines, rail lines, and private clubs. This story was furthered by S. C. Herbst, who owned the "Old Fitz" brand from the 1880s through Prohibition, and Pappy Van Winkle, who purchased the brand during Prohibition and made it his signature label. However, it was revealed by Pappy's granddaughter, Sally Van Winkle Campbell, in her 1999 book, *But Always Fine Bourbon—Pappy Van Winkle and the Story of Old Fitzgerald*, that in fact John E. Fitzgerald was not a famous distiller at all. He was in reality a treasury agent who used his keys to the warehouses to pilfer Bourbon from the finest barrels.[5]

Whiskey enthusiasts relish these histories, and women have become absolutely crucial to finding stories and plastering them on packaging and advertisements to help sell whiskey brands.

Around Shapira Latts's return to Heaven Hill, whiskey companies began hiring women at all levels of marketing and PR positions. Whether they were marketing managers over brands or starting whiskey-focused PR firms like Laura Baddish in 2000, the marketing- and PR-oriented ladies almost created a monopoly in spirits promotions. To work in marketing, Shapira Latts told me, "You have to have a little bit of passion for pop culture and creativity to wonder why blue might work better than red. Men just in general may be less excited about those sorts of things. This sounds silly, but who spends more time coloring with crayons when they're kids: boys or girls? Beyond the analysis and the strategic thinking, which are really at the core of what we do in marketing, the more creative things just appeal more to women."

Women born into whiskey also seem to have a great propensity for preserving their family's whiskey history. Gabriela Quirarte's grandfather once ran the Juarez, Mexico, D. M. Distillery and maintains the archives of her grandfather's correspondence, deeds, and historic bourbon collections, including a series of letters from the U.S. government requesting that Mexican distillers stop using the term *bourbon* after Congress declared it America's spirit in 1964. She's talked to newspaper reporters and whiskey writers in her quest to keep the distillery's memory alive.

As her grandfather's legacy was being forgotten and passed over by new brands such as Maker's Mark and Blanton's Single Barrel, Sally Van Winkle Campbell self-published *But Always Fine Bourbon* in 1999. At the time, Pappy Van Winkle meant little to the outside world. "It was way before bourbon was cool again," Campbell told me.

The Old Fitzgerald distillery, also known as the Stitzel Weller Distillery, was sold in 1972, a painful moment for the Van Winkle family.

Like many people in their thirties, Campbell looked at her childhood and realized that the distillery was a playground, a "paradise to use, and it was so painful for the family when it sold. We could hardly talk about it for a long time." Twenty years after the closure, Campbell decided to visit the old buildings. "It looked like a different place; it was devastating. I realized that the feeling of that fabulous company, the family atmosphere, and what they did was going to be lost if I didn't write something," she said.

Campbell searched for old photographs, letters, articles, scrapbooks, and other materials that might help preserve her grandfather's distillery. "I didn't want the family history to be lost for my grandchildren," she said. But Campbell had no idea how important her book would be to her grandfather's legacy and her brother's quest to make Pappy Van Winkle bourbons important again. After she paid for a designer, editor, and printing of *But Always Fine Bourbon*, major whiskey magazines wrote positive reviews about the book, and visitor centers could not keep the book in stock.

Meanwhile, her brother, Julian Van Winkle, used his uncanny ability to blend bourbons to create the world's most sought-after whiskey.[6] Julian releases about 7,000 cases a year, ranging from the Old Rip Van Winkle to Pappy Van Winkle twenty-three-year-old, and they are sold as soon as they show up in liquor stores. His bourbons follow the mantra that the Pappy said years ago: "We make a fine bourbon, at a profit if we can, at a loss if we must, but always a fine bourbon."

Campbell does not make, market, or sell the whiskey to liquor stores, but she wrote one of the best-selling bourbon books of all time in an effort to keep her grandfather's memory alive. Now in its fourth printing, *But Always Fine Bourbon* helped her brother resurrect the Pappy Van Winkle name, giving a powerful history book to supplement her brother's fine whiskey talents. "My grandfather was gone, my father was gone, my uncle was gone, my aunt was almost gone. . . . It was a miracle that the whole thing ever came to fruition." After the book's publication, Campbell received hundreds of letters from people Pappy Van Winkle worked with. Now "Pappy is famous and my brother's bourbons are famous."

Jack Daniel's Lynne Tolley also carried on her family whiskey. Her great-great-uncle, Jack Daniel, died in 1911 and left the Lynchburg, Tennessee, distillery to his nephews. Had Jack bequeathed the distillery to his niece, Lynne's grandmother, Tolley says she might have become a billionaire. But that doesn't stop her from telling her family's heritage and becoming a Jack Daniel's master taster.

In the early 1980s, Tolley worked her way into the tasting room. Now she's one of five tasters on Jack Daniel's premium products, such as the single barrel select, and she is the proprietress of Miss Mary Bobo's Boarding House, near the distillery. She's enjoyed her career with one unrealized dream: "I would pursue being a distiller if I weren't so old."

Another legendary brand, Willett, has always employed women, dating back to Mary Willett in the 1930s. Today Britt Chavanne, the granddaughter of Thompson Willett and daughter of Even Kulsveen, is helping Willett reach its rightful place in bourbon lore. The distillery stopped making whiskey in the 1970s, and in 1984 Even Kulsveen, Willett's son-in-law, started purchasing whiskey from other distilleries and bottling it under the Kentucky Bourbon Distillers name. The company brokered whiskey and bottled for other distilleries, while promoting its Willett, Noah's Mill, Old Bardstown, and Johnny Drum brands.

In January 2012 Kentucky Bourbon Distillers changed its name to the Willett Distillery Company and recommenced distillation operations. Instead of the towering stills found at Jim Beam and Heaven Hill, Willett is Kentucky bourbon's elegant craft distillery operating a pot still that cranks out beautiful whiskey. Britt Kulsveen Chavanne runs the business side and should be credited with the smaller brand's marketing power, landing equal coverage to Jim Beam in the likes of the *Wall Street Journal* and DrinkSpirits.com. She works with her husband, brother, and father, admitting that family business partners "complicate" things, but "everybody is working toward the same goal and everybody has such a passion for it."[7]

Hollis Bulleit grew up in a household with a start-up whiskey. In the late 1980s, Tom Bulleit, a former tax attorney and Vietnam War veteran, resurrected his ancestor's whiskey. "All we talked about was bourbon when I was growing up," Hollis told me. Today Bulleit is one of the most important brand ambassadors in the bourbon business. She travels the world with her father pitching their bourbon to bartenders and creating the modern speakeasy scene. An outspoken lesbian, Bulleit has also singlehandedly won over the gay market, perhaps the most affluent spirits enthusiasts of all demographics. "Bar trends are being influenced by shows like *Mad Men* and the forgotten times of your grandparent's cocktail hour," she told the lesbian magazine *Curve*. "I'm hoping that the general consumer is up for a more complex and mature experience with the brown spirits."

After Bulleit's themed parties, where guests dressed in extravagant clothing of the times, several whiskey distillers copied her idea and threw *Mad Men* or Prohibition-era parties. Hollis Bulleit is most responsible for tapping into modern popular culture's fascination with Prohibition stories and 1960s advertising executives. But she says she's still Daddy's little girl. "We are naive and authentic; my dad and I are partners. Every time we give a pitch, it's real."

THE EXECUTIVES

From the middle management positions, such as the Woodford Reserve brand manager Laura Petry, to William Grant's CEO Stella David, women are leading major whiskey brands in every U.S. and international market. They're also in the male-dominated positions, such as Diageo's CFO Deirdre Mahlan and Brown-Forman's vice president of operations Jill Jones.

Earning $1.8 million in 2012, Deirdre Mahlan oversees the financial records for Diageo, the world's largest spirits company, including Captain Morgan, Johnnie Walker, Smirnoff vodka, Guinness beer, Crown Royal Canadian whisky, Bailey's, Bulleit Bourbon, and Jose Cuervo tequila. In 2012 Diageo earned $5.1 billion before taxes. Formerly working in senior finance positions for spirits company Seagram and Sons, Mahlan is considered the spirits industry's top financial officer and was named to Cranfield University's prestigious "100 Women to Watch" list in 2009. "Deirdre is a superb financial strategist, a dynamic leader, and a trusted adviser. She understands the beverage alcohol business," said Ivan Menezes, president and CEO of Diageo North America, in 2009.[8]

While Mahlan oversees the financial angle, Jill Jones ensures Brown-Forman's production runs smoothly and is economically feasible for such brands as Jack Daniel's, Woodford Reserve, Chambord Liqueur, Korbel, and Southern Comfort. But, like Mahlan, Jones finds that her job comes down to accounting. "Everything in the operation eventually has to become a number," Jones told me. When Jack Daniel's is being dumped from barrels into tanks, Jones's team analyzes the yield numbers. If the numbers are off, they immediately seek the answers.

Was it the malt? What's happening with the barrels en route? What's happening, period? On a new whiskey requiring a new barrel type, she might ask: "If we're going to use a new barrel for this project, what kind of filtration are we going to put in place? I come up with a question that the engineers will say, 'You know, you're not a scientist, but sometimes you ask the darnedest questions.'" Jones asks these probing questions of her site managers and engineers from Beijing to Dubai at Brown-Forman's eighty facilities. Her team innovates and improves, from increasing the speed on the bottling line to saving whiskey from leaking from the barrel.

For example, her team has helped save Brown-Forman money with its whiskey barrel. Every year that a barrel ages whiskey in a hot Kentucky warehouse, some 3 to 5 percent is lost to evaporation, the "angel's share." Although she would not go into details, due to the "proprietary" nature of Brown-Forman's barrel-making procedures, Jones said they have reduced the amount of whiskey loss. Whiskey companies are often secretive about these "proprietary" methods, because, well, the competition steals the idea and does the same thing and takes credit for it. Both Jill Jones and Deirdre Mahlan work for large publicly traded companies that must answer to stockholders. Their efforts can increase or decrease stock price.

When explaining what William Grant & Sons offers to whiskey drinkers, William Grant CEO Stella David is quick to point out that her company is not publicly traded. "Personal connections are still important," David said. William Grant & Sons owns Glenfiddich, Tullamore Dew, Hendricks Gin, and many others. Stella David feels no pressure from stock brokers. "When you talk about being committed to the long term, people think that means you're slow. The opposite is true, though. We do commit to the long term, but we act with a huge amount of agility and pace. We have to try to do things in a different way. If you don't do it differently, then there's no point in existing, is there?"[9]

One of David's strategies was to ride the Irish whiskey wave when William Grant purchased Tullamore Dew Irish whiskey for €171 million and later acquired a fifty-eight-acre site for a €35 million distillery expansion. The new state-of-the-art pot still whiskey and malt whiskey distillery brings whiskey production back to the town for the first time since the original distillery closed in 1954. Tullamore Dew, which was growing on average 15 percent annually, became Stella David's priority in the past three years and paramount to William Grant's growth. It was also a favored development for Ireland, and the *Irish Times* credited Stella David with "pressing the button" on the move despite sluggish Irish economy. For the William Grant CEO, it was all about the whiskey. "At the end of the day, to be able to produce it in Tullamore itself is a huge attraction. Taking the brand back to its original home felt compelling," she said.[10]

Anna Malmhake also understands the importance of Irish whiskey and the country's heritage. She is the chairman and CEO of the Irish Distillers, a subsidiary of Pernod Ricard. Malmhake is the leader of the world's no. 1 Irish whiskey in Jameson and many highly decorated brands, including Redbreast, Powers, and Green Spot. During her short tenure—she was named the CEO in late 2011—Malmhake has already returned a once beloved Irish whiskey. Yellow Spot, taken off the shelves in the 1960s, is a twelve-year-old Irish whiskey aged in bourbon, Spanish sherry, and Spanish Malaga wine casks. Yellow Spot's return was a welcome surprise to the whiskey media, especially after Irish Distillers committed to annual releases. "We are delighted to welcome Yellow Spot back into the portfolio. . . . We're confident that it will heighten the rekindled interest we see in single pot still whiskies around the globe," Malmhake said.[11]

Despite women running two major whiskey companies and making significant decisions at every level, women whiskey executives face the same "Oh, wait, you're a woman" stigma that Bessie Williamson endured in the 1960s. Women are no longer novelties to the whiskey boardrooms. They run too many of these companies to be considered gimmicks.

15

Organizing the Whiskey Effort

Today, a whiskey enthusiast can travel to just about any major metropolitan area and find a restaurant offering a whiskey dinner. From Brooklyn's Char No. 4 pairing High West Utah whiskey with smoked trout to Boston's Endicott House matching Talisker ten-year-old with braised lamb shank, restaurants are treating whiskey much like wine. Celebrity chefs Charles Phan, Emeril Lagasse, and Anthony Bourdain are among culinary rock stars who have publicly professed their love for drinking and cooking with bourbon, while food trucks and fast food joints have used bourbon's marketing power to draw customers.

Ten years before this culinary craze, Kentucky chef Ouita Michel, owner of the Holly Hill Inn and a graduate of the Culinary Institute of America in Hyde Park, added the whiskey to chutneys, crème fraiche fumet, brines and barbecue sauces. "The most common comment I get from people about cooking with bourbon is, 'I can't taste the bourbon.' If you're going to simmer a sauce for two hours, guess what? You're really not going to be able to taste the bourbon," Michel told me. "That's why I finish with bourbon in a demi-glace or sauce." The Woodford Reserve chef-in residence is among a small group of chefs who created the unwritten rules for cooking with bourbon with the most important rule: Use a lot of bourbon if you want to taste it.

She also represents a new wave within the bourbon business, a sophistication that would not exist without the organic growth of consumer whiskey interests and organizations: From the barrel to the still, people want to touch, taste, eat, learn and see everything there is about the spirit. The national cooking trend stands as a glowing reminder of how far whiskey enthusiasm has come.

In the 1980s, the average whiskey dinner meant Jack & Coke with a hamburger and french fries. There was no sophistication toward whiskies, and few realized the potential. Whiskey was served neat, on the rocks, in Coke, or in the occasional cocktail, and the spirits companies largely targeted the trades for tastings, ignoring consumers at the ground level. Whiskey makers relied on the positive magazine reviews, print advertising, and retailer point-of-purchase materials to reach consumers. Up until 1996, whiskey companies did not advertise on television. Lost in this twentieth-century consumer outreach was the old-fashioned tasting.

Nobody had made a consensus effort to set up special whiskey tastings, but that changed when John Hansell and his wife, Amy Westlake, pursued organizing consumer tastings.

With a built-in audience from their *Malt Advocate* magazine, now *Whisky Advocate,* the couple had the audience to create a special event with whiskey tasting booths for the public. However, nobody had done this before, and few people gave the idea a chance. One legendary whiskey writer told Hansell: "No way it will work or be successful."

When they opened talks with a New York Marriott, they were taking an "absolute huge risk. . . . If we weren't successful at this, we failed in front of our subscribers, in front of our advertisers, and in front of all the press in New York City," Westlake told me. "The risk was so great, the risk of failure, the risk of financial ruin, because you have to guarantee the hotel. You're going to pay them a *bazillion* dollars before you even sell a ticket, before you sell a booth."

In 1998 John and Amy were doing business as sole proprietors. Their lawyer took a look at the contracts with the whiskey distillers and asked, "Are you guys insane? You're not incorporated?" The couple could lose their house, bank accounts, retirement savings, and everything else if a court found them personally liable in the event something happened, such as a drunken driver killing a family on his way home. They became incorporated and reworked all contracts with the whiskey companies.

Their first WhiskyFest ran out of tickets one month before it even started. Although PR people assured Westlake high demand was a good thing, she did not want to disappoint loyal readers and tried to accommodate as many people as possible. The Marriott room was packed with eager whiskey drinkers ready to taste something they had never had before or to meet the distillers who made the products they loved so dearly. Meanwhile, something else was happening: the distillers were treating WhiskyFest like a collegiate alumni gathering. "No one had brought the whiskey guys together for one event, and they were really excited to be a part of it and to have the chance to interact with each other," Westlake said.

Amy and John walked away knowing they were onto something similar to the beer festival phenomenon. "There were no whiskey festivals," Westlake said. But WhiskyFest was much more than drinking to get drunk, which is the usual outcome at a beer festival. WhiskyFest held seminars and tastings and educated consumers about why rye spices up bourbon and how peat makes a Scotch smoky. This was not for intoxication. WhiskyFest was all about education from the palate and beyond. For the first time, an American event celebrated all whiskies and all whiskey makers.

And every year WhiskyFest grew. Amy and John pursued WhiskyFests in new markets. However, despite their success in New York, people did not always understand the concept. When Amy was flying to meet with a retailer in San Francisco to help promote WhiskyFest to his customer base, he canceled on Amy, telling his secretary: "I have no interest in meeting with her." Westlake said some retailers understood the concept; others barely gave her two minutes. But she pressed on. After Hansell came up with the show idea and helped run the first two, he stepped back into his full-time role as the editor and publisher of *Malt Advocate*. Westlake essentially became the CEO of WhiskyFest.

WhiskyFest Praise

"It's the Holy Grail of whiskey events. You can try so many whiskies, some that cost $150 to $200 a bottle. The only problem is that it isn't long enough. The only time I missed WhiskyFest was when I tore my quadriceps muscle and had to have surgery the day of the event."—Peter Silver, Greenwich Village, 2004

By 2004, the event had been copied by others, and no respectable retailer or distiller would turn down a WhiskyFest opportunity. As one distillery PR person told me: "They created something that attracts the most loyal whiskey enthusiasts. We would be stupid to ignore it." WhiskyFest now partners with restaurants and retailers to create a local Whiskey Week, encouraging area consumer participation and drawing a great deal of local press. With up to thirty events in the city, ticket buyers call up to find out what's going on ahead of time to make special plans. This has built a word-of-mouth growth somewhat unimaginable.

For Westlake, there is no doubt an unrivaled feeling of accomplishment, but there are still the headaches. "My biggest scare the first couple of years was someone would do something stupid," she said.

To alleviate the possibilities of the occasional irresponsible drinker, Westlake selected cities with good public transportation and made sure whiskey companies only poured a quarter ounce to consumers. "We were worried that after a few hours, the attendees would be really wasted if we didn't control the flow of whiskey," she said. But leave it to one whiskey maker to break the rule. At the first WhiskyFest, when people walked up to the Wild Turkey table, master distiller Jimmy Russell filled their glasses to the brim. The pouring rule has been dubbed the "Jimmy Russell" rule, and he's followed it at all thirty-two WhiskyFests. But other than that, WhiskyFest has run without hiccups and is the most successful consumer distilled beverage event in the country. Whiskey makers launch products here, and "it's one of the only places where we can interact with so many core customers," said Fred Noe, master distiller for Jim Beam and the great-grandson of Jim Beam. John Hansell and Amy Westlake's efforts to create the first true large-scale whiskey event for consumers changed the industry.

The whiskey consumer market, from plumbers and carpenters to doctors and lawyers, grew exponentially, and global companies realized whiskey drinkers were more passionate about their spirits than vodka or gin fans. As WhiskyFest has grown, so have Scotch whisky, Irish whiskey, and bourbon whiskey. The event has become a venue for brands to launch new products and to discuss ideas with consumers. Without WhiskyFest reaching affluent audiences and creating partnerships with restaurants, the world may not know of the joys of pairing a rich rib eye with bold bourbon. Hansell and Westlake gave whiskey exposure that the distillers could never accomplish with the restrictive post-Prohibition serving laws.

After the first WhiskyFest, Riannon Walsh created Whiskies of the World in San Francisco. Before this whiskey show, Walsh started the Irish whiskey brand Cloonaughall Distillers with eighty-five acres of land at the crest of the Connemara Mountains. She had access to amazing water and open space for distillation. Walsh made connections with biodynamic farmers to acquire the purest barley and even established coach lines for tourism. "The main thing for me was that we would have made it possible for Ireland to finally put out a truly high-end whiskey. . . . There is some good Irish whiskey out there. But overall, most exported Irish whiskey was mediocre," Walsh told me. "We had a taste profile that was aiming toward what I felt would be most appealing in the U.S. market."

The dot.com crash hit, and 60 percent of the Cloonaughall's funds dried up. Walsh tried to secure other monies, refusing to give up. "I just kept trying, and trying, and trying, and trying, and it was . . . this is just it. My husband at the time basically said: 'You've got to refocus, or you're going to lose yourself over this, financially and otherwise.'"

Her total refocus became Whiskies of the World. She transferred her passions and energy from Cloonaughall to this new whiskey show.

"I was sitting on the porch feeling horrible about the distillery project, thinking, 'I have to do something, and it has to be whiskey, and it has to be something that will make me really feel like I'm bringing something to people just as the distillery would've done.' It was a really sunny June day, and I just remember saying to my husband, 'I'm going to do a whiskey show,'" she said.

For no reason other than the fact she loved the city, Walsh pursued San Francisco and set the Bay Area's current whiskey craze into motion. Before long, all the major magazines, even *Playboy*, were on board to promote the event. She started selling tickets in the fall of 1998 for a March 1999 show. After the first event, Walsh noticed women only made up some 3 percent, and so she made it her priority to target women, who "hold the purse strings in most families. . . . Whiskey wasn't genteel enough for women. It was impolite for women to be drinking whiskey. It was time to cut that crap and change that attitude."

At Whiskies of the World, Walsh made sure the whiskey was presented as handcrafted and not a vehicle for intoxication. She hoped to lose the image among women that whiskey was fuel for a bar fight. "All the vendors had to sign a contract saying that every tasting table—they were only allowed three people behind each table—had to have at least two people who were trained whiskey people. In other words, they couldn't call up Betty Boop's Bar Hire and send out some half-naked girl to pour whiskey," she told me.

Even though Walsh helped whiskey brands, such as Compass Box Scotch whisky, break into the U.S. market, her greatest accomplishment is the fact that women made up 50 percent of the Whiskies of the World in 2009, the year before she sold the show. "I started the Best

Dram Whisky Club, which was part of a special benefit for ticket buyers. They got all these perks, and it really helped me reach out to the spouses. We found some different ways to get women to come even if they said they never had whiskey, and we started to turn them into whiskey drinkers," Walsh said.

Meridith May, whose *Patterson's Beverage Journal* (now *Tasting Panel*) was Whiskies of the World's first media sponsor, told me: "Riannon Walsh was a true pioneer." The year Walsh stepped away, another long-time whiskey professional was about to realize a dream she had had since 1998. Peggy Noe Stevens was a master taster for Brown-Forman and helped the company launch Woodford Reserve. During her tenure at Brown-Forman, she came up with the idea to start a women-only club for bourbon lovers. More than ten years after the idea struck, she created Bourbon Women in 2011, because "bourbon did not have the margarita" for women in a growing cocktail culture. In the early to mid-2000s, cocktail making rode to stardom on the heels of the celebrity chef movement. By 2005, bartenders were frequently called mixologists, a term first used in the 1800s, and were mastering craft cocktails. Major metropolitan areas like New York and San Francisco were selling $12 to $16 cocktails, made from homemade syrups and garden-grown herbs. Bartenders were revisiting the classics, like the Old-Fashioned and the Manhattan, putting their own spins on whiskey recipes and attracting women to once men-only drinks.

Before this cocktail movement, the majority of women found bourbon unapproachable, Stevens told me. "Women might remember bourbon as their father's drink. It was just one of the drinks they were never served in growing up. All of a sudden, you have this great cocktail culture, Stevens told me. Renowned female bartenders like Las Vegas's Patricia Richards and Chicago's Bridget Albert helped make whiskey more appealing in cocktails to women, but Stevens pursued a ground-level approach to making bourbon more approachable, creating Bourbon Women, a consumer organization similar to the American Wine Society. This empowerment of female drinkers deeply resonated with many founding members. Mary Quinn Ramer, a founding board member from Lexington, told the Associated Press: "I think there's this sense of relief that finally we were at a point where we can be taken seriously as women who enjoy bourbon and the lifestyle that accompanies it. That it's just not for men anymore."

Whereas WhiskyFest and Whiskies of the World attracted consumers for education, Bourbon Women's intent is to educate only women while giving bourbon companies the opportunity to market to them. With 300 members within its first year and satellite chapter requests all over the country, Bourbon Women is out to show ladies that bourbon is elegant and lady-like, while teaching the distillers that women should be a marketing priority. Stevens's connections to the industry have made the latter strategy an interesting one, especially since she knows what it's like inside the marketing room discussions. Women have long been ignored as a potential target audience, she told me. "Women are kind of hard now to ignore, but it all boils down to bourbon has always been seen as a men's market—the marketing priority. You only have so many marketing dollars."

This mind-set of capturing women with marketing dollars is nothing new. Marketers work with so-called mommy bloggers, and consultants make millions educating companies to appeal to women. Stevens, who is now an image-branding consultant, is taking those same principles used in other industries to help bourbon companies win women. "I don't want to be looked at as a social club that's strictly for women. There're plenty of those. There are also plenty of women's associations and organizations where you listen to business speakers. Bourbon Women is unique."

Her goal is to create focus groups across the country for women of all knowledge sets to try out new products, judge advertising, and discuss events that would appeal to them. "We have formally brought this group together to be taken seriously," she said. Stevens tried similar tactics when working for whiskey companies, but her strategies were not taken seriously because marketing dollars were earmarked for men. Now whiskey companies are listening because women have organically become whiskey drinkers.

Female-only Scotch whisky clubs are popping up all over the world. In New Delhi, the Spirit of Nero—India's first women's whiskey club—sponsored whiskey workshops. "Women are emerging as excellent aficionados of whiskey," writes Sandeep Arora, an Indian whiskey connoisseur and lifestyle consultant.[1] Arora said his general whiskey appreciation sessions draw at least 40 percent of female audiences.

Whiskey women clubs are in Venezuela, Japan, and China, across Europe, and all over the United States. An array of social media connect women and whiskey, including Wild Turkey's parent company Campari's "Women & Whiskies" interactive Facebook page, which was created "to help women come together to teach, learn, and further appreciate this mighty brown spirit. With help from world-class whiskies, we will embark on this flavorsome journey together. Just for us ladies!" Campari's women-targeted marketing is exactly what dozens of female whiskey veterans have always tried to do.

In the 1990s, several female marketers, including Peggy Noe Stevens, tried to convince male counterparts that women would make a sizeable consumer base if targeted. To this day, the lack of advertisements targeting women puzzles female whiskey enthusiasts. Huffington Post writer Brooke Carey observed Jameson and Bushmills ads clearly indicating "real men drink Jameson" and "Bushmills, it seems, is just one of the bros." When Jack Daniel's targeted women, Carey wrote, it was to use the whiskey in a cookie recipe. "Because the only way women will consume hard liquor is if it's in dessert," she wrote on Huffingtonpost.com.

In addition to men drinking one-quarter more than women, the "old school" whiskey executives may still fear fallout from marketing to women. The distilled spirits industries once agreed not to include women in ads or to advertise on television to prevent an anti-alcohol advertising attack similar to those in the 1950s. In a November 1958 edict, the Distilled Spirits Institute (now the Distilled Spirits Council of the United States) told its membership: "In no instance, may women be shown holding a drink in an advertisement and no illustrations of women unless they are dignified, modest, and in good taste."[2]

But as the woman's role changed in the American household and beer created stellar television ads that cut into whiskey's market share, the spirits industry knew it needed to update its advertising methods. The television ad ban "turned out to be not the world's greatest decision, because television ads became the central crossroads of communication in our society," Frank Coleman, senior vice president of public affairs and communications for the Distilled Spirits Council of the United States (DISCUS) told me. "Beer ramped up its television advertising profile, which coincided with spirits losing market share, particularly in the late eighties and the nineties."

DISCUS lifted the ban on showing women holding a drink in November 1987, saying the "good taste" measure applied to all sexes, and allowed spirits TV advertising nearly ten years later. In 1996 Crown Royal purchased ad time on a Corpus Christi, Texas, TV station. The Crown Royal ad led to larger regional television stations, cable stations, and increased advertising in markets that companies would have never considered, such as NASCAR, baseball, and morning talk shows. When opponents challenge the broadcast advertising of spirits, the Federal Trade Commission has said liquor is no different than beer and deserves the same First Amendment rights.

Distilled spirits companies lifted the self-imposed bans against television ads and marketing to women. But instead of pursuing this consumer base with existing products, whiskey companies have created new flavor profiles and brands to reach women.

16

For Women, by Women

Wild Turkey executives found themselves in a boardroom, asking, "How do we appeal to women?" In the 1970s master distiller Jimmy Russell said most women thought bourbon was too strong, and he figured Wild Turkey bourbon would make a nice flavored product. Many Irish whiskey brands had created sweetened products, most notably Locke Irish Whiskey's Honey Liqueur, and early American whiskey distillers created liqueurs to make the spirit more palatable. But those were long forgotten when Wild Turkey came out with American Honey in the late 1970s. The flavored whiskey concept was foreign to drinkers. "It was basically a bourbon flavor for the ladies to start out with; we wanted to get the ladies involved. Nowadays, as many men drink it as the ladies do," Russell told me.

Wild Turkey honey and more than 350 flavored Vodkas, from cotton candy to bubble gum, opened up the conversation for flavoring whiskies. Whiskey purists tend to scoff at this category, saying it may not be legal to flavor whiskey and still call it whiskey. But the U.S. Alcohol and Tobacco Tax and Trade Bureau (TTB) permits flavored whiskey as long as the product meets the legal requirements.[1]

Diageo, Jim Beam, Pernod Ricard, Campari, and Brown-Forman—the parent companies of the best-selling whiskey brands—are publicly traded and constantly seeking value for shareholders. At the turn of the millennium, it became clear that whiskey brands were alienating women from marketing tactics. Women were only customers when their husbands purchased whiskey.

After Wild Turkey, Jim Beam came out with Red Stagg, becoming an overnight success, and Evan Williams introduced a honey line that has sold well. By 2009, dozens of honey- and cinnamon-flavored whiskey brands were on the market, and an entirely new genre of flavored whiskies was becoming the fastest-growing category. From Bushmills Irish Honey to cinnamon Early Times Fire Eater, flavored whiskeys have become the new entry-level whiskey. According to industry statistics, the flavored whiskey segment grew 136 percent from 2010 to 2011, and the first quarter of 2012 saw flavored spirits sales increase 155 percent.[2]

The most popular flavor, by far, is honey. "The consumer perception of the word *honey* is going to be smoother, sweeter, more palatable, if you will, for a non-whiskey drinker. So by taking that approach of a little bit of honey and a whole lot of Jack Daniel's, we were able to appeal to a broad range of consumers, including women," Casey Nelson, brand manager for Jack Daniel's Tennessee Honey, told me.

Though the flavored whiskeys reach new audiences and are within the TTB parameters, critics have questioned whether they will damage the whiskey purity or continue to sell well. Many women in the industry believe that targeting women with flavored whiskies is sexist and perpetuates the idea that a woman could never understand the unaltered spirit's complexities. "I just wish we would focus on educating women about the great whiskies that are out there instead of making flavored ones," one executive told me. Heather Greene, whiskey sommelier for the Flatiron Room in New York, believes the flavored whiskey category disregards a woman's acute senses. "Why would you make products of the lowest common denominator to target women?" Greene asks.[3] This is the same question many analysts have asked, with the European Centre for Monitoring Alcohol Marketing commenting: "Apparently alcohol producers believe that if you want to attract women you have got to make your alcoholic beverages sweet."

Still, super female tasters like Greene and Bourbon Women founder Peggy Noe Stevens frequently find whiskey nuances that men might miss. For example, in large tastings, legendary bartender Joy Perrine says she almost always picks up fruits that men do not detect. "I'm always one of the few who pick up pineapple," Perrine says. That's not to say men cannot pick up these nuances; the fruity and perfume notes come much more naturally to women than men.

Studies show that ovulation leads to a surge of estrogen and increases sensitivity of the olfactory region. "Smells activate a greater region in the brain in women than men," said Tim Jacobs, professor at Cardiff University, in 2002.[4] Jacobs's findings have been confirmed in several studies since. In studying brains, Columbia University finds that men use mostly the left side of their brain for verbal reasoning, while women use both cerebral areas for visual, verbal, and emotional responses. The collective research indicates that the balanced brain usage makes women better at sensing emotional messages and gives them better verbal skills. Women have a "more acute sense of smell, taste, and hearing," Columbia University reports.[5]

A 2009 study published in the *Flavour and Fragrance Journal* even discovered women's sense of smell is so great that it is difficult for them to ignore body odor. "Our studies indicate that human sweat conveys information that is of particular importance to females," said Charles Wysocki, a behavioral neuroscientist at Monell Chemical Senses Center in Philadelphia. "This may explain why it is so difficult to block women's perception of sweat odors."[6]

Though no study indicates women can taste whiskey better than men, women are on nearly every whiskey tasting panel in the world. Before the whiskies go to the bottle, these super tasters analyze for impurities and promotional flavor notes. From Bushmills's all-women tasting panel to Maker's Mark's woman-led tasters, distilleries trust the noses of women over men.

Behind the bar, women bartenders take the female taster's palate to the next level. Like a chef with the perfect ingredients, mixologists have opened new doors for whiskey by using complementary flavor profiles to create whiskey cocktails for consumers who may not appreciate the spirit.

As the director of mixology for the Wynn Las Vegas, Patricia Richards is one of the most important spirits buyers in the world. When she puts a cocktail on a Wynn Las Vegas or Wynn Encore menu, Hong Kong billionaires and Hollywood starlets see her creations, and her discovery of products can mean mega exposure to a brand. In 2011 she created the Sinatra Smash cocktail for Wynn's new restaurant, Sinatra: five or six fresh blackberries, two ounces of fresh sweet and sour mix, ⅓ ounce of Sonoma Vanilla infused simple syrup, ½ ounce Briotett Crème de Cassis, and two ounces Gentleman Jack Tennessee whiskey.

Despite its connection to Las Vegas and Frank Sinatra, Jack Daniel's had lost its cocktail power in Sin City. Few, if any, bars featured creative Jack Daniel's cocktails in 2011. Furthermore, Jack Daniel's customers typically drink the whiskey on the rocks or with Coke, and bartenders have generally cut back on Jack Daniel's cocktails in lieu of hipper, edgier cocktail whiskeys, such as Bulleit, Woodford Reserve, and Redemption Rye. Richards's Sinatra Smash was featured in several magazines, and the Wynn promoted the drink all over the world. When she made this cocktail, Richards reminded bartenders that the Tennessee whiskey was not to be forgotten and influenced an uptick in Jack Daniel's cocktails.

For most new age cocktails, the female bartenders tend to make them sweeter than the typical dry vermouth Manhattans. Award-winning bartender Tiffanie Barriere, at Atlanta's One Flew South, uses brown sugar in a lot of bourbon cocktails, a trait common among southern bartenders. "We southerners like to run our fingers in the bottom of the pot and lick our fingers, and we especially love it when our cocktails are sweet," Barriere told me.

In Portland, mixologist Suzanne Bozarth uses a blackcurrant liqueur to sweeten a Tennessee whiskey cocktail she named "Tennessee Rose." *New York Magazine* gave Julie Reiner credit for reviving the sweeter classic cocktail "Athol Brose #3," a Glenfiddich and honey syrup cocktail with a cream float and nutmeg. Women behind the bar have contributed to making mixology or bartending a career rather than just a job. Patricia Richards was the first woman named the director of mixology for a major hotel, and Julie Reiner went from serving cocktails in Honolulu to becoming the owner and beverage director of Manhattan's Flatiron Lounge and Brooklyn's Clover Club. Southern Wine and Spirits regional director of mixology Bridget Albert designed President Obama's 2008 Inauguration cocktail, "The American Dream."

With so many high-profile female bartenders sweetening up whiskey drinks and winning a plethora of awards, it's hard to believe that women were not allowed behind some American bars just fifty years ago, and now they are among the leaders in the burgeoning mixology industry with fun organizations like the Ladies United for the Preservation of Endangered Cocktails bringing greater attention to a woman's ability to make cocktails. Of course, the growth of women in the spirits business does not stop behind the bar.

Women hold every position in the distillery business and are even taking the entrepreneurial leap to start their own distilleries. In 2008 hobbyist distiller Cheryl Lins created the Delaware Phoenix Distillery in Walton, New York, an area that was once highly populated with farm distilleries. Lins started making absinthe. "Whiskey was the only other spirit that interested me from its historical standpoint, being an American spirit and a spirit that was made in my community. Those were rye and wheat whiskey, dating back to some of the earliest settlers in this area between 1795 and 1830," Lins told me. "I really wasn't a whiskey aficionado or big whiskey drinker, but it interested me." That interest has led to Lins becoming one of the most beloved and elite smaller distillers in the world. Her Rye Dog whiskey won a gold medal at the San Francisco World Spirits Competition and was rated 96 out of 100 by CocktailEnthusiast.com. Lins used the 1818 Catherine Frye Spears Carpenter sour mash recipe as a whiskey guide.

While not all women making whiskey are digging through the archives for old recipes, they are making a difference in the independent distillery community. Samantha Unger Katz created the Ladies of American Distilleries to "accommodate the growth of women involved in the strategic development of boutique distilleries." In an April 2012 event called the Manhattan Cocktail Classic, the Ladies of American Distilleries worked with the Boston chapter of the Ladies United for the Preservation of Endangered Cocktails to show the spirits community that "from mold-breaking saloon owners to current-day cocktail mavens, women have had a vital, though often overlooked, impact on the evolution of bars and cocktails."[7] Women like Nicole Austin, owner and distiller at King's County Distillery in New York City, are on a mission to show the world they are as effective distillers and bartenders as men. Riannon Walsh, who consults with budding distillers, estimates women make up half of the new interest in creating new distilleries.

Since the founding of Bourbon Women in 2011, women have started American moonshine, Irish *poitín*, blended Scotch, and French whiskey brands. In Ashville, North Carolina, a woman named Troy Ball created Troy and Sons Distillers, making corn whiskey. "Our product is made in the tradition of 100 percent corn whiskey, like heritage moonshine," Ball told *Garden and Gun Magazine*. "We take extra time and produce lower quantities so we don't sacrifice flavor. We distill in a way that retains the natural flavors of the corn."

Irish-born and raised, U.S. resident Ashlee Casserly wanted to see her beloved native spirit, poitín, in the United States. "I've worked in the food and drink industry for some time and am frankly surprised and a bit disappointed that Ireland has attained notoriety for its drinking culture, while very little attention has been paid to its rich cultural history associated with food and drink. Although Guinness and Irish whiskey have gained attention here in the United States, there are whole histories that are ignored or swept aside," Casserly told me. She grew up on a farm in central Ireland with poitín always around. "I fondly remember going with my dad to pick up a few bottles of poitín for Christmas. Although he never really knew where it was coming from, he always managed to get a great batch," she remembers.

With more than 320 craft distilleries opening since 2000 in the United States and the country's burgeoning local food movement, Casserly saw an opportunity to bring home the craft spirit of Ireland. In 2012, she pursued capital on the crowd-funding website Kickstarter. Within six months, Casserly raised more than $40,000 to start importing 1661, which she named after the year of the Irish tax law that made it illegal. "I am humbled that I am making my own attempt at reviving this spirit. I have seen the desire for craft products grow, seemingly without bounds, in the past decade," Casserly said. "Ireland deserves a rightful place alongside many other countries in terms of its deep appreciation for local ingredients."

Like Casserly, Carin Castillo pursued funds on Kickstarter in December 2012 to pursue her dream of creating a Scotch whisky. A former app designer and global creative director for Reuters, Castillo realized the male stereotype when she and girlfriends ordered Scotch neat. "The bartender came back and then tried to hand them behind us, looking for the men he thought we had ordered them for. When he realized it was for us, he tried to hide a little smile as he walked back to some other customers." Castillo said.[8] She raised $45,000 in five weeks for Sia, a blended Scotch named after the Gaelic number 6. Castillo's blended whisky has one thing going for it—Scotch sales are always steady.

Allison Patel chose to gamble on whiskey from France, a country known more for its wine. "France actually has an amazing distilling history. Cognac, armagnac, and calvados are all amazing brandies. I thought, why not put the distilling to use in whiskey? I wanted to develop an artisanal whiskey expression in the Cognac region," Patel told me.

Patel works with a third-generation cognac distiller to grow the barley in the Cognac area and distill as they would a Cognac. The single malt is finished in cognac barrels, giving it a fruit-forward touch with the undeniable aroma of dried apricot. Bottled at 80 proof, Brenne French Single Malt whiskey is one of the world's most distinctive products because it is distilled in Charentais copper stills, a form of the alembic still invented by Maria the Jewess.

Patel's Brenne French whiskey has only been on the market since October 2012, and she's already facing supply issues. With only three French whiskies available in the U.S. market, Brenne is poised to become a bright spot in the microscopic category. She hopes to build upon the whiskey love people have found for Japanese and India whiskey. And the fact is, the whiskey market is ready, but this single malt would not exist without Patel's entrepreneurial spirit, an infectious idea of Brenne whiskey being a "one woman whiskey show," she says.

Casserly's hope for poitín resurgence, Castillo's entry-level blended Scotch, and Patel's attempt of resurrecting a forgotten, or perhaps unknown, French whiskey industry show how important women are to the future of whiskey. Casserly's creamy poitín and Patel's softer single malt will open new doors for other women looking to take the entrepreneurial leap, showing banks that it is more than possible for whiskey companies owned by women to succeed.

This female entrepreneurial enthusiasm really should come as no surprise. After all, women were among the first distillers. But the fact that women organizations have had to be formed to make this point shows how forgotten women are to whiskey history. It's also a subtle reminder that women were held back in society for a long time, and sexist rules purveyed the landscape. To this day, the whiskey industry has faced severe sexual harassment claims, ranging from a woman claiming an industry executive stuck his hand up her skirt to a blogger who was debating the virtues of a particular brand when the elder whiskey writer in the room patted her on the head and said, "There, there, honey, let's let the men talk about this." These are typically isolated incidents and not a representation of the industry, but it shows that even the progressive whiskey business is not beyond sexism.

More than 90 percent of the women interviewed for this book said they had never been sexually harassed. When asked, Helen Mulholland, master blender of Bushmills Irish Whiskey, said, "I have never come across anything at all in my entire career, at all."

Sexual harassment may be rare in whiskey, but there's no denying men still hold the most coveted positions. At the moment, there are no female master distillers in Kentucky, and even though several Scottish women hold the master blender title, blender jobs greatly skew toward Scottish men.

Furthermore, many top-selling whiskey brands are named after men: Jack Daniel's Tennessee whiskey, Jim Beam bourbon, and Johnnie Walker blended Scotch whisky lead their respective categories. Will there ever be a whiskey line named after a woman? Perhaps the Helen Mulholland Reserve? Or the Rachel Barrie Select? How about the Marge Samuels Wheat Whiskey? Then again, a whiskey woman may not want the brand named after her. If there's one thing I have learned from researching this book, women prefer giving credit to their team members. Mulholland told me: "It would be a huge honor to have a whiskey named after you. But one person doesn't deserve the honor."

Neither does one gender deserve all the spirit's glory. The whiskey business has an amazing opportunity to promote its female heritage. Despite the popular notion that the brown spirit is a man's drink, whiskey would not exist without women greatly contributing to the creations of beer and distillation, women opening distribution channels, women illegally transporting whiskey, and women growing, creating, and saving now-iconic whiskey brands. These undeniable facts contradict the industry's masculine labels, which perpetuate historically inaccurate depictions of women. Furthermore, the blatantly false accusation that women are just now warming up to drinking whiskey arrogantly discounts the women in early Scotland, Ireland, and America who used whiskey to entertain guests. In the 1899 book *Memoirs of a Highland Lady*, Elizabeth Grant (1797–1830) wrote: "Decent gentlewomen began the day with a dram. In our house the bottle of whisky, with its accompaniment of a silver salver full of small glasses, was placed on the sidetable with cold meat every morning."

Cold meat aside, why doesn't the whiskey industry recognize its female heritage? The events leading up to and during Prohibition have scarred the world's view of women working in bars or for whiskey companies. The righteous female arguments for Prohibition overshadowed important whiskey women, such as Bessie Williamson, who helped change the American palate from blended whisky to single malt Scotch, and Elizabeth Cumming, who built the most important distillery for Johnnie Walker. After Prohibition, whiskey brands did not want to market to women for fear of the saloon prostitution perceptions resurfacing. To this day, the whiskey and women sexual connotation lives in the lyrics of Buck Owens's "Cigarettes, Whiskey, and Wild Wild Women," David Allen Coe's "Whiskey and Women," and Toby Keith's "Whiskey Girl."

But society's majority is no longer misogynistic men or temperance women. It's time for whiskey companies to reconnect with their female heritage.

Although they faced societies that did give them equal rights, women were as important to whiskey as men were in every facet of the business. We can no longer ignore a woman's place in this spirit category's history. It's time to celebrate women.

Let the race for a woman-named whiskey begin.

ACKNOWLEDGMENTS

There are so many people to thank for this book, but my acknowledgments should begin with Peggy Noe Stevens. If she had not founded the group Bourbon Women, *Whiskey Women* would not have occurred to me.

As I researched this incredibly vast subject matter, I realized this was the type of work scholars spend twenty years studying. I knew if I were to research this alone, I would miss many important women. I had to find a team on a shoestring budget. Well, really, I had no budget.

Thank you to Beth Dempsey, for giving me access to ProQuest's incredible database, which helped me find many important women bootleggers.

Bushmills supported my travel to Ireland, which allowed me to spend time in archives, libraries, and the Bushmills distillery.

Kristina Bedford, CEO of Ancestral Deeds, helped me discover female distillers in thirteenth-century apothecaries and translated Latin texts that contained the word *aqua vitae*.

John McGee, the founder of Wheech Scottish Ancestry Services, assisted with my Scotland research, especially with Dalmore and Laphroaig. Fortunately, he is easily bribed with a dram of Islay whisky.

The following archives were quite helpful in my quest to find whiskey women: Public Record Office for Northern Island in Belfast; Filson Historical Society in Louisville; National Library of Ireland in Dublin; Kentucky Historical Society; National Archives of Ireland; National Archives in Chicago; Anne Carrol of the A. K. Bell Library in Perth, Scotland; and, especially, the National Records of Scotland, whose Alison Lindsay went above and beyond in accessing and explaining the 1494 Exchequer Rolls of Scotland.

I'd also like to thank Mike Veach, Robin R. Preston, and Chet Zoeler, for helping me discover hard-to-find early American female distillers.

The extraordinarily talented Kate Vance assisted during her University of Louisville internship. Kate helped me find the post-Prohibition laws that prevented women from working in bars. She proved that college students can do research beyond Google.

A big thanks to my pal Richard Auffrey, for reading the book's first five chapters.

This book is in great factual shape thanks to my outstanding copyeditor, Elaine Durham Otto.

Thanks to the following publicists for assistance: Buffalo Trace's Amy Preske, Diageo's Gillian Cook, Brown-Forman's Rick Bubenhofer, and Maker's Mark's Mathew Evins.

A huge thanks goes out to Mary Ellyn Hamilton of the Oscar Getz Museum of Whiskey History. She took time away from grant writing to flip through old dusty photos with me. Our toil yielded this book's cover photo.

My former agent, Neil Salkind—I hope you're enjoying retirement—found the fine people of Potomac Books, an imprint of the University of Nebraska Press. A big thanks goes to University of Nebraska Press editor Bridget Barry, for the direction and the talented crew who designed this book. Perhaps the greatest gratitude is owed to Potomac's Sam Dorrance and Elizabeth Demers, for deciding to publish *Whiskey Women*.

To Sara Roeske, Gretel Sharpee, Mary Flynn, Jessika Ross, Blair Larson, and Autumn Grimsley: Thank you for opening my eyes to how women can always do a job just as well as or better than men. In our long year together you six young women changed my views on life more than you'll ever know.

NOTES

1. BEFORE WHISKEY

1. Wort is used for making Scotch whisky. The grains are separated, and only the liquid is distilled. Bourbon, on the other hand, does not separate the grains. Bourbon distills the whole fermented grain mash.
2. Cuneiform, 4000 BC, from the excavations at Tep Gawra, northern Iraq, University of Pennsylvania Museum of Archaeology and Anthropology.
3. Hartman and Oppenheim, *On Beer and Brewing Techniques in Ancient Mesopotamia*, 12.
4. "Terracotta Plaque with an Erotic Scene," 1800 BC, British Museum.
5. Leick, *Sex and Eroticism in Mesopotamian Literature*, 95
6. Miguel Civil, trans., "A Hymn to the Beer Goddess and a Drinking Song," in Studies Presented to A. Leo Oppenheim (Chicago: Oriental Institute of the University of Chicago, 1964).
7. Dickie, *Magic and Magicians in the Greco-Roman World*, 179.
8. Winter, *Roman Wives, Roman Widows*, 152.
9. Jochens, *Women in Old Norse Society*, 107.
10. M. E. Moseley, D. J. Nash, P. R. Williams, S. D. DeFrance, A. Miranda, and M. Ruales, "Burning Down the Brewery: Establishing and Evacuating an Ancient Imperial Colony at Cerro Baul, Peru," *Proceedings of the National Academy of Sciences* 102, no. 48 (November 29, 2005): 17264-71.
11. Unger, *Beer in the Middle Ages and the Renaissance*, 225.
12. Prioreschi, *A History of Medicine: Medieval Medicine*, 168.
13. Will of Stephen de Barnade, 1306, TNA, Catalogue Reference E 40/2362.
14. Bennett, *Ale, Beer, and Brewsters in England*, 18.
15. Brewery Lawsuit 1493-1500, Court of Chancery: Six Clerks Office: Early Proceedings, Richard II to Philip and Mary, C 1/234/43, National Archives, London.
16. Ian S. Hornsey, *A History of Beer and Brewing* (Cambridge : Royal Society of Chemistry, 2003), 333.
17. Corpus cum Causa Petition, Chancery Rolls 1475-85, translated by Ancestral Deeds, C /1/66/296, National Archives, London
18. MacFarlane, *Witchcraft in Tudor and Stuart England*, 153.
19. Marchant, *In Praise of Ale*, 504.
20. See Bennett, *Ale, Beer, and Brewsters in England*.
21. Peter Damerow, "Sumerian Beer: The Origins of Brewing Technology in

Ancient Mesopotamia," Cuneiform Digital Library Journal, http://cdli
.ucla.edu/pubs/cdlj/2012/cdlj2012_002.html.

22. Abigail Tucker, "The Beer Archaeologist," *Smithsonian Magazine*, July/
August 2011.

23. One new theory based on recent archaeology finds is that the Chinese
made beer around 7000 BC.

24. Rayner-Canham and Rayner-Canham, *Women in Chemistry*, 1.

25. Kremers and Urdang, *Kremers and Urdang's History of Pharmacy*, 7.

26. In *A Short History of the Art of Distillation* (1970), 2, Barnes writes of the
alembic device Maria is thought to have invented: "a tube for transporting the distillate and vapors and the receiving flask." More advanced designs of the alembic still are available throughout the world.

2. THE FIRST DISTILLATIONS

1. Rayner-Canham and Rayner-Canham, *Women in Chemistry*, 2–4.

2. Forbes, *A Short History of the Art of Distillation*, 384.

3. Rayner-Canham and Rayner-Canham, *Women in Chemistry*, 3–4; Holmyard, *Alchemy*, 48.

4. Apotheker and Sarkadi, *European Women in Chemistry*.

5. Patai, *The Jewish Alchemists: A History and Source Book*, 61.

6. Forbes, *A Short History of the Art of Distillation*, 21.

7. Schreiner, *History of the Art of Distillation and of Distilling Apparatus*, 29.

8. Prioreschi, *A History of Medicine: Medieval Medicine*, 351.

9. "Aqua Vitae Instructions," in *The Red Book of Ossory*, Representative
Church Body Library, Dublin, 1317–60, 62. Latin to English translation
by Ancestral Deeds.

10. Markham and Best, *The English Housewife*, 125.

11. A. L. Martin, *Alcohol, Sex, and Gender in Late Medieval and Early Modern
Europe*, 26.

12. Leonard Guthrie, "Lady Sedley's Receipt Book, 1686, and Other Seventeenth-Century Receipt Books," *Proceedings of the Royal Society of Medicine* 6 (1913): 150–73.

13. McIntosh, *Working Women in English Society*, 53.

14. Singer and Williams, *A History of Technology*, 2:144.

15. Bodin, *On the Demon-Mania of Witches*, 181.

16. Hugh, "Distilleries of Nelson County," 362.

17. Evans, Salih, and Bernau, *Medieval Virginities*, 157.

18. Chambers and Chambers, *Chambers's Miscellany of Instructive & Entertaining Tracts*, 18:4.

19. Burns, *Witch Hunts*, 145.

20. Goodare et al., "The Survey of Scottish Witchcraft," http://www.shca
.ed.ac.uk/witches/ (archived January 2003, accessed 5-14-2013).

21. Sandby, *Mesmerism and Its Opponents*, 105.

22. This number was tallied from the following sources: London livery company apprenticeship registers, 1531–1685, Brewers Company collections, MXCC10, the National Archives London; Patrick Wallis, "Apothecaries' Company 1617–69," London Livery Company Apprenticeship Registers, vol. 32, Society of Genealogists, 2000, 12–36.

3. TOUGH IRISH WOMEN

1. Ure, *A Dictionary of Arts, Manufactures, and Mines*, 396.
2. Ó Cléirigh, *Annals of the Kingdom of Ireland by the Four Masters from the Earliest Period to the Year 1616*, 785.
3. H. Ferneley to Toby Bonnell on the mode of making usquebaugh, September 4, 1671, National Library of Ireland, MS_UR_011879.
4. *Clogher Record* 4, no. 3 (1962): 203–4.
5. A nineteenth-century translation of a poitín recipe:

   Place oats and barley in sacks in a boghole and allow to thoroughly soak in water.

   Pull from boghole and spread grain over the floor until it begins to sprout. {This is the malting process.}

   Kiln dry.

   When that process is finished, partially hand bruise grain.

   Throw malted grain in a vat of water and ferment. {There is no mention of yeast, but it's likely yeast was added here.}

   Pour into the still. The still consists of a tin vessel on the top of which is a wooden portion called a cap that feeds the arm that feeds the worm, a copper pipe 24 yards in length with coils. Its contents are boiling, steam passes into the cap and through the arm and worm where it is converted into liquid and trickles out of the spout into the skillet.

   It should be distilled a third time. Note: "To keep joints under the cap and worm air tight, a thick paste of oatmeal is layered over the joinings."
6. Cusack, *An Illustrated History of Ireland*, 203.
7. G.B., "On the Early Use of Aqua-Vitae in Ireland," *Ulster Journal of Archaeology* 6 (1858): 291.
8. An ad for whiskey made the front page of the *London Journal* on March 7, 1729.
9. "Home Affairs," *London Read Weekly Journal*, February 19, 1737.
10. *London Read Weekly*, May 27, 1738.
11. Manning, *Donegal Poitín: A History*, 8.
12. Rev. Edward Chichester, "Oppressions and Cruelties of Irish Revenue Officers," *Christian Parlor Magazine*, Boston, 1818, 3.
13. Manning, *Donegal Poitín*, 50.
14. "Collection of Legal Documents Relating to Illegal Poteen Making in County Carlow," edited by Excise Agency, 1818.
15. Chichester, *Christian Parlor Magazine*, Boston, 1818, 7.

16. Manning, *Donegal Poitín*, 27.

17. Manning, *Donegal Poitín*, 33.

18. "The Poteen Evil," *Irish Times*, March 11, 1932, 5.

19. "Justice Blames the Women: The Poteen Evil in Donegal," *Irish Times*, September 9, 1932, 5. This statement was made 100 years before the context of the quote, but the author makes the reasonable conclusion that judges in the 1800s viewed women in much the same way as they did in the early 1900s.

20. Manning, *Donegal Poitín*, 53.

21. Manning, *Donegal Poitín*, 64.

22. Chichester, "Oppressions and Cruelties," 46.

23. "On Illicit Distillation in Ireland," in Select Committee on Irish Grand Jury Presentations, Reports, Also Accounts and Papers Relating to Ireland, 1816, 111.

24. William Tate, "On Reform of the Excise of Department," *Tait's Edinburgh Magazine* 4 (1837): 232.

25. Diner, *Erin's Daughters in America*, 27.

26. Public Records Office of Northern Ireland, 2012.

27. Forbes, *A Short History of the Art of Distillation*, 22–23.

28. Cornelius Soule Cartée, "Answer to Kate Kearney," in *The Souvenir Minstrel: A Choice Collection of the Most Admired Songs, Duets* (Philadelphia: Marshall, Clark, 1833), 66.

29. Edward Newman, "Notes on Irish Natural History, More Especially Ferns," *Magazine of Natural History* 4 (1840): 72.

30. "The Chronicle of the British & Irish Baptist Home Mission, Extracts from the Secretary's Notes, Taken during the Late Visit to Ireland," *Baptist Magazine*, January 1872, 638.

31. Great Britain, Parliament, House of Commons, *The Consequences of Extending the Functions of the Constabulary in Ireland to the Suppression or Prevention of Illicit Distillation*, 1854, 96, 243.

32. "Captures in Dublin: Women Carrying Rifles," *Irish Times*, February 6, 1923, 6.

33. "Stills and Poteen in Court," *Irish Times*, January 4, 1934, 5.

34. From The Emigrants of Ahadarra, in *The Works of William Carleton*, 2:497.

35. Interview with Bushmills master distiller Colum Egan, 2012.

36. Muspratt, *Chemistry, Theoretical, Practical, and Analytical*, 94.

37. "Bushmills, Bundle of Copy Deeds, Memorandum and Articles," Public Records Ofice of Northern Ireland, 1801–1891.

38. *Supplement to Colonies and India*, June 5, 1889, 4.

39. Bielenberg, *Locke's Distillery*, 45.

40. All anecdotes, quotes, and information about the Locke tribunal come from the account books, correspondence, and miscellaneous papers

stored at the National Library of Ireland. Call number Ms. 20,00 and 20,275. For more on Locke Irish Whiskey, an excellent book is *Locke's Distillery: A History*, by Andy Bielenberg. For anybody willing to spend a weekend at the National Library of Ireland, the Locke tribunal records are handwritten and bound together in four large leather binders.

41. My interview with Steven Teeling appeared in "The Test of Time," *Whisky Magazine*, October 2012.

4. EARLY SCOTCH WHISKY WOMEN

1. One of the most highly contested claims in Scotch whisky history is where Friar John Cor lived. Many published accounts credit Cor with coming from the Lindores Abbey, but according to the National Archives of Scotland, this error dates back to two pieces of information published by one of its former employees. All that is known for sure is that he was from Fife.

2. Scotland Exchequer, *Accounts of the Lord High Treasurer*, 1473-1498, 373.

3. Seal of Cause granted by the City of Edinburgh and confirmed by James IV, 1506, *Society of Antiquaries of Scotland*, 261.

4. David, *Extracts from the Records of the Burgh of Edinburgh*, 1557-71, 262.

5. M'Laren, *Rise and Progress of Whiskey Drinking in Scotland*, 20.

6. Comrie, *History of Scottish Medicine*, 64.

7. "The Definition of Whiskey in Olden Times," *Lancet* 1 (1905): 240.

8. In Burns, *Works*, 417.

9. Great Britain, Board of Inland Revenue, "Report of the Commissioners of Inland Revenue on the Duties under Their Management, for the Years 1856 to 1869 Inclusive," 12.

10. Coyne, *Ireland: Industrial and Agricultural*, 499. Despite its title, the 1902 text offers an in-depth coverage of illicit distillation throughout the United Kingdom.

11. Spiller, *Cardhu*, 32-33.

12. Barnard, *Whisky Distilleries of the United Kingdom*.

13. Spiller, *Cardhu*, 24.

14. Spiller, *Cardhu*, 23.

15. National Archives of Scotland, reference CS 318/345.

16. "Sequestration Processes: Margaret Sutherland, Parks of Inshes, Inverness-shire, 1865," National Archives of Scotland, General Register House, Edinburgh, CS318/8/345.

17. Master distiller Richard Patterson interview.

5. EARLY AMERICAN WOMEN

1. Ewell, *Medical Companion*, 257.

2. Huish, *The Female's Friend, and General Domestic Adviser*, 452-53.

3. Taylor, *On Poisons, in Relation to Medical Jurisprudence and Medicine,* 326.
4. B. Achelor, "Ague Treatment," *St. Louis Medical Journal* 11 (January 1884): 449.
5. Johann Georg Hohman, "To Make Good Eye Water," *Faithful & Christian Instructions,* 1850, 16.
6. *Virginia Gazette,* March 4, 1773.
7. Meyers and Perreault, *Colonial Chesapeake,* 209.
8. Carpenter Family Papers, 1780–1860, Kentucky Historical Society.
9. "Currente-Calamosities to the Editor," *Southern Literary Messenger* 5 (1839): 96.
10. Gould, *American First Ladies,* 67.
11. Bear and Stanton, *Jefferson's Memorandum Books,* 1:519.
12. Yetman, *Voices from Slavery,* 232.
13. Nancy Morgan Hart's heroism has been well documented. *Revolutionary Women* and *Patriots in Petticoats* are two respected books that cite her patriotism. Georgia named Hart County after her. Hart is also the grandmother of Lucretia Hart Clay, who married future U.S. presidential candidate Henry Clay.
14. Washington et al., *Writings of George Washington from the Original Manuscript Sources, 1745-1799,* 11:144.
15. Colonel Reed to President of Congress, July 25, 1776, in *American Archives,* ed. Force, 1:576.
16. Smith, *Medical and Surgical Memoirs,* 363.
17. Wiley, *Life of Johnny Reb,* 40.
18. Varhola and Varhola, *Life in Civil War America,* 124.
19. Pember, *A Southern Woman's Story,* 30.
20. This anecdote was shared in Paul Pacult's *American Still Life,* 27. Additional material came from my interview with Fred Noe, Jim Beam master distiller and descendent of Jacob Beam, and Jacob Myer's will.
21. Tariff bill, *Register of Debates in Congress,* April 15, 1828.
22. Eli Huston Brown III Collection, Filson Historical Society, Louisville.
23. These licenses were discovered on pre-pro.com, which contain more than 20,000 liquor wholesale licenses from 1860 to 1920 and more than 2,800 distilleries. This database was built using Treasury Department records collected for the Snyder Whiskey Research Center.
24. Kay Baker Gaston, "George Dickel Tennessee Sour Mash Whiskey: The Story behind the Label," *Tennessee Historical Quarterly* 57 (Fall 1998): 150–66.
25. Zoeller interview.
26. "The Mountain Moonshiner," *Forest and Stream,* July 14, 1906, 689.
27. Arkansas Traveler, "A Woman Distiller, Arrested for the Illicit Manufactur of Whiskey," *Sunday Herald,* June 21, 1885, 6.

28. "A Woman Moonshiner, Mollier Miller, the Head of a Once-Desperate Gang," *Hartford Republican*, October 5, 1894, 1.

29. "A Woman Moonshiner, Betsy Mullens Carries on Her Business in Defiance of Raiders," *Hartford Republican*, March 5, 1897, 4.

30. "Woman of 80 a Moonshiner, Arrested after a Struggle in Mountains of West Virginia," *Boston Globe*, January 2, 1907, 10.

31. Shirley, *Belle Star and Her Times*, 65.

6. THE TARGETED AND EARLY MARKETERS

1. Villard, *John Brown*, 97.

2. *The History of Prostitution* by William W. Sanger, et al., and *Whiskey and Wild Women* by Cy Martin served as the chief sources for this section. They are equally important books. *The History of Prostitution* gives a great statistical look at why women sell their bodies, while *Whiskey and Wild Women* offers anecdotal tales.

3. Martin, *Whiskey and Wild Women*, 59.

4. Martin, *Whiskey and Wild Women*, 67–68.

5. Sanger et al., *History of Prostitution*, 373, 606.

6. For more on the Nancy Boggs floating bordello owner, see Karl Klooster, "Legend & Lore: Nancy Boggs' Barge," *Oregonian*, May 23, 1988.

7. "The Social Evil: A Practival View of Female Depravity. Debauchery in Paris and European Cities. The Evil in This City—Statistics and Facts for the Legislature. What Is and What Is Not—Remedial Measures," *New York Herald*, February 7, 1870.

8. Tait, *Magdalenism*, 164.

9. New York prostitutes sold more than $2 million in liquor in 1857. The data for 1847 is not available, but I make a reasonable conclusion the numbers were similar. The net revenue for each of the four states is referenced in Sparks, Bowen, and Sange, *American Almanac of Useful Knowledge* 18 (1847). Further Indiana revenues are found in the 1848 *Annual Report of the Officers of State of the State of Indiana*, 189.

7. TEMPERANCE WOMEN

1. History looks at Prohibition as an American black eye, but it is important to remember the issues that led to the law. Starting with histories written in the 1800s, such as *History of the Temperance Movement in Great Britain and Ireland* by Samuel Couling and *History of Woman Suffrage* by Elizabeth Cady Stanton and others, I began to understand the emotional complexities that came along with alcohol in that time. Reading those histories also helped me discover Theobald Mathew, whom I believe shaped the first winning argument for Prohibition.

2. "Extracts from His Various Speeches at Dublin: Of Irishmen in America," *American Temperance Union* 4, no. 7 (July 1840): 110.

3. Maguire, *Father Mathew: A Biography*, 464.

4. Clay, *Works of Henry Clay*, 3:102.

5. Lady Emeline Stuart Hartley, "Results of Petitioning: Voice of the People," *Journal of the American Temperance Union* 12–14 (1848): 145.

6. Stanton, *History of Woman Suffrage*, 1:473.

7. Clubb, *Maine Liquor Law*, 5.

8. Stanton, *History of Woman Suffrage*, 1:167.

9. Murdock, *Domesticating Drink*, 25.

10. Harper, *Life and Work of Susan B. Anthony*, 1:108.

11. Williams, *Prohibition and Woman Suffrage*, 3.

12. Nation, *Use and Need of the Life*, 165–66.

13. Nation, *Use and Need of the Life*, 172.

14. "Carry Nation in an Old Veterans' City Cigar Store," *Elyria Chronicle*, November 25, 1907, 1.

15. Butler-Andrews, "That Little Hatchet," in *Nation, Use and Need of the Life*, 408.

16. Snedon, "The Hatchet Crusade," in *Nation, Use and Need of the Life*, 413.

17. James Burran, "Prohibition in New Mexico, 1917," *New Mexico Historical Quarterly* 48 (April 1973): 140–41.

18. Current, *Wisconsin: A History*, 54.

19. Gordon, *Women Torch-Bearers*, 167.

20. Gordon, *Women Torch-Bearers*, 170.

8. WOMEN MOONSHINERS AND BOOTLEGGERS

1. Thayer, "Whisky, Oceans of Whisky, And Not a Chance to Sell It," *Boston Globe*, December 21, 1919, E8.

2. Letter from R. A. Dowling to W. L. Weller & Sons, December 8, 1926. This letter is from the private collection of Sally Van Winkle Campbell, the granddaughter of Pappy Van Winkle. Other Dowling correspondence is held at the Stitzel-Weller collection in the United Distillers archive in Louisville.

3. "Aged Woman Moonshiner Stands Guard in Lonely Hills to Defy Officers," *Tulsa Daily World*, August 17, 1920.

4. "Woman Moonshiner Taken at Kenosha," *La Crosse Trubune and Leader-Press*, November 25, 1920, 5.

5. "White Woman Moonshiner," *Biloxi Daily Herald*, October 3, 1923.

6. Associated Press. "Woman Moonshiner Given Three Months," *Hattiesburg American*, March 2, 1922, 7.

7. "Woman Moonshiner Gets Leniency from Donahey: Made Liquor in Order to Feed Children Deserted by Father, Her Defense," *Charleston Daily*, November 30, 1924, 1.

8. "President Harding Frees Muskegon Woman Bootlegger," *Marshall Evening Chronicle*, October 10, 1922, 1.

9. "Woman Moonshiner Pleads for Her Boy," *Biloxi Daily Herald*, January 18, 1924.

10. "Judge Would Deport Woman Moonshiner," *Chicago Tribune*, February 10, 1923, 5.

11. Associated Press, "Woman Makes Booze to Keep Her Husband at Home at Night," *Billings Gazette*, May 10, 1925, 7.

12. The World Almanac & Book of Facts, 1929, 304.

13. Subcommittee of the Committee on the Judiciary, 69th Senate, National Prohibition Law, April 5–24, 1926.

14. "Moonshine Mary Is Convicted in Death," *New Castle News*, March 19, 1924, 1.

15. "American Poteen: Where Prohibition Has Failed," *Irish Times*, May 6, 1925, 7.

16. "Women Bootleggers Foxy: Keeps Oklahoma Officers Busy Trying to Catch Females Who Sell Whisky to Indians," *Washington Post*, May 28, 1911.

17. "How Are We Going to Handle Woman Bootlegger?" *Boston Daily Globe*, April 22, 1922, E8.

18. "Officials Face Problem of Eliminating 'Women Bootlegger,'" *Hamilton Evening Journal*, December 17, 1924, 20.

19. "Woman Bootlegger Problem That Is Worrying Dry Agents," *Linton Daily*, Marcy 27, 1922, 1.

20. "Woman Bootlegger Is a Serious Problem: Pretty Girl Is Useful as Liquor Camouflage," *Charleston Daily Mail*, January 6, 1924.

21. United Press, "State, Federal Officers Drawn into Investigation of Protective Payments; Woman Bootlegger Says State Senator Endorsed Check to Fix Case," *Moorhead Daily News*, November 20, 1931, 1.

22. There are more than a dozen published reports of this alleged female bootlegger in Zanesville, Ohio. Most stories originated from the February 19, 1930, Associated Press article "Blonde Sought as Bootlegger in Zanesville: Capture of Plane Landed with Liquor Leads to Search for Woman." It's unknown if she was ever captured.

23. "Alcohol Company and 27 Indicted; Special Grand Jury Names Federal-Agent and 'Queen of the Bootleggers,'" *New York Times*, January 16, 1926, 1.

24. "Views from Two Cities: A Young Woman Bootlegger Says She Made Nearly $30,000," *Mitchell Evening Republican*, January 27, 1925, 4; Society for American Baseball Research, SABR.org.

25. Jana G. Pruden, "The Only Woman Hanged in Albert," *Edmonton Journal*, 2011. Online: http://www.edmontonjournal.com/news/hanged/lassandro.html.

26. Regarding the Lassandro trial, letters and court documents can be found at the Library and Archives of Canada under "Lassandra or Lassandro,

Florence," R188–54–4-E and "Emilio Picariello alias Emperor Pic and Florence Lassandro—Coleman, Alberta—Murder," under HQ-681-K-1.

27. "English Girl Owner of Noted Rum Ship," *New York Times*, September 12, 1925, 3.
28. Goodwin, *The Fitzgeralds and the Kennedys*, 444. Okrent disputed the Kennedy bootlegging business in Last Call.
29. Lythgoe, *The Bahama Queen*, 87.
30. "Miss Lythgoe Queen of the Bootleggers,'" *Gleaner*, October 25, 1922, 5.
31. McCoy, *The Real McCoy*, 78.
32. Lythgoe, *Bahama Queen*.
33. "Bootlegger Queen," *Gleaner*, September 25, 1923, 11.
34. "Miss Lythgoe Queen of the Bootleggers," *Gleaner*, October 25, 1923, 5.
35. Gertrude Lythgoe, "Chance to Share Latin Republic Offered Woman of Rum Runners; Many Suitors Propose by Mail," *Winnipeg Free Press*, June 14, 1924, 7. Several Free Press readers criticized the newspaper's editor for running these letters.
36. "Rum Runner Queen Freed," *Indiana Evening Gazette*, December 9, 1925, 1.
37. Virginia, Swain, "She Craves Peace and Safety after Gold-Strewn Career," *Ogden Standard-Examiner*, May 30, 1926, 6.
38. "Woman's Profits as a Bootlegger Put at $5,000," *Evening World*, August 24, 1921.
39. "Bustle Squeezers: That Is What Women Bootleggers Are Called in Montana," *Hutchinson News*, April 2, 1930, 6.
40. "Few Women in Bootleg Game," *Morning Herald*, November 19, 1926, 11.
41. In the photo provided by Independent Stave Company (see photos), women are doing the very type of work that New York law enforcement officials said they could not. I believe women were so detrimental to law enforcement's efforts to stop bootlegging that they had to use propaganda to shift public opinion about women bootleggers. As the press looked to crown another "Queen of the Bootleggers," the government tried to reinforce traditional views of women.
42. "Woman Bootlegger Problem That Is Worrying Dry Agents," *Linton Daily Citizen*, March 27, 1922, 1.
43. The famous La Romanée appellation makes 900,000 bottles a year. See Terroir-France.com.

9. REPEAL WOMEN SAVING WHISKEY

1. Wheeler et al., "Topics of the Day: First Returns in the Digest's Nationwide Poll," *Literary Digest*, July 15, 1922, 5–7.
2. "Cross-Currents in the Digest's Prohibition Poll," *New York Morning Telegraph*, August 12, 1922, 6.

3. Pauline Morton Sabin, "I Change My Mind on Prohibition," *Outlook*, June 13, 1928, 254.
4. "Leader of 1,000,000 Wets," *Charleston Daily Mail*, November 27, 1932, 13.
5. "Prohibition and The League of Nations—Born of God or The Devil—Which? The Bible Proof," 1930 press release, Women's Organization for National Prohibition Reform, Pennsylvania Division Records, Hagley Museum and Library, 1928–33.
6. Root, *Women and Repeal*, 13.
7. Maxine Davis, "Thinks Plank Is Temperance," *Oelwein Daily Register*, June 30, 1932, 1.
8. Schapsmeier and Schapsmeier, *Political Parties and Civic Action Groups*, 477.
9. "Women's Part in the Repeal of the Probi Law," *Thomasville Times Enterprise*, November 11, 1933, 3.
10. Brown, *Ratification of the Twenty-First Amendment*, 298.

10. THE POST-PROHIBITION LEGAL BATTLES

1. The 1950s served as a uniting decade of the entire alcohol industry. While temperance supporters sought to ban alcohol advertising numerous times, brewers, distillers, and winemakers worked together for a common cause. Their togetherness was evident in similar messages during the legislative hearings that shaped the future of alcohol advertising.
2. Committee on Interstate and Foreign Commerce, *Advertising of Alcoholic Beverages*, 85th Cong., 2nd sess., April 22, 23, 29, and 30, 1958, 217.
3. *Advertising of Alcoholic Beverages*, 45.
4. *Advertising of Alcoholic Beverages*, 257.
5. *Advertising of Alcoholic Beverages*, 314.
6. Sagert, *Flappers*, 49.
7. Shteir, *Striptease*, 111.
8. Patterson, *The American New Woman Revisited: A Reader*, 1894–1930, 15.
9. Cobble, *Dishing It Out*, 166.
10. Marion Porter, "Solo Women Get Only Drop of Sympathy from Barmen," *Louisville Courier-Journal*, August 29, 1945, 2.
11. Burrell, *Women and Political Participation*, 75.
12. Select Joy Perrine Cocktail, Summer of '92 Blueberry Sour:
    2 ounces of blueberry infused 1792 Ridgemont Reserve Bourbon Whiskey
    1 tablespoon brown sugar syrup
    1 tablespoon blueberry syrup
    2 ounces lemonade
    Shake over ice, garnish with blueberries and lemon wedge.

13. The Joy Perrine anecdote originally appeared in "Mixing before It Was Cool: Joy Perrine Is a True Pioneer behind the Bar," by the author, *Tasting Panel Magazine*, December 2011, 38.

11. POST-PROHIBITION WOMEN BOOTLEGGERS

1. "Timely Baby Foils Law with Cushing Woman Bootlegger," *Ada Evening News*, November 9, 1955, 2.
2. Wright, Hamilton, "Woman Bootlegger, 64, Gets 6 Months in Jail," *Abiline Reporter-News*, B1.
3. "Father Complains Son, 15, Drunk; Hold Woman as Bootlegger," *Carroll Daily Times Herald*, February 23, 1951, 1.
4. U.S. District Court for the Northern District of Ohio, Eastern Division, United States of America v. Lillian Marie Poles, Aka Lillian Stancel Poles, Aka Ludmila M. Fretch, in CR 63-252, edited by Eastern Division Northern District Court of Ohio, 18. National Archives, Chicago, 1963.
5. Norman Hayden interview.
6. Jim Nesbitt, "Making Georgia Shine: There Still Are Stills Up There in Those Hills," *Chicago Tribune*, April 6, 1986, A3.
7. Associated Press, "Woman Moonshiner Recalls First Arrest on Her Birthday," *Hartford Courant*, May 2, 1980, C39.
8. In an interview, Wild Turkey distiller Jimmy Russell spoke fondly of Popcorn Sutton, a legendary moonshiner.

12. WHISKEY'S PROGRESSIVE SIDE

1. Since this book's intent is to explain the women's role in whiskey, I did not elaborate on the Bottle-in-Bond Act of 1897's importance to American whiskey. The law was a solution to rectifiers coloring whiskey, adding water and other liquids to make a whiskey barrel last longer. In the October 1897 issue of *Practical Druggist and Pharmaceutical Review* on page 145, the editor wrote: "The law is well considered and it is in the interest of honesty and will put an end to much deception." For further reading on the Bottle-in-Bond Act and bourbon history, see Michael R. Veach, *Kentucky Bourbon Whiskey: An American Heritage,* or Chuck Cowdery, *Bourbon, Straight: The Uncut and Unfiltered Story of American Whiskey.*
2. Don and Petie Kladstrup's *Wine and War: The French, the Nazis, and the Battle for France's Greatest Treasure* is a great book chronicling French winemakers during World War II.
3. National Parks Service: Women's History Project.
4. "Partners in Winning the War: American Women in World War II," National Women's History Museum, http://www.nwhm.org/online -exhibits/partners/2.htm.

5. The 1992 film A League of Their Own starring Tom Hanks and Geena Davis greatly captures women baseball players' importance during World War II.

6. Arnesen, *Encyclopedia of U.S. Labor and Working-Class History*, vol. 1, A-F, 1206.

7. U.S. Statistics, *Bureau of Labor, Monthly Labor Review*, 1952, 1.

13. THE LADY OF LAPHROAIG

1. Unless otherwise noted, Laphroaig quotations, references, facts, and figures are from the Laphroaig Distillery collections at the University of Glasgow Archives or the personal "Bessie Williamson" collection of *History of Laphroaig* and LaphroaigCollector.com archivist Marcel van Gills Offringa.

2. Rumors certainly existed that Ian and Bessie had an affair, but Laphroaig was a small town. People interviewed for this book said Ian had few friends and probably just enjoyed her company.

3. In Bessie's paperwork, the Allied ship mentioned was the SS Moor, but no record could be found of this boat otherwise. The American SS Robin Moor was sunk by German U-boats in 1941, and the British SS Eastmoor was destroyed in 1942. The USA Morris was a destroyer and would not have transported cargo in 1944. Either she wrote "S.S. Moor" in error, or the ship's records are lost.

4. Eddy Gilmore, "Normal Woman in Liquor Business for Past 29 Years," *Hattiesburg American*, December 17, 1962, 6B.

5. Gils and Offringa, *Legend of Laphroaig*, 72.

14. MODERN WOMEN

1. National Center for Education Statistics, "The Educational Progress of Women," in The Condition of Education 1995, NCES 95-768.

2. See scotch-tasting-bums.com.

3. See http://www.glenmorangie.com/our-whiskies/signet.

4. See MissWhisky.com.

5. "Heaven Hill Distilleries Announces the Launch of Larceny Kentucky Straight Bourbon Whiskey," press release, July 23, 2012.

6. Julian Van Winkle won the coveted James Beard Award in 2011 for the Wine and Spirits Professional. He has his grandfather's gift for blending "but always fine bourbon."

7. DrinkSpirits.com interview with Britt Chavanne.

8. Press release, "Deirdre Mahlan Named Senior Vice President and CFO of Diageo North America," August 11, 2009.

9. Olly Wehring, "The Wehring Interview—William Grant & Sons." In just-drinks.com, 2011.

10. Ciarán Hancock, "Whiskey Galore for Tullamore," *Irish Times*, June 1, 2012.

11. Martin Crymmy, "Relaunch of Yellow Spot Part of Yearly Expressions," TheDrinksBusiness.com, May 25, 2012.

15. ORGANIZING THE WHISKEY EFFORT

1. Ishani Duttagupta and Neha Dewan, "First Exclusive Women's Whisky Club to Host Whisky Appreciation Session," *Economic Times*, October 12, 2011.

2. "Code of Responsible Practices," DISCUS, November 1958.

16. FOR WOMEN, BY WOMEN

1. According to the U.S. Alcohol and Tobacco Tax and Trade Bureau, flavored whiskey is "flavored with natural flavoring materials, with or without the addition of sugar, bottled at not less than 30% alcohol by volume (60 proof). The name of the predominant flavor shall appear as part of the class and type designation, e.g., 'Cherry Flavored Whiskey.' Wine may be added but if the addition exceeds 2.5% by volume of the finished product, the classes and/or types and percentages (by volume) of wine must be stated as part of the class and type designation."

2. "Step Right Up! Introducing Early Times Fire Eater; Flavored Spirits Are Growing," brochure, Brown-Forman, 2012; Brandy Rand, "Bourbon's New Frontier: The Innovation Path Leads to Growth," *Beverage Media Group*, August 29, 2012.

3. There currently are no whiskey sommelier certification courses. In wine, several sommelier courses exist to further the education of wine and tasting. Heather Greene says she hopes one day to initiate a whiskey sommelier course.

4. "Women Nose Ahead in Smell Tests," BBC.co.uk, February 4, 2002.

5. Columbia University, "Male Vs. Female: The Brain Differences," http://www.columbia.edu/itc/anthropology/v1007/jakabovics/mf2.html.

6. Charles J. Wysocki et al., "Cross-Adaptation of a Model Human Stress-Related Odour with Fragrance Chemicals and Ethyl Esters of Axillary Odorants: Gender-Specific Effects," *Flavour and Fragrance Journal* 24, no. 5 (2009): 209–18.

7. "LUPEC Takes NYC, Dig Boston," http://digboston.com/experience/2012/04/lupec-takes-nyc-2012/.

8. "Sia Scotch: The Spirit of Entrepreneurship—Literally," ActSeed.com, 2012.

BIBLIOGRAPHY

Apotheker, Jan, and Livia Simon Sarkadi. *European Women in Chemistry*. Weinheim, Germany: Wiley-VCH, 2011.

Arnesen, Eric. *Encyclopedia of U.S. Labor and Working-Class History*. 3 vols New York: Routledge, 2007.

Barnard, Alfred. *The Whisky Distilleries of the United Kingdom*. 1887; reprint, New York: A. M. Kelley, 1969.

Bear, James A., Jr., and Lucia C. Stanton, eds. *Jefferson's Memorandum Books: Accounts, with Legal Records and Miscellany, 1767–1826*. 2 vols. Princeton NJ: Princeton University Press, 1997.

Bennett, Judith M. *Ale, Beer, and Brewsters in England: Women's Work in a Changing World, 1300–1600*. New York: Oxford University Press, 1996.

Bickerdyke, John. *The Curiosities of Ale & Beer: An Entertaining History*. London: Field and Tuer, 1886.

Bielenberg, Andy. *Locke's Distillery: A History*. Dublin: Lilliput Press, 1993.

Bodin, Jean. *On the Demon-Mania of Witches*. Translated by Randy A. Scott. Toronto: Centre for Reformation and Renaissance Studies, 1995.

Brown, Everett Somerville. *Ratification of the Twenty-First Amendment to the Constitution of the United States: State Convention Records and Laws*. Clark NJ: Lawbook Exchange, 2003.

Burns, Robert. *The Works of Robert Burns; with His Life*. 8 vols. Edited by Allan Cunningham. London: Cochrane and McCrone, 1834.

Burns, William E. *Witch Hunts in Europe and America: An Encyclopedia*. Westport CT: Greenwood Press, 2003.

Burrell, Barbara C. *Women and Political Participation: A Reference Handbook*. Santa Barbara CA: ABC-CLIO, 2004.

Carleton, William. *The Emigrants of Ahadarra*. In vol. 2 of *The Works of William Carleton*. New York: Collier, 1881.

Chambers, William, and Robert Chambers. *Chambers's Miscellany of Instructive & Entertaining Tracts*. New and rev. ed. 10 vols. London: W. and R. Chambers, 1872.

Clay, Henry. *The Works of Henry Clay, Comprising His Life, Correspondence, and Speeches*. Vol. 3. Edited by Calvin Colton. New York: A. S. Barnes, 1857.

Cléirigh, Mícheál Ó. *Annals of the Kingdom of Ireland by the Four Masters from the Earliest Period to the Year 1616*. Dublin: Hodges, Smith, and Co., Grafton-Street, 1856.

Clubb, Henry Stephen. *The Maine Liquor Law: Its Origin, History, and Results.* New York: Fowler and Wells, 1856.

Cobble, Dorothy Sue. *Dishing It Out: Waitresses and Their Unions in the Twentieth Century.* Urbana: University of Illinois Press, 1991.

Comrie, John D. *History of Scottish Medicine.* London: Welcome Historical Medical Museum, 1860.

Corren, H. S. *A History of Brewing.* North Pomfret VT: David and Charles, 1975.

Couling, Samuel. *History of the Temperance Movement in Great Britain and Ireland; from the Earliest Date to the Present Time.* London: W. Tweedie, 1862.

Coyne, William P. *Ireland: Industrial and Agricultural.* Dublin: Brown and Nolan, 1902.

Current, Richard Nelson. *Wisconsin: A History.* New York: W. W. Norton, 1977.

Cusack, Mary Francis. *Illustrated History of Ireland: From the Earliest Period.* London: Longmans, Green, 1868.

David, Sir James. *Extracts from the Records of the Burgh of Edinburgh.* Edinburgh: Scottish Burgh Records Society, 1557-71.

Department of the Treasury Alcohol & Tobacco Tax & Trade Bureau. *The Beverage Alcohol Manual: A Practical Guide.* Washington, DC: Government Printing Office, 2007.

Dickie, Matthew W. *Magic and Magicians in the Greco-Roman World.* London: Routledge, 2001.

Diner, Hasia R. *Erin's Daughters in America: Irish Immigrant Women in the Nineteenth Century.* Baltimore: Johns Hopkins University Press, 1983.

Evans, Ruth, Sarah Salih, and Anke Bernau. *Medieval Virginities.* Toronto: University of Toronto Press, 2003.

Ewell, James. *The Medical Companion.* 3rd ed. Philadelphia: Printed for the author by Anderson and Mechan, 1816.

"Extracts from His Various Speeches at Dublin." *Journal of the American Temperance Union* 4, no. 7 (July 1840): 110-11.

Forbes, Robert James. *A Short History of the Art of Distillation; from the Beginnings up to the Death of Cellier Blumenthal.* 2nd rev. ed. Leiden: Brill, 1970.

Force, Peter. *American Archives: Consisting of a Collection of Authentick Records, State Papers, Debates, and Letters and Other Notices of Publick Affairs, the Whole Forming a Documentary History of the Origin and Progress of the North American Colonies; of the Causes and Accomplishment of the American Revolution; and of the Constitution of Government for the United States, to the Final Ratification Thereof. In Six Series.* 9 vols. Vol. 1. Washington, 1848.

Gils, Marcel van, and Hans Offringa. *Legend of Laphroaig.* Odijk, Netherlands: Still, 2007.

Goodwin, Doris Kearns. *The Fitzgeralds and the Kennedys.* New York: Simon and Schuster, 1987.

Gordon, Elizabeth Putnam. *Women Torch-Bearers: The Story of the Woman's Christian Temperance Union.* Evanston IL: National Woman's Christian Temperance Union Publishing House, 1924.

Gould, Lewis. *American First Ladies: Their Lives and Their Legacy.* New York: Routledge, 2001.

Grant, Elizabeth. *Memoirs of a Highland Lady: The Autobiography of Elizabeth Grant, 1797–1830.* New York: Longmans, Green, 1899.

Guthrie, Leonard. "Lady Sedley's Receipt Book, 1686, and Other Seventeenth-Century Receipt Books." *Proceedings of the Royal Society of Medicine* 6 (1913): 150–73.

Harper, Ida Husted. *The Life and Work of Susan B. Anthony: Including Public Addresses, Her Own Letters and Many from Her Contemporaries during Fifty Years.* 2 vols. Indianapolis: Bowen-Merrill, 1899.

Hohman, John George. "To Make Good Eye Water." In *The Long Lost Friend, or Faithful & Christian Instructions.* Harrisburg, PA, 1850.

Holmyard, Eric John. *Alchemy.* New York: Dover, 1990.

Huish, Robert. *The Female's Friend, and General Domestic Adviser.* London: George Virtue, 1837.

Indiana. *Annual Report of the Officers of State of the State of Indiana.* Indianapolis, 1848.

Jochens, Jenny. *Women in Old Norse Society.* Ithaca: Cornell University Press, 1995.

Kladstrup, Don, and Petie Kladstrup. *Wine and War: The French, the Nazis, and the Battle for France's Greatest Treasure.* New York: Broadway Books, 2001.

Kremers, Edward, and George Urdang. *Kremers and Urdang's History of Pharmacy.* 4th ed. Revised by Glenn Sonnedecker. Philadelphia: Lippincott, 1976.

Leick, Gwendolyn. *Sex and Eroticism in Mesopotamian Literature.* London: Routledge, 1994.

Lythgoe, Gertrude, and Robert McKenna. *The Bahama Queen: The Autobiography of Gertrude "Cleo" Lythgoe, Prohibition's Daring Beauty.* Mystic CT: Flat Hammock, 2007.

M'Laren, Duncan. *The Rise and Progress of Whisky Drinking in Scotland.* Glasgow: Scottish Temperance League, 1858.

Macfarlane, Alan. *Witchcraft in Tudor and Stuart England: A Regional and Comparative Study.* New York: Harper and Row, 1970.

Maguire, John Francis. *Father Mathew: A Biography.* London: Longman, Green, Longman, Roberts, and Green, 1863.

Manning, Aidan. *Donegal Poitín: A History.* Published by author, 2003.

Marchant, W. T. *In Praise of Ale: With Some Curious Particulars Concerning Ale-Wives and Brewers, Drinking Clubs, and Customs.* London: George Redway, 1888.

Markham, Gervase, and Michael R. Best. *The English Housewife*. Kingston: McGill-Queen's University Press, 1986.

Martin, A. Lynn. *Alcohol, Sex, and Gender in Late Medieval and Early Modern Europe*. Houndmills, Basingstoke, Hampshire: Palgrave, 2001.

Martin, Cy. *Whiskey and Wild Women: An Amusing Account of the Saloons and Bawds of the Old West*. New York: Hart, 1974.

McDougall, John, and Gavin D. Smith. *Wort, Worms & Washbacks: Memoirs from the Stillhouse*. Glasgow: Angels' Share, 1999.

McIntosh, Marjorie Keniston. *Working Women in English Society, 1300-1620*. Cambridge: Cambridge University Press, 2005.

Meacham, Sarah Hand. *Every Home a Distillery: Alcohol, Gender, and Technology in the Colonial Chesapeake*. Baltimore: Johns Hopkins University Press, 2009.

Murdock, Catherine Gilbert. *Domesticating Drink: Women, Men, and Alcohol in America, 1870-1940*. Baltimore: Johns Hopkins University Press, 2002.

Muspratt, Sheridan. *Chemistry, Theoretical, Practical, and Analytical: As Applied and Relating*. Vol. 1. Glasgow: William Mackenzie, 1859.

Nation, Carry Amelia. *The Use and Need of the Life of Carry A. Nation*. Topeka: F. M. Steves & Sons, 1908.

Okrent, Daniel. *Last Call: The Rise and Fall of Prohibition*. New York: Scribner, 2010.

Patai, Raphael. *The Jewish Alchemists: A History and Source Book*. Princeton: Princeton University Press, 1994.

Patterson, Martha. *The American New Woman Revisited: A Reader, 1894-1930*. New Brunswick: Rutgers University Press, 2008.

Pember, Phoebe Yates. *A Southern Woman's Story*. New York: G. W. Carleton, 1879.

Penney, *Five Hundred Employments Adapted to Women: With the Average Rate of Pay in Each*. Philadelphia: John Potter, 1868. 148.

Prioreschi, Plinio. *A History of Medicine: Medieval Medicine*. Lewiston NY: Edwin Mellen, 2003.

Rayner-Canham, Marelene F., and Geoffrey Rayner-Canham. *Women in Chemistry: Their Changing Roles from Alchemical Times to the Mid-Twentieth Century*. Washington DC: American Chemical Society and Chemical Heritage Foundation, 1998.

Root, Grace C. *Women and Repeal: The Story of the Women's Organization for National Prohibition Reform*. New York: Harper, 1934.

Sagert, Kelly Boyer. *Flappers: A Guide to An American Subculture*. Santa Barbara: Greenwood, 2010.

Sandby, George. *Mesmerism and Its Opponents; with a Narrative of Cases*. 2nd ed. London, 1848.

Sanger, William W. *The History of Prostitution: Its Extent, Causes, and Effects throughout the World*. New York: American Medical Press, 1895.

Schapsmeier, Edward L., and Frederick H. Schapsmeier. *Political Parties and Civic Action Groups*. The Greenwood Encyclopedia of American Institutions. Westport CT: Greenwood, 1981.

Schreiner, Oswald. *History of the Art of Distillation and of Distilling Apparatus*. Vol. 6. Edited by Edward Kremers. Milwaukee: Pharmaceutical Review, 1901.

Scotland Exchequer. *Accounts of the Lord High Treasurer, 1473–1498*. Edited by Thomas Dickson. Vol. 1. Edinburgh: Authority of the Lords Commissioners of Her Majesty's Treasury, under the Direction of the Lord Clerk Register of Scotland by HM General Register House, 1877.

Select Committee on Irish Grand Jury Presentations. *Reports, Also Accounts and Papers, Relating to Ireland*. Vol. 9. London: House of Commons, 1816.

Shirley, Glenn. *Belle Starr and Her Times: The Literature, the Facts, and the Legends*. Norman: University of Oklahoma Press, 1982.

Shteir, Rachel. *Striptease: The Untold History of the Girlie Show*. New York: Oxford University Press, 2004.

Singer, Charles Joseph, and Trevor I. Williams. *A History of Technology*. 8 vols. Oxford: Clarendon, 1954–58.

Smith, Nathan R. *Medical and Surgical Memoirs*. Baltimore: W. A. Francis, 1831.

Snedon, Carrie Chew. "The Hatchet Crusade. " In *Nation, Use and Need of the Life*, 413.

Sparks, Jared, Francis Bowen, and George Partridge Sange. *The American Almanac and Repository of Useful Knowledge*. Vol. 18. Boston: Charles Bowen; Collins and Hannay, 1847.

Spiller, Brian. *Cardhu: The World of Malt Whisky*. John Walker & Sons, 1985.

Stanton, Elizabeth Cady, Susan B. Anthony, and Matilda Joslyn Gage, eds. *History of Woman Suffrage*. 3 vols. Rochester ny: Susan B. Anthony, 1887.

"The Stomachic Usquebaugh," *Whitehall Evening Post*, February 8, 1750, 2.

Tait, William. "On Reform of the Excise of Department." *Tait's Edinburgh Magazine* 4 (1837).

Tait, William. *Magdalenism: An Inquiry into the Extent, Causes, and Consequences of Prostitution in Edinburgh*. Edinburgh: P. Rickard, 1840.

Taylor, Alfred S. *On Poisons, in Relation to Medical Jurisprudence and Medicine*. Philadelphia: Lea and Blanchard, 1848.

Tynan, Katharine. *The Dear Irish Girl*. Chicago: A. C. McClurg, 1899.

Tyron, Thomas. *A New Art of Brewing Beer, Ale, and Other Sorts of Liquors*. 1690.

Unger, Richard W. *Beer in the Middle Ages and the Renaissance*. Philadelphia: University of Pennsylvania Press, 2004.

U.S. Bureau of Labor Statistics. *Monthly Labor Review* 75 (October 1952): 516.

Van de Water, Frederic Franklyn. *The Real McCoy*. Garden City NY: Doubleday, Doran, 1931.

Varhola, Michael O., and Michael O. Varhola. *Life in Civil War America*. 2nd ed. Cincinnati: Family Tree, 2011.

Villard, Oswald G. *John Brown, 1800–1859: A Biography after Fifty Years*. New York: Houghton Mifflin, 1910.

Washington, George, John Clement Fitzpatrick, David Maydole Matteson, and U.S. George Washington Bicentennial Commission. *The Writings of George Washington from the Original Manuscript Sources, 1745–1799; Prepared under the Direction of the United States George Washington Bicentennial Commission and Published by Authority of Congress*. 39 vols. Vol. 11. Westport CT: Greenwood, 1970.

Wiley, Bell I. *The Life of Johnny Reb, the Common Soldier of the Confederacy*. Indianapolis: Bobbs-Merrill, 1943.

Williams, Albert. *Prohibition and Woman Suffrage: Speech of Hon. Albert Williams, of Ionia, Michigan, made at Charlotte, Mich., October 9th, 1874*. Lansing, October 9, 1874.

Winter, Bruce W. *Roman Wives, Roman Widows: The Appearance of New Women and the Pauline Communities*. Cambridge: Wm. B. Eerdmans, 2003.

Yetman, Norman R. *Voices from Slavery: 100 Authentic Slave Narratives*. Mineola NY: Dover, 2000.

INDEX

Distillers Company Limited of Edinburgh, 34–35
distributors, 93
divorce, 65
Dixon, Callie, 104–5
D'Orazio, Angela, 135
Douglass, Frederick, 64
Dowling, Mary, 72–73, 111–12
Dr. Bull's Cough Syrup, 56–57
drunk driving, 95
drunkenness, 2, 3; in army, 45; arrests because of, 74–75; attributed to Irish, 63; divorce for, 65; science of, 95
dry counties, 67–68, 93, 104, 105
Duffy's Pure Malt Whiskey, 57–58
Dunmore Distillery, 37
duties on foreign spirits, 49

Eccless, Florence, 28
Egyptians, xiii, 2–3, 10
Elizabeth I (Queen of England), 17
Elizabeth II (Queen of England), 127
Elliott, Margaret, 19
Ellis, Grace, 97–99
Emmons, Minnie, 104
Endicott House, 144
English Chronicle, 13–14
Equal Rights Amendment, 102
equal rights for women, 101, 102
Essex Witch Records, 5
European Centre for Monitoring Alcohol Marketing, 154
Evans, Julia, 69
Evan Williams, 137, 153. *See also* Heaven Hill
evaporation, 142
excise agents, 19–22, 53, 73; tactics of, 19–20; violence toward, 21, 45. *See also* Revenue Police
executives, 141–43
Ezelle, Mrs. R. L., 94

Faithful & Christian Instructions, 42
Federal Alcohol Administration Act of 1935, 94

The Female's Friend, 41
First Amendment, 152
Fitzgerald, John E., 137
Fitzgerald family of Ireland, 18
Flatiron Room, 154
flavor, 1, 36, 121, 124, 126, 130–31
flavoring whiskey, 153–54, 178n1
Flavour and Fragrance Journal, 155
Folkingham, Cyril, 5
Food and Fuel Control Act, 70
"For Your Children's Sake," 90–91
Four Roses, 72
French whiskey, 158–59
Fretch, Ludmila M., 105–6
Friends, Society of, 66
Fucaloro, Lena, 105
fur trade, 58

Gallowhill Distillery, 36
gambling, 69
Garrison, William Lloyd, 64
gay market, 140–41
George Dickel Distillery, 52
Germans, bias against, 70
Gilseth, Mary, 77
Glenfiddich, xii, 156
Glenmorangie Distillery Company, 38, 131, 135; Sanalta PX, 131; Signet, 131
Glenturret Distillery, 37
Goesaert v. Cleary, 100
Grant, Elizabeth: *Memoirs of a Highland Lady*, 160
Great Depression, 91
"Great Whore Invasion," 58–59
Greeks, 3
Greene, Heather, 154, 178n3
Guild of Surgeon Barbers, 31, 32
Guinan, "Texas" (Mary Louise Cecilia), 99
G&W Distillers, 110

Haig's, 81
Hamilton, Alexander, 46
Hansell, John, 145–47
Harding, Warren G., 74
Harriman, Mrs. E. Roland, 89